Spiritual Criminals

Spiritual Criminals

HOW THE CAMDEN 28 PUT THE VIETNAM WAR ON TRIAL

Michelle M. Nickerson

The University of Chicago Press   Chicago and London

Publication of this book has been aided by the Meijer Foundation Publication Fund, which supports books of enduring interest in the disciplines of American political history, political science, and related areas.

The University of Chicago Press, Chicago 60637
The University of Chicago Press, Ltd., London
© 2024 by The University of Chicago
All rights reserved. No part of this book may be used or reproduced in any manner whatsoever without written permission, except in the case of brief quotations in critical articles and reviews. For more information, contact the University of Chicago Press, 1427 E. 60th St., Chicago, IL 60637.
Published 2024
Printed in the United States of America

33 32 31 30 29 28 27 26 25 24   1 2 3 4 5

ISBN-13: 978-0-226-82803-9 (cloth)
ISBN-13: 978-0-226-83438-2 (paper)
ISBN-13: 978-0-226-82804-6 (e-book)
DOI: https://doi.org/10.7208/chicago/9780226828046.001.0001

Library of Congress Cataloging-in-Publication Data

Names: Nickerson, Michelle M., author.
Title: Spiritual criminals : how the Camden 28 put the Vietnam War on trial / Michelle M. Nickerson.
Other titles: How the Camden 28 put the Vietnam War on trial
Description: Chicago : The University of Chicago Press, 2024. | Includes bibliographical references and index.
Identifiers: LCCN 2023053694 | ISBN 9780226828039 (cloth) | ISBN 9780226834382 (paper) | ISBN 9780226828046 (ebook)
Subjects: LCSH: Vietnam War, 1961–1975—Protest movements—United States. | Catholics—Political activity—United States.
Classification: LCC DS559.62.U6 N525 2024 | DDC 364.1/31—dc23/eng/20231201
LC record available at https://lccn.loc.gov/2023053694

♾ This paper meets the requirements of ANSI/NISO Z39.48-1992 (Permanence of Paper).

In memory of Ronald W. Nickerson (1944–1965) of the U.S. Army First
Infantry Division, Killed in Action in South Vietnam, and dedicated to
E. Allen Nickerson, a sole surviving son

CONTENTS

List of Figures ix

Introduction 1

Part I: The Catholic Left 11

1. A Movement within a Movement 15
2. Civil Disobedience 38
3. One Big Catholic Movement Family 55

Part II: Exit 4 to Camden 73

4. Camden Calls the Catholic Left 75
5. Where's Bob? 97

Part III: Putting the Vietnam War and the FBI on Trial 121

6. Research, Preparations, and Communion 123
7. A Prosecution Disarmed by Loving Kindness 145
8. No Guilt, No Apologies 160
9. Aftermath and Results 177

Conclusion: Is There Anything Left of the Catholic Left? 197

*Acknowledgments 203   List of Abbreviations 207
Notes 209   Index 247*

FIGURES

1. Likelihood of Service 19
2. Draft Avoiders 20
3. Thomas Merton at Gethsemani 31
4. Dorothy Day 41
5. Nuns at the Selma March 45
6. Daniel Berrigan 48
7. Woodstock Wedding 65
8. Map of Camden 28 and Puerto Rican Uprising Sites of Action, 1971 86
9. Camden Federal Building 90
10. Joseph Rodriguez Walks through Riot Smoke 92
11. FBI Surveillance Photo of Kathleen Ridolfi and Rosemary Reilly 94
12. Draft Board with Broken Filing Cabinets 95
13. Arrest Photo of Sara Tosi 98
14. Camden 28 Mugshots 99
15. William Davidon and Bob Williamson at a Rally 102
16. Robert Hardy 116
17. Father Michael Doyle Preparing for Ash Wednesday Service 135
18. Handwritten Jury Research Note 141
19. Handwritten Juror Note 152
20. Kathleen Ridolfi Teaching Law at Santa Clara University 182

INTRODUCTION

Through the bars of his cell, Bob Williamson could register the priest's disgust. Williamson's big, blue eyes regarded the pastor of his family's church in Runnemede, New Jersey, who stopped by that day on behalf of the inmate's parents. The visitor came mainly to see how the young man was enduring jail and to tell him how much Williamson had disappointed his mother. August 1971 found the twenty-two-year-old in the Atlantic County jail, where he waited for release on bail after federal authorities arrested him for breaking into a draft board. Though eager for the bond that would free him from lockup, Williamson felt certain that his future days on the outside were limited. The FBI had caught him and seven other burglars red-handed. The government, moreover, had collected an abundance of evidence on their plans to commit the crime even before the raiders broke into the draft board. The coconspirators, twenty-eight in all, faced the possibility of up to forty-seven years in prison.

Williamson and the other trespassers did not breach the federal building in Camden because they wanted to steal something, but rather to interfere with the government's ability to wage war. They were political radicals trying to stop, or at least slow down, the wheels of the draft that was plucking up young American men to fight and die in Vietnam. They knew the stakes of their crime. These activists embarked on a risky political action indicative of the burning outrage that characterized so much opposition to the war. They were also aware that they could land in prison for decades. Williamson and his cohorts did not regard themselves as criminals. They broke the law to achieve the humanitarian goal of stopping the violence in Indochina. Many assumed the responsibility because they saw it as a spiritual act. As treacherous and extreme as this break-in had been, it was one among scores of such raids committed by radicals in the movement known as Catholic Resistance.

Robert Williamson was one of the Camden 28, a group of defendants who found themselves in a world of legal trouble after conducting one of these raids of a draft board in 1971. Their story includes not only a burglary, an arrest, a trial, and its outcomes, but also the chain of events that prompted the raid in the first place. A combustible mix of political movements, foreign policy decisions, and theological developments led the defendants to take this chancy course of action, gambling their personal freedom by breaching federal facilities. For many, the work started in their college years. They did not merely arrive on their Catholic university campuses, sign up for classes, and start casing federal buildings, however. Their outrage over the war in Vietnam set them on a path to nonviolent resistance that included a series of stepping stones in a process that warrants examination.

On deciding to join others in this lawbreaking, these radicals embarked on experiences that made their lives very different from those of their parents. They actively sought such personal transformation. The activists could not anticipate, though, that the trial itself would become the capstone ending to this chapter of their days. With their appearance in court in that February 1973, the Camden 28 launched a historic defense that swept the judge, jury, courtroom marshals, journalists, and gallery of observers into the thrall of its drama. The three months of arguments, motions, and testimony moved even the adversaries representing the government.

Students of American history rarely learn about Catholic Resistance, also known as the Catholic Left. The draft board raids, which were developed by radicals as a form of creative nonviolent protest, played a significant role in the success of the Vietnam-era peace movement. At the time, the media reported on the movement's activities along with the rest of its news about protests. Local weeklies, the religious press, and national newspapers covered the burglaries as well as the angry responses of government officials who had to deal with the mess and re-create the destroyed or stolen documents. Reporters sat in the galleries of courtrooms where these trials took place, watching the defendants turn the proceedings into forums for denouncing the war. Despite the documentary record left by journalists, however, the Catholic Left does not feature prominently in histories of the Vietnam War era. The most sweeping and detailed documentary series on the period, *The Vietnam War,* by Ken Burns and Lynn Novick, features no material about the movement in its eighteen-hour investigation. The omission is

INTRODUCTION

understandable given the small number of people in the Catholic Left, but unfortunate given how effectively these activists exposed the war's horrors.[1]

Dominated by priests, nuns, and lay Catholics, this movement within a movement drew adherents to its bold but nonviolent strategy for stopping the war. Catholic Resistance developed the raids as its modus operandi to damage property for the sake of saving people. As they liked to say when explaining all the broken door locks, filing cabinets, and office chairs: "Some property has no right to exist."[2] By no means sanctioned by bishops or linked to the operations of any diocese, this loose network of a few hundred men and women broke into draft boards mostly along the East Coast and Midwest. They warrant the attention of historians because they, in cooperation with other participants in the larger peace movement, forced the war to end by relentlessly exposing its atrocities and making the draft unsustainable.[3]

This war of nonviolent direct action stymied the government in a number of ways. Activists overwhelmed officials, who became caught in a daunting cycle of indictments, charges of contempt, lengthy trials, and media frenzies. Conscientious objectors brought draft boards to court for the inconsistent and racially biased process by which the committees evaluated applications. Men in uniform clogged military courts by deserting or refusing to follow orders. The government had to fight its own people in order to fight the war in Vietnam.

Politicians in both political parties at first capitalized on the opportunity to punish the rebellious hippies, who became easy targets. "Hanoi Jane" Fonda and other foul-mouthed youths angered mainstream Americans by disparaging the men who were fighting as well as the government that handed them their guns. Putting protesters into their place became a successful campaign strategy, especially for Republicans. California governor Ronald Reagan rallied conservatives who were angry at campus radicals with his promise to "clean up the mess at Berkeley."[4] Exasperated officials in the Selective Service System used their power to beat back the insubordination with the instrument of "punitive reclassification," whereby one day a draft-card burner enjoyed 2-S deferment status as an enrolled university student, but the next day found him with a 1-A fit-to-serve classification and a call from his draft board.[5]

Punishing protesters did not help the military the way it helped politicians, however. Demonstrations paid dividends for antiwar activists by the 1970s. The more militant the resistor, the less likely he was to serve. Vowing to radicalize fellow GIs in Vietnam or fellow inmates in prison, opponents dared their draft boards to call them up or jail them for refusing service. Others—more than 100,000 men—won dismissals from conscription by taking their draft boards to court for rule violations. Two scholars of the Vietnam War–era draft determined that about 570,000 men violated the draft in some way that could have resulted in prison sentences of at least five years. That figure represents about one-fifth the number of Americans who served in Vietnam during the war.[6] The government pursued only about twenty of those cases, however, both because this litigation became unpopular and because it could not keep up. Fighting the war became increasingly difficult as more men, including those at the front lines, refused to fight. "The overburdened military justice system," note L. M. Baskir and W. A. Strauss, "gave 130,000 servicemen undesirable discharges as plea bargains, sparing the armed forces the expense of trying and imprisoning" soldiers who deserted or violated the military code of conduct in some way.[7]

This is the story of peace activists who deliberately made themselves part of that problem for the government. The Camden 28 defendants included Kathleen "Cookie" Ridolfi and Anita Ricci from South Philadelphia. Ridolfi was one of the eight who broke into the draft board, along with the Reverend Michael Doyle, a recent immigrant from Ireland whose public comments on the war kept him in trouble with the archdiocese. Ricci assisted with the raid planning and casing of buildings. Rosemary ("Ro Ro") Reilly of Long Island was also in the federal building that night, while her sister Joan Reilly kept watch across the street. The Ohioan Bob Good, a former seminarian whose brother died in Vietnam, joined Doyle, Williamson, Ro Ro Reilly, and Ridolfi in the office, as did Jesuit priest Rev. Peter Fordi, VISTA volunteer Paul Couming, and the former Franciscan brother Michael Giocondo.[8] Recent Columbia University law graduate Frank Pommersheim watched from the roof of a nearby apartment building while his girlfriend, Anne Dunham, stood lookout next to Joan Reilly and two other activists, Marge Inness and Barry Musi. Inness and Musi had come down from Boston to help. The leader of the action, John Peter Grady, monitored operations from a nearby rowhouse owned by the Lutheran minister Milo Billman. Terry Buckalew and Keith Forsyth of Philadelphia, the Reverend Ned Murphy of New York, Sara Tosi and Lianne Moccia of Boston, and veteran John Swinglish of Washington, D.C., also waited in Billman's house with a local man, Mel Madden, to help transport the raiders to safety after the action. Five other people—the Jesuit Reverend Edward McGowan of New York and student Jayma Abdoo, as well as locals Martha Schemeley, Dr. William Anderson, and Eugene Dixon—assisted with the raid though they were not present in Camden on the night of the action.

The Camden 28 made their impact in the late stages of the war, seven

INTRODUCTION

years after President Lyndon Johnson's Gulf of Tonkin Resolution committed U.S. military forces to aid the struggling pro-U.S. regime of South Vietnam (Republic of Vietnam). By the time of the 1971 raid in Camden, Americans had soured on the ongoing conflict. Tens of thousands of U.S. soldiers had been killed in action when the 1968 Tet Offensive revealed that, contrary to rosy reports from the White House, the South Vietnamese and their U.S. ally were losing ground to the communist National Liberation Front (NLF). That same year, the anxious nation watched the streets of Chicago erupt during the Democratic National Convention as helmeted police officers battered protesters with batons and loaded handcuffed marchers into paddy wagons. The peaceful nonviolent opposition launched by activists on university campuses in the early 1960s had, by the end of the decade, sprouted newly militant revolutionary wings, like the bomb-planting Weather Underground.[9]

Urban uprisings further heightened the political tensions and social upheaval in this period, as fires, shattered windows, and flying bullets devastated neighborhoods across the country from Newark, New Jersey, to Detroit and Los Angeles. Camden suffered this fate as well. By coincidence, the city erupted in what became known as the "Puerto Rican riot," a racial uprising that continued for days and overlapped with the night of the Camden 28 raid. The ransacked federal offices, in fact, lay amid the downtown buildings that were most damaged by the unrest. Two police officers triggered the riot that scorched Camden's main streets when they pulled over a Puerto Rican driver for suspected drunk driving and proceeded to kick him into unconsciousness. Some of the resistors never made it to the action because they failed to penetrate the law enforcement wall that put the entire city on lockdown during the riot.[10]

Profound changes disrupting the global Catholic Church shaped the Camden 28 story as well. The Second Vatican Council, which convened in Rome over the early 1960s, put Catholicism on a path of major reforms. The Pope, bishops, cardinals, and Vaticanologists used the word *aggiornamento* prolifically at the council between 1962 and 1965 to refer to the church's "opening up" and engagement with the world.[11] Vatican II liberalized everything from the basic liturgy of worship and the role of laity in the church to the acknowledgment of truth in other faith traditions. Political radicals in the American church had hoped to ride the council into a new era of social organization, where the patriarchal hierarchy might give way to a horizontal form of leadership that either welcomed women into the priesthood or eliminated the category of "priesthood" altogether.[12] They took the opportunity to forge new models of communal family with each other along with new models of ministry. They openly broke the church's laws that prohibited marriage for clergy and nuns, expecting (or at least hoping) that other Catholics would follow their lead.

These radicals were naive in thinking that the larger church would liberalize to this extent. Priests and nuns who married had to leave their orders. In rare instances, the church excommunicated them. In their bold attempt to radically reshape Catholicism, however, they exuded a steady idealism that drew the younger, less religious, generation to them. The college-age Catholics showed less interest in the church itself but trusted these priests, nuns, and missionaries—many of whom were literally their teachers—to maintain core spiritual commitments. Secular arguments against war, racial segregation, and capitalist exploitation moved the younger Catholics into closer alignment with their nonreligious cohorts on university campuses. They still gravitated to their spiritual elders as grounding moral forces, especially at the end of the 1960s as the secular Left seemed to unravel.

The church's tentacles also reached into the group's dynamics with what scholars refer to as the "Catholic Imagination." A conceptual framework for understanding the order of the world shaped by centuries of church tradition, the Catholic Imagination is born partly from religious instruction and partly from culture. It is a mentality shared by people raised in the orbit of the church, which is based on common routines in spaces of worship and socialization. Aspects of Catholicism like the celebration of mysteries and devotion to saints have shaped how Catholics see the world and relate to the people around them. The liturgy and the church's other worship rituals reinforce this vision.[13]

Scholars who study the impact of the Catholic Imagination focus mainly on its manifestations in literature, music, art, and other forms of cultural representation. History shows us, however, that living, breathing historical figures exhibited the Catholic Imagination in their political demonstration as well. Whether pouring blood onto draft files, sitting around the table for a "last supper" before actions, or burning the Pentagon Papers to use for Lenten forehead ashes, Catholic Resistance activists drew on church rituals to mark the sacred imperative behind their actions. The Catholic Imagination was more than symbolic. It recognized possibilities for bringing the real presence of Christ into the world.[14] Activists even used their trials as occasions for celebrating spiritual community, where they took every opportunity possible to name and acknowledge the humanity of those in the courtroom.

The ways in which the Catholic Left embodied political activism made them somewhat different from other radicals but, ironically, helped them adopt the countercultural lifestyles of the larger peace movement. Histories of Vietnam War protest rarely probe the spiritual dimensions of radicalism. In most accounts, the New Left, represented by organizations like the Students for a Democratic Society, appears on the scene as a secular peace front advancing radical humanist concepts over religion. Indeed, the decline in national religiosity is often said to have begun in the sixties. The Maoist-turned-conservative David Horowitz became a popular figure on the American Right in the early 2000s with his attacks on Left-wing atheists, advancing a compelling 1960s origin story for Christianity's shrinking relevance. From the feminists who established Women's Studies departments to the Black Panthers, whom he accuses of murdering his friend Betty Van Patter, Horowitz identifies the New Left as anti-Semitic and anti-Christian killers of religion who were handicapped by "utopian anti-God illusions" borrowed from communism. His case made sense, especially to baby-boomer Republicans, who rallied behind the cold warrior Ronald Reagan when the California governor and later president of the United States admonished the "beatniks, radicals, and filthy speech advocates" on university campuses.[15]

The New Left was not antireligious, and it indeed created space for serious contemplation and reverence of the metaphysical. This respect for the sacred first came to the larger Vietnam generation of American youths through Black churches in the southern freedom struggle. The direct actions launched by the civil rights movement raised the political consciousness of Catholic Leftists, who took those lessons and fused them with the Catholic Social Teaching (CST) they knew from their own upbringing and catechism. Martin Luther King Jr. and Ralph David Abernathy Sr. were early models from the civil rights movement that was captivating the larger nation. These ministers drew from the Gospels to create a vision of economic and racial justice as well as world peace. Catholics also turned to the examples of the Catholic Worker Dorothy Day and the Trappist monk Thomas Merton to understand their Christian obligations to humanity. These overlapping visions burned bright in the hearts of activists, some of whom embraced Scripture but many of whom did not.[16]

The bloody battles against racial discrimination in the 1960s jolted awareness of disparities between Black and white, but also between drafted and deferred. Within the four walls of their communal living spaces, where they called each other "brother" and "sister," these idealists created bona fide moments of group transcendence together and carried that feeling into marches, rallies, and other public gatherings. Some sang "We Shall Overcome" and other spirituals; all sang from the political soundtrack of Bob Dylan, Joan Baez, Jimi Hendrix, and other folk and rock musicians. Believers and nonbelievers bent together to the work of alleviating hunger, poverty, and violence without much concern over differences of epistemology. Deliberately eschewing material prosperity, they chose to live close to the poverty line.

The Catholic spiritual undercurrent of this movement dovetailed with radical ideologies driving much of the New Left. While mainstream Catholics did not welcome communism or free love sexuality in their ranks, CST lent itself to Leftist critiques of capitalism. The sixties generation of activists, particularly those who broke the law, took significant risks with their lives out of deep convictions that they could take on the market economy and military-industrial complex. They strove to realize visions of communal societies where life came before profit and military dominance.

Though journalists chose the title "Catholic Left" to describe these religious activists who opposed the war, its participants did not sit comfortably alongside everyone on the Left side of the political spectrum. These peace protesters shared a deep mistrust of the "liberal" part of the Left. They critiqued the liberal political-economic order that made the United States a superpower after World War II and blamed the expansion of the federal government, tied as it was to the obscene wealth accumulation of American corporate executives, for the decline of morality and spiritual conviction. "Christian anti-liberalism," as one scholar names this "idiom," became a compelling political religion that encompassed activists across denominations who challenged the overarching logic of Western liberalism. They pushed back against the state by cultivating their own intentional communities and, when necessary, breaking laws they deemed unjust.[17]

By 1970 the twenty-somethings had taken over and the religious leaders who started the Catholic Left found their influence gradually waning. The Camden action took place during the end stages of Catholic Resistance, when people with tenuous connections to the Catholic Church outnumbered the religious. Many knew each other from the worlds of Catholic primary and secondary schools, seminaries, and universities. They rebelled against these structures while protesting the war. The priests, nuns, and lay members of Catholic Resistance thus yielded dominance to a younger and far less pious contingent of draft board raiders. This rising generation came to the work of activism through their Catholic elders but joined forces with their contemporaries in making the Left secular. Having embraced Christian nonviolence and liberation theology as guiding principles, they saw no need to hold onto the "Christian" or the "theology" in moving these ideals forward. Drawn out of the parochial world of their Catholic upbringings into the larger realm of global concerns, they recognized the imperative of legitimating other faith traditions and building community around shared commitments to basic human rights. Focusing one's life on peace and the common good no longer required the guide rails of Catholic Social Teaching by 1970.

The crucible of dissent in those decades included another important element that animated Catholic Resistance, especially the younger, college-age generation—feminism. A deceiving band-of-brothers swagger characterized the public image of the movement, as represented most often by the charismatic Berrigan brothers, Philip and Daniel. This bravado masked the significant participation and impact of women. These were New Left women who joined enthusiastically in the risk-taking, partying, and overall insubordination against the powers that be. Their political awareness developed as the middle-class liberal women's movement prompted by Betty Friedan's *Feminine Mystique* was joined by myriad expressions of feminism, from the radical Redstockings of New York to the Black womanists who challenged the white dominance of the women's liberation movement. For these women, working in the shadow of, and in many instances sleeping with, their male cohorts in Catholic Resistance forced a reckoning about patriarchy in the church and society.[18]

The Camden 28 story does not start in one place; it has multiple origins. It was an idea discussed by a group of South Jersey friends seeking to take a bolder stance against the Vietnam War in 1971. It sprang also from the pen of Pope Leo XIII when he wrote the encyclical *Rerum novarum* in 1893, which guided CST over the next century. It took shape from the early "simple supper" discussions hosted at Catholic Worker Houses of Hospitality in the 1930s. And it germinated in the seminary halls of Woodstock College on New York City's Morningside Place, where young Jesuit novitiates excitedly contemplated the new directions in which their superior, General Pedro Arrupe SJ, steered the order. When activists launched the first draft board raid of Catholic Resistance in 1967, they seized on a body of spiritual thought cultivated by these forebears.

The different trajectories ultimately intersect in 1973 at the historic Camden 28 trial. By executing a pro se defense in which many of the defendants gave statements and questioned witnesses, the 28 instrumentalized their large number into a powerful asset. It took three months, but their steady appearances inside and outside the jury box became occasions to express kindness and make personal connections. The trial was unorthodox in several ways that worked to the advantage of the defense. The 28 pursued a long-shot strategy of proudly admitting their crime to convince the jury to acquit based on its moral underpinnings. The multiple questions asked by jurors were unconventional also, as were the hours of testimony by witnesses who spoke about the atrocities in Vietnam. Indeed, the judge himself shocked participants and observers alike with the extraordinary latitude he extended to the defendants in making their case against the war and the government. At the end, he gave the jury unprecedented instructions to consider the outrageous extent to which FBI agents used their power to coax the defendants into committing the crime.

Judge Clarkson Fisher thus brought one of the most important political trials of the twentieth century to a close and marked one of the final moments in the longest peace movement of American history. Its impact can only be understood by peeling away the layers of political history, theological traditions, and personal stories that prompted women and men to raid a draft board in 1971.

PART I

The Catholic Left

Lianne Moccia remembers a conversation with her father after the FBI arrested her for assisting with the Camden raid. "Those damn Jesuits," he said; "They ruined you."[1] The Italian American bookie who raised his family in Revere, Massachusetts, had sent his daughter to an elite private Catholic high school and then to Fordham, a Jesuit university in the Bronx. He was livid when she dropped out to participate in the antiwar movement. The philosophy major had been hanging around campus in the summer of 1969 when she encountered one of her schoolteachers in the university cafeteria. The former nun Anne Walsh introduced Moccia to a group of friends who had raided a draft board in the Bronx. She told Moccia all about the movement and invited her to help with mailings and fund-raising. "So, I started probably the next day," remembers Moccia, who excitedly hopped on a bus to the North Bronx and to her future.[2]

Over the next several months, Moccia made movement work into a full-time job. The North Bronx headquarters, called "Iron Mountain," was an Episcopal church where the draft board raiders set up operations in a large hall. Moccia processed mass mailings to supporters. She also helped with the upkeep, cooking, and cleaning to maintain the space. Moccia was enthusiastic about helping with the 1971 raid in Camden when its organizers put the plans in motion because it included her friends from New York and Boston. "My people were all there," she explained in a later interview. Since she was broke, she hitchhiked down the New Jersey Turnpike to a rest stop near Exit 4, where she waited for another activist to fetch her and transport her to a movement apartment in Camden.

Arrested with the other twenty-seven after the raid, Moccia continued to fight with her father in the months after she left jail because she disobeyed his command to stay away from Camden. Then he died.[3]

To Moccia's horror, her father had a heart attack shortly after Christmas 1972. By the time of his death in January, Moccia had become disillusioned with Catholicism, especially its hierarchy. The budding feminist was done with priests. She remembers feeling angry that some of the clergy from the Camden action traveled to Massachusetts to support her and her family. "Again," she remembers, they were "getting the honor and the attention" when this was her father's funeral. They cocelebrated a High Mass with local priests at St. Anthony's church in Revere, a replica of an Italian basilica replete with marble and statues. At the same time, she observed that these men became a powerful source of consolation to her family. As she watched them giving genuine "solace and comfort" to her mother, she thought about telling her family that "these aren't the priests that you . . . these aren't priests like you think."[4]

Lianne Moccia developed a complicated relationship with the people who radicalized her, and the church that had incubated their political consciousness. The priests who said her father's funeral Mass had built the Catholic Left from the church's social teachings. Nuns and laywomen had been just as important as priests, though they found themselves relegated to secondary roles even after performing the riskiest work. An older generation of late-twenty- and thirty-somethings started and led the movement—women such as Moccia's former teacher Anne Walsh. Some had recently returned from Latin America, Africa, or other parts of the world to apply lessons learned in the mission fields to America's social problems.

Animated by the freedom struggle unfolding in the American South, these seasoned radicals pivoted to antiwar protest after the 1964 escalation in Vietnam. The younger baby-boomer generation, which included Lianne Moccia, attended lectures by this vanguard generation, which were often held at the prayer vigils and peace demonstrations that had become radicalizing spaces of Catholic universities. Deeply impressed by what they heard in these talks, many students came to believe that stopping the war in Vietnam was more important than going to class. As the conflict dragged on, their friendships and romances carried them through the fury. Moccia came to the viewpoint that "these aren't priests like you think" by experiencing the downside of these relationships.

This radical spiritual ferment paradoxically thrived in an antimodern subculture. Indeed, understanding the relationship between Catholicism and the American Left requires an exploration of this social justice history that unfolded alongside ongoing tensions between the church and social progress. For much of its long life, the Vatican had sought to insulate Catholics from transformational forces like science, technology, and capitalism as protection against possible corruption to the soul.

Moccia and other feminists had to contend with church authorities who regarded developments like the women's movement and sexual liberation warily, as dangerous threats to traditional values.

While developing this criminally nonviolent approach to disrupting military induction, the Catholic Left put the "social" into "social movement." They tramped around, couch surfed in living rooms, or moved in with one another. Movement ideals mixed with sex and communal living to engender feelings of kinship that, in many instances, substituted for the families who rejected their choices. Some of the Catholic Leftists fell in love and got married, including priests and sisters who forfeited their membership in religious orders to do so. Sexual dalliances flourished in the heady atmosphere of love, drink, and drugs. Some religious simply left the clergy or convent as the movement swept their lives in other directions away from the institutional church. And it all started with four Christian men at a draft board in Baltimore.

CHAPTER ONE

A Movement within a Movement

The first Catholic Left action did not attract much attention outside activist circles, though it did provide a valuable lesson. The government, it turns out, did not duplicate draft records. The raiders executed their demonstration mainly to highlight the class disparities inherent in the Vietnam conscription system. Its ceremonial aspects—the Catholic elements—were paramount in their minds. They did not much hope that their quick, four-person demonstration would do much to disrupt the induction process. Philip Berrigan, the primary instigator, had consulted with a civil rights lawyer ahead of time, before working out the details with three friends: teacher and writer Dave Eberhardt, United Church of Christ minister James Mengel, and artist Thomas Lewis.[1]

On October 17, 1967, in the middle of the business day, the team forced their way into a draft board located on the first floor of the Baltimore Customs House. This stately government building sat just north of the city's Inner Harbor.[2] With Lewis serving as lookout, the others entered the six-story structure with its striking beaux art edifice. They first approached a clerk to file a request, as a distraction. After the woman turned her back, Berrigan, Eberhardt, and Mengel followed her to the cabinets, where they hurriedly pulled out drawers and poured blood (mostly from a poultry plant but mixed with a pint of their own) on the files. The women staff members screamed and tried to shut the opened drawers while pulling the men away from the records. Standing near the location where assassinated president Abraham Lincoln had lain in state a century earlier, one of the federal employees wrestled in vain with the tall, white-haired Berrigan as the much stronger priest emptied materials onto the floor. Members of the press, who had followed the trespassers into the office, documented the entire confrontation with the police before the FBI arrived. The action took all of thirty seconds.[3]

Only afterward did Berrigan, Mengel, Eberhardt, and Lewis discover that they had damaged the sole copies of those files. Once the records disappeared, the impact was permanent. The Selective Service Office, in other words, did not maintain a centralized system for maintaining draft files. The staff had to reassemble nearly all the missing materials from scratch. This realization delighted the activists, who recognized a vulnerability they could exploit with nonviolence. By stealing or shredding the paper trail, they could interfere with the government's conscription operations, which might slow the wheels of induction and quite possibly save the lives of draftees.[4]

The religious men who broke into the Customs House that mild fall day did not trespass with visions of future nighttime burglaries, which the Catholic Left ultimately undertook.[5] Their intent was merely to use religious symbols for the purposes of political demonstration. The Baltimore Four poured blood, according to Philip Berrigan, to "anoint" the files. They invited observers and let law enforcement officers arrest them to involve others in this ritual of consecration.[6]

The press statements prepared ahead of time outlined the political and religious purpose of their action, evoking aspects of the Catholic Imagination. Over the next year those features became defining elements of the emerging movement. The Baltimore raid attracted attention because of these spiritual gestures, especially from opponents of the war who were eager to make a bolder statement with their own activism. The unique combination of blood, prayers, and priests raised heads. The precirculated memo described the raid as a "sacrificial and constructive act" of penance for the waste of American and Vietnamese lives, in which all Americans were complicit. Confronting "the idolatry of property and the war machine that makes property of men," they asserted that "America would rather protect its empire of overseas profits than welcome its black people, rebuild its slums and cleanse its air and water." They concluded by calling on peacemakers to join them in escalating the resistance in this way.[7] Before leaving the scene in handcuffs, the Reverend Mengel offered a Bible to one of the office clerks. She accepted the gift, but only so she could hit him over the head with it.[8]

Though Mengel was Protestant and the raiders invoked broad Christian principles of peace straight from the Bible, the event's drama derived from its ritualistic Catholic features, like the church's traditions surrounding the incarnation. Non-Catholic Christians had discarded these practices long ago. The Reformation had cast the centuries-old Eucharistic process of "eating the body" and "drinking the blood" of Christ as morbid and cultish remnants of the medieval church-states. Sacramentalism, which had long been frowned on by Protestants since the day Luther penned his ninety-five theses, lived on in the Catholic way of ritualizing the death of Jesus.[9]

By pouring blood on files, the activists drew from deep theological underpinnings to make a point about the violence in Vietnam. In Catholic liturgy, the Eucharist represents a sacrament in which ordained clergy convert bread and wine into the body and blood of Christ. This "transubstantiation" reenacts the biblical last supper when Jesus Christ prepared his disciples for his coming execution on the cross. Most Protestant denominations continued to celebrate communion as part of their religious services, but as a memorial of the Last Supper rather than a conversion of Eucharistic substance. Not only does the Catholic Mass unfold around the sacrament as the central element of liturgy, but it also elevates the "mystery" surrounding this process into a sacred force that imbues God into the substance of all living things.[10]

This sacramental worldview stands out as a defining characteristic of the Catholic Imagination, though it would be misguided to imagine that every Catholic has believed in the mystical process of transubstantiation in the same way. Writer Thomas Howard describes sacramentalism as the "physical" point where divinity touches humanity.[11] Sacramentalism pervaded Catholic culture of the twentieth century. Like other Christians, Catholics recognized the historical Jesus of Nazareth as the son of God, through whom divinity took human form. Catholic theology and spiritual practice, however, extended this recognition of divinity into all aspects of life, recognizing God's physical existence in the material world.[12] As sociologist Andrew Greeley noted, "Our imagination is necessarily sacramental because it believes that God is hiding everywhere—like Richard Wilbur's Cheshire smile, which sets us fearfully free—to reveal the love with which He passionately pursues."[13]

By the time of the Customs House raid in 1967, the Catholic Imagination had found creative expression in the American public sphere for decades. An enthusiasm for reforming and invigorating Mass rituals spread at the turn of the twentieth century in a development that became known as the "liturgical movement." Its ideas animated Catholics to bring the spirit of the Sunday Mass into the other six days of the week by addressing social concerns. Indeed, the growing immigrant church of the United States celebrated the incarnation in every aspect of life, from home and school to work and social gatherings.

These new attitudes about religious life also found expression through the formation of new institutions created by Catholics. Some of these organizations operated within the managing structure of the archdiocese and others functioned independently. In a movement known as

"Catholic Action," lay Catholics worked together to do God's work in society not by evangelizing non-Catholics, but by embarking on community projects. They eagerly ventured beyond the world of the parish confines to address larger social and economic problems.[14]

Though most of this work unfolded on the ground in American cities and beyond, the Vatican was watching. In 1943, Pope Pius XII fanned the fervor of the liturgical and action movements with his encyclical *Mystici Corporis Christi* (Mystical Body of Christ), which declared that all of humanity constituted one body with Christ as the head. "As the Mystical Body," writes historian Karen Johnson, "laypeople joined Christ in his sacrifice by placing themselves metaphorically on the altar during Mass, and then entered the world with this sacrificial attitude, strengthened by having partaken Christ's literal body and blood."[15] Johnson documents how this excitement for the Mystical Body prompted Catholics in Chicago to launch a flurry of projects over the 1920s and 1930s. Animated by the Catholic Worker movement, which developed during the Great Depression, one project known as "Friendship House" brought Black and white Christians together for interracial community work.[16]

By consecrating the draft board files with blood in 1967, the religious intruders in the Baltimore Customs House started a new practice that drew power from this Catholic sacramentalist worldview. In these "hit and stay" raids, as they came to be known, activists damaged conscription records openly in the fluorescent light of the office workday and submitted publicly to law enforcement after the bloody-but-nonviolent anointing was said and done. They deliberately sought arrest. As they had hoped and anticipated, news of the Baltimore Customs House raid rippled quickly through the webbed friendships of radical Catholics, especially as observers learned that draft boards did not typically duplicate files.[17] They had discovered a way to strike at disparities baked into the American system of induction.

The Baltimore Four thus started a movement within a movement. They introduced the Catholic Imagination into the political landscape of the antiwar protest that had already been underway for several years. Peace activists, mainly university students, had been demonstrating against American involvement in Vietnam since the United States expanded troop deployments in 1964. As frustrations with the lingering war grew in the latter part of the decade, their attention turned increasingly to the Selective Service System as a focal point of dissent.

Opponents of the war attacked the unjust classification system through which local communities executed the draft process. "1A" designated men whom draft boards deemed most fit to serve by virtue of their youth and fitness. It also became a marker of lower social and economic status, however, since affluent men had the resources and knowledge to avoid this classification. The sorting system, which became known as "channeling," sent some men off to fight in Indochina while diverting more privileged youths to safer national guard duties or protective educational institutions. Though most of those who served in Vietnam enlisted for duty, about 20 percent of troops were draftees. By the end of 1965, the Selective Service System was conscripting between 35,000 and 45,000 men every month, more than five times the monthly calls of 1962 and 1963.[18] In 1966, 1967, and 1968, the agency drafted approximately 300,000 men each year.[19] In the end, 15 million men of draft age avoided service through loopholes in the classification system (see figures 1 and 2).[20]

Men started burning their draft cards in public as a form of protest against the Vietnam War in 1966. They did not suddenly develop the idea to stage these public conflagrations on their own, however. World War II–era peace activists had introduced this tactic almost twenty years earlier. The first such demonstration reportedly took place at a 1947 event sponsored by the War Resistors League that drew about four hundred

	Military Service	Vietnam Service	Combat Service
Low-Income	40%	19%	15%
Middle-Income	30%	12%	7%
High-Income	24%	9%	7%
High-School Dropouts	42%	18%	14%
High-School Graduates	45%	21%	17%
College Graduates	23%	12%	9%

FIGURE 1. Likelihood of Service

Much of the protest against the Vietnam War focused on the system of induction, which privileged white, educated men with means through a process known as "channeling." Two social scientists who studied the Vietnam draft, L. M. Baskir and W. A. Strauss, illustrated its racial and economic disparities with graphs and tables reprinted here from their 1978 book *Chance and Circumstance: The Draft, the War, and the Vietnam Generation.* The "Likelihood of Service" table, reprinted here, breaks down the odds of being drafted by income and education levels. From L. M. Baskir and W. A. Strauss, *Chance and Circumstance: The Draft, the War, and the Vietnam Generation* (New York: Knopf, 1978), 9.

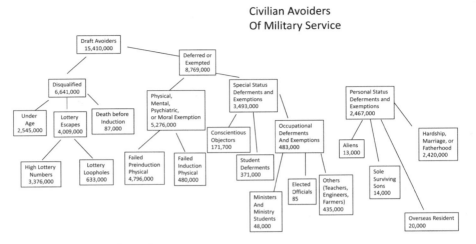

FIGURE 2. Draft Avoiders
The "Civilian Avoiders of Military Service" tree, featured in L. M. Baskir and W. A. Strauss, *Chance and Circumstance*, and partially reprinted here, shows the multiple ways in which registrants could secure deferments or exemptions from service in Vietnam by demonstrating that their occupation, educational status, or health conditions should excuse them. The decentralized nature of the draft process enabled men with connections and resources to take advantage of these loopholes. From L. M. Baskir and W. A. Strauss, *Chance and Circumstance: The Draft, the War, and the Vietnam Generation* (New York: Knopf, 1978), 30–31, fig. 2, 278–82.

people. Crowds watched men burn their own draft cards. That did not stop the draft, though. Even after World War II had ended, the Selective Service System continued operations, and within a year Congress legislated the first peacetime draft system into existence.[21] Activists resumed the draft-card burnings and turn-ins after President Lyndon Johnson started the Vietnam War inductions nineteen years later. Most of those who spoke up described how their own personal conscience prevented them from participating in a brutal war lacking a principled justification. Many also mentioned the race and class disparities of the draft.[22]

"I am a pacifist.... I do what I believe as an individual. I believe in the law but when the law violates my conscience," declared David Reed in front of the Boston Courthouse before lighting his draft card with a portable gas-burning stove in 1966. Reed could not finish making his statement, though, because a mob of angry high-school students jumped him mid-sentence.[23] David O'Brien of Boston wrote to his own draft board in similar terms, explaining, "I could never serve in the armed forces in any capacity for I consider the existence of the war machine the furthest step taken toward the demise of mankind, not only physically but morally."[24] Though white men dominated the draft-card demonstrations, much of their protest focused on the inequities built into the American system of conscription, which disproportionately impacted economically marginalized Black men. Gary Graham Hicks, a Black member of the Committee for Non-Violent Action (CNVA), lamented out loud while burning his own card that "we couldn't even guarantee a fair election in Mississippi."[25]

These demonstrations generated momentum in the antiwar movement of the 1960s by drawing attention to the numerous loopholes in the draft, especially its long list of designations for deferral or exemption from service. Some, like 4A, designated registrants who had already completed service or were "sole surviving" sons. Though permitted to serve if they wanted to enlist, draft boards did not call up these brothers of fallen soldiers. The 2S men were students and 2Ds were seminarians. The 2A deferrals also excused men in civilian occupations deemed essential enough by the file readers to excuse them from battle.[26]

Draft boards had more than twenty classifications from which to choose, which created wide latitude for boards to bestow favor on men from advantageous backgrounds. A survey conducted by Lawrence M. Baskir and William A. Strauss revealed that men from low-income backgrounds were twice as likely to serve in Vietnam as their more affluent peers.[27] The military's own postwar studies showed that enlisted men with college degrees had a 42 percent chance of serving in Vietnam, as compared with 70 percent of enlisted men who dropped out of high school. Two sociologists who studied the draft in Chicago learned that men from neighborhoods with low levels of education in the city were four times more likely to die in Vietnam than those from better-educated parts of the city.[28]

The classification loopholes that attracted so much scrutiny did not originate in the 1960s. The problem started decades earlier but became more acute over the decade because Vietnam did not inspire young men across class categories to enlist en masse as they had in World War I and World War II. The government officials who established the system imagined that community members, who were closer to the day-to-day events of their neighborhoods, could perform a civic duty by conscripting from a population familiar to them, what the Selective Service director, Lewis Hershey, described as "little groups of neighbors."[29] These unpaid volunteers, however, had the burden of classifying hundreds or thousands of men in their meetings, which typically occurred once or twice a month. When left to their own decisions, they fell into a pattern of "channeling" men from disadvantaged backgrounds into combat.[30]

As critics mounted opposition to this system, the government quickly reformed the process between 1969 and 1971. Officials instituted a draft lottery that impartially drew birthdates to determine the order of call for men born between 1944 and 1950. Though this modification did make it harder for draft boards to channel, affluent and educated men still had more resources to dodge or defer than men who were less fortunate. The 1971 amendments to the Selective Service law also adjusted the age range for induction. By only giving lottery numbers to men in the calendar years of their nineteenth birthday, the new draft law excluded an entire nation of eighteen-year-old male college freshmen from service.[31]

The lottery might have helped Richard Nixon in the 1972 presidential election by exempting new voters, but it did not dampen the fervor of the draft resistance movement.[32] Between 1965 and 1972, about 25,000 men burned or destroyed their own draft cards. The gesture was not merely symbolic, as it posed serious risks of imprisonment or induction as retaliation. Although the Justice Department only prosecuted fifty men for destroying draft cards, it indicted more than 25,000 men for violating draft law in this period, sending 4,000 of them to prison. About 370 of those who were convicted served five or more years.[33] When radical pacifist David Gutknecht refused to register for the draft in 1967, his local board in Minnesota retaliated by reclassifying him and ordering the activist to report for service.[34] Historian Michael Foley reports that 75 percent of the draft resisters who responded to his questionnaire noted that boards punitively reclassified them.[35]

Almost seven months after the Customs House action in 1967, resistors launched another raid in the nearby Maryland community of Catonsville. The group targeted a draft board office housed in the Knights of Columbus Hall. This location provided both the symbolic significance and spatial features that, its organizers hoped, would attract public notice. By choosing a building belonging to a Catholic fraternal order, the demonstrators could highlight the role of church complicity in Vietnam bloodshed. Located in a suburb, it stood next to an open grassy space that ideally accommodated the public outdoor display for the journalists invited to document the spectacle. This time, nine raiders seized the draft files, stuffed them into wire trash bins, doused them with napalm, and ignited a blaze. As cameras rolled and flash bulbs clicked, the activists stood side-by-side facing the flames and black smoke. After crossing themselves, three of the men said prayers. All nine tossed lit matches into the fire to show their individual and collective responsibility for the act before clasping hands and reciting the Our Father. Within five minutes, police officers arrived, took statements, arrested the nine, and took them to jail.[36]

Unlike the original Baltimore Four raid, the Catonsville Nine action captured and sustained media attention. This event generated the enthusiasm that carried the movement into 1973. Reporters covered the group's activities during their time in county lockup, where their inability to post bail kept them incarcerated as they awaited indictment. The jailhouse fast in the men's unit made for great copy, especially with quotes from the sympathetic Catholic warden, who told reporters that the prisoners' fast mimicked that of Jesus Christ after his baptism. "It's a religious thing," he explained to a *Newsweek* interviewer, "like Christ in the wilderness."[37] The six male defendants communed with each other in their spacious cellblock, where the accommodating warden provided four cubicles, an open sitting area, and tables at which they worked diligently to keep the action going. Marjorie Melville and Mary Moylan could not partake in the group activities because they were by themselves in the women's unit upstairs.[38]

In addition to hosting evening seminars for their fellow inmates and assembling a ten-foot collage of news clippings about peace politics, the men churned out writing for the outside world. They turned the Baltimore County Jail into a publicity machine. David Darst issued a public letter about the symbolic and literal intents of their action. With their "iron wrench" that pried open filing cabinets, they sought to "monkey wrench" the draft system. In a gesture that directly alluded to Martin Luther King Jr.'s writing campaign from a Birmingham cell, Philip Berrigan penned a "Letter from a Baltimore Jail," which first appeared in the journal *Christianity and Crisis* that summer. The essay elaborated on the many reasons why he and his cohort felt the need to destroy property.[39]

Newspaper coverage intensified as the court moved the defendants through the stages of due process. Much of the reportage favored the nine raiders and much of it condemned them. Judge Edward Northrop sparked mass outrage when, on the day of the Catonsville indictment, he handed down harsh sentences to Tom Lewis and Philip Berrigan for their role in the Baltimore Customs House raid—six years in Pennsylvania's Lewisburg prison. The *Boston Globe* lobbed a stinging critique of the court for the severe punishment of two peace activists who were hardly "a moral threat."

A positive buzz reportedly arose among youths who admired the brazen act of defiance against the government. One student activist at the University of Pennsylvania called them outrageous—in a good way. "These people are crazy," he wrote. "Crazy like Jesus. Crazy like Che

Guevara. Crazy like all of us said we would be had we lived in Germany under Hitler."[40] A Johns Hopkins student active in Students for a Democratic Society (SDS) lauded the "courage" of the Catonsville Nine in an interview with the Baltimore *Evening Sun* and predicted that they would succeed in making their point. He also underscored the importance of priests who could "lend an air of respectability" to the actions.[41] John Deedy, managing editor of *Commonweal*, praised the nine in the "News and Views" section of the Catholic periodical where he observed, "The world would be better off with more rather than fewer Berrigans, and it will profit from their witness, impractical though this may occasionally appear to be."[42]

The Catonsville Nine also drew significant publicity from scathing attacks in the Catholic press. A group of alumni from a Benedictine seminary in Indiana criticized the raiders in the diocesan newspaper of Indianapolis. In a letter to the editor of the *Criterion*, they reported how "stunned" they were "to find people we are supposed to look to for advice and understanding, and to whom our children will look to [*sic*]—our clergy—are advocating complete rebellion and rejection of the duties, and rights contained within our citizenship."[43]

National and local news sources expressed a range of responses to the action, reflecting a split among Catholics in their views about the war in Vietnam. "The very public and very illegal nature of the raids in Baltimore and Catonsville," notes scholar Penelope Moon, "called into question Catholic patriotism and initiated a debate among Catholics over what constituted acceptable Catholic behavior and what it meant to be a loyal American."[44] The celebrated southern writer Walker Percy equated the actions of the Catonsville Nine with those of the Ku Klux Klan. In *Commonweal*, for which he wrote frequently, the convert to Catholicism said he "would be hard-pressed to explain to a Klansman why he should be put in jail and the Berrigans set free."[45]

The denunciations of unpatriotic, rebellious activity as failures to fulfill duties of citizenship come from a deep place in church tradition. Catholics historically supported war efforts to show that they could be loyal to their governments. This behavior reflected a common insecurity among people who, as a religious minority that acknowledged the Pope's authority in far-off Rome, had to demonstrate their allegiance to state leaders. When Catholic radicals faced this rebuke of their disloyalty in the 1960s, they were dealing, not merely with Cold War nationalist fervor but with a centuries-old inheritance of church-state relations. They reckoned with an expressive patriotism that became a distinguishing characteristic of mainstream Catholic culture in the United States. By denouncing the president, the FBI, and the U.S. military, radicals thus rejected a defining feature of the religious community that had raised them.

Centuries of church doctrine also justified soldiering for Catholics. Theologians first started articulating ideas about the appropriate relationship between Catholics and secular potentates in the first century. This "just war" tradition first appeared in the works of Augustine and found further articulation by Thomas Aquinas in the thirteenth century. In the early fifth century, Augustine described war as a "miserable necessity."[46] Aquinas argued that state leaders should exercise authority to make decisions about wars and outlined criteria for discerning whether situations warranted applications of violence. Augustine drew from both the Old Testament and the New to show that, while peace was the goal, warfare sometimes represented an unavoidable means to achieving peace.[47] Aquinas elaborated on this assertion by enumerating the conditions that made a war just, namely, that it had to be declared by a lawful public authority, waged in the interest of peace and the common good, unharmful to civilians, proportional to the threat it annihilated, and deemed likely to succeed.[48]

Since the era of Constantine and the Holy Roman Empire, then, Catholicism made room for state-sponsored militarism in its teachings. Church officials drew from this theology in subsequent centuries as they blessed warriors headed into battle, most notably during the Crusades waged between the years 1000 and 1300. Indeed, by flexing the definitions of "just" and "common good," the church perpetrated violence liberally throughout the ages, especially when it justified the slaughter of nonconformists.[49]

The explosion of political tensions in early twentieth-century Europe presented an opportunity for faithful immigrants to demonstrate fealty to their new home of America. This form of patriotic support for U.S. forces in World War I became a means by which Catholics, though inwardly focused on their own ethnic immigrant enclaves, could demonstrate civic participation in their adopted nation.[50] Led by Cardinal James Gibbons of Baltimore, American bishops endorsed universal military training in a 1917 letter to President Woodrow Wilson after Congress declared war on Germany. "We are all true Americans," they declared, "ready as our age, our ability, and our conditions will permit, to do whatsoever is in us to do, for the preservation, the progress and the triumph of our beloved country."[51] The Knights of Columbus, moreover, provided religious and recreational opportunities to soldiers overseas and stateside as the National Catholic War Council formed to assist the U.S. government with providing services. This group ultimately became the United States Conference of Catholic Bishops (USCCB), one of the most important organizations governing the U.S. church today.[52]

Catholic customs of patriotic participation in warfare continued throughout the twentieth century into the Vietnam War era. Church officials in the United States made it difficult for laymen to avoid military service on the basis of principle. The bishops of the United States mostly refused to support conscientious objectors (COs).[53] They had already decided in 1939, before the U.S. declaration of war, that when draft legislation came before Congress, they would maintain their opposition to the conscription of priests and seminarians but not lay Catholics.[54]

The bishops' stance on conscription put Catholics at odds with the American "peace churches," which had been incorporating nonviolence into their theology since the nineteenth century. From the prophet Isaiah ("They shall beat their swords into plowshares") to the Gospel stories of Jesus ("Blessed are the peacemakers"), the Bible repeatedly exhorts readers to repudiate violence.[55] A handful of Christian religious communities that were planted in nineteenth-century America, namely, the Quakers, Mennonites, and Church of the Brethren, made peace a central defining tenet. In the twentieth century, leaders in these churches developed ideas for what became known as Civilian Public Service (CPS) camps, also known as "Peace Camps." These alternative service programs, which were supervised by the federal government, performed humanitarian duties for the nation. The men worked without pay and with their expenses covered, not by the government, but by their own churches. Catholic men were underrepresented among the COs, but they could avoid the conflict by working in two locations for nonmilitary service, Camps Stoddard and Warner. Unlike the Quaker, Mennonite, and Brethren camps, Catholic CO camps operated without financial backing from the church.[56]

Protestant peace theology also informed a tradition of "Christian nonviolence" during World War I through the operations of an antiwar organization called Fellowship of Reconciliation (FOR). FOR represented a "radical religious vanguard" that adopted nonviolence as an "active process of interpreting religion in the modern world" rather than "a fixed dogma," notes historian Kip Kosek. Led by internationally known figures like A. J. Muste, the pacifist fellowship denounced all violence as anti-Christian. In its many decades of existence, FOR cultivated an ecumenical theology that welcomed traditions such as Gandhian nonviolence. It remained distinctly Christian, however, in its ritualism. Kosek describes these "acts" as theatrical by definition. FOR made nonviolence into "a calculated performance attuned to the sympathies of audiences."[57]

Catholic support for American wars continued into the Vietnam era, in large part due to the power of Cardinal Francis Spellman, archbishop of New York. Spellman supported the war in Vietnam until the day he died in 1967. He called for "total victory." When the United States commenced hostilities in Vietnam, the archbishop was the most influential Catholic in the United States, with national and international political ties dating back decades. Spellman had been interested in Vietnam since the early 1950s, when he supported the presidency of a Catholic, Ngo Dinh Diem. Watching Diem's refugees flee from the communist north pushed Spellman to back the American intervention. North Vietnamese leader Ho Chi Minh's communism blinded the cardinal, like many others, to the mass annihilation of the Vietnamese perpetrated by the United States to win this ideological battle.[58]

Spellman was powerful, but his attitudes about the war did not represent the entire magisterium. The Catholic Church, as an international body led by the Vatican in Rome, did not take a unified stand on the Vietnam War. The Pope unequivocally denounced the war in Indochina, but his many cardinals, bishops, and priests who represented the church officialdom did not line up behind him. In 1965, Paul VI made a historic trip to the United Nations, where he doubled down on his institution's responsibility to establish global peace, telling delegates that it was a sacred duty placed in their hands.[59] Paul issued the encyclical *Christi Matri*, which reminded Catholics of the special blessings invoked by praying the rosary to the Virgin Mary in the month of October. But now, he urged, there was a pressing need to pray for negotiations and peace. He pressed world leaders to "bring about the necessary conditions for the laying down of arms before the possibility of doing so is taken away by the pressure of events. Those in whose hands rests the safety of the human race should realize that in this day and age they have a very grave obligation in conscience."[60]

The division between the Pope and Spellman over Vietnam represented, to some degree, a disagreement among Western liberal Catholics over the meaning of human rights and how the teachings on social justice should dictate the church's approach for promoting that goal. Many of the faithful aligned themselves with the hawkish, anticommunist foreign policy posture of the previous president, the Catholic John F. Kennedy. Kennedy became a beloved figure on the world stage for his bold declarations and assertions of power against communist aggressors. While his "Ich bin ein Berliner" speech demonstrated the United States' elevation to leader of the free world, it also symbolized the arrival of Catholics into the cultural and political elite. Kennedy and Spellman operated at the forefront of this establishment at the outset of the 1960s.[61]

Spellman also became powerful because he led the American church in its prime. The economic boom and baby boom of the 1950s sparked a parish construction boom as well. The pluralist zeitgeist also made it possible for Catholics to participate in mainstream society more than ever before while a nationwide religious revival boosted membership in many different religious groups.[62] Church and synagogue attendance increased by 30 percent in the 1950s, going beyond the population increase of 19 percent.[63] White evangelical Christianity entered a postwar revival led by the charismatic Billy Graham.[64] Congress put "under God" into the Pledge of Allegiance in 1954 and put "In God We Trust" on newly minted coinage.[65] The mainline Protestantism that had dominated the American political and social establishment for centuries had been eroding, but Jews, Mormons, Catholics, Black evangelicals, and born-again white people forged an energized religious culture around a fused concept of "Judeo-Christianity."[66]

The church had an outsized impact in this period also because Catholics entered American culture through new media and imagery. Catholic characters in movies, like the nineteenth-century peasant saint Bernadette, represented purity, loyalty, and morality. Americans celebrated these values in the wartime era. Catholic veterans accessed benefits of the GI bill to lift their family into the middle class by attending college or university and by buying a single-family home in one of the new housing developments. Many earned union wages, which included health insurance and a pension, in automobile-manufacturing plants. Unlike their childhoods in city parishes, these postwar Catholics raised their children in a less insulated world, where they tended to mix with Protestants in their neighborhood associations and public-school activities. They socialized in commercial spaces where they would not have been recognized as Catholic, and where the cornucopia of entertainment, shopping, and dining experiences welcomed their dollars. In places like southern New Jersey's Cherry Hill Mall, which opened on the site of a former sixteen-acre farm near Camden in 1961, Catholics and Protestants grew increasingly indistinguishable from each other over the years.

Spellman was the church's version of an economic growth liberal, against whom the fledgling Catholic Left defined itself. Spellman criticized Pope John as incompetent while denouncing the adoption of vernacular languages in the Mass liturgy (instead of Latin) and openly supporting the war in Vietnam. Known as "Cardinal Moneybags" for his financial skills, Spellman adroitly negotiated better interest rates with banks for his church expansion spree in the New York archdiocese and consolidation of parish-building programs. Spellman was the builder of churches, schools, and hospitals in this period. When Eleanor Roosevelt criticized the use of federal funds given to parochial schools, Spellman lashed out at the former first lady, calling her "anti-Catholic." Spellman preferred Nixon over Kennedy, the first Catholic to ever serve as president, because he opposed Kennedy's liberalism. When asked to send a delegation of nuns and priests to the civil rights march from Selma to Montgomery, Alabama, however, he agreed. He also fought against racial discrimination in public housing in New York City.[67]

The politically centrist Spellman disliked activists, especially Daniel Berrigan. In late 1965, the Jesuit spoke at the funeral Mass for Roger LaPorte, who famously lit himself on fire to protest the war. Berrigan infuriated Spellman by comparing LaPorte to Christ, who was killed by the "violence of others." That same year, Spellman traveled to Vietnam and spoke to American troops while wearing full military regalia. To punish Berrigan, the cardinal exiled the him to South America for several months.

The growing ranks of Catholic radicals who opposed the war in Vietnam stung Spellman like a thorn in his vestments. He did not like the way they challenged authority, especially *his* authority, even as he voiced his own dissent against the Pope. Catholic radicals also challenged the very structures and boundaries of the church by working through organizations outside its reach. In their opposition to hierarchy, however, radicals like Daniel Berrigan drew from a corpus of church texts to counteract the long-standing Catholic tradition of sanctioning combat.

Catholicism offered a wealth of teaching that supported arguments for peace. Even as the just war tradition endured into the 1960s, the church had established a body of documents that served Catholics who were opposed to the escalation in Vietnam. The draft board raids became popular because the priests, nuns, lay Catholics who launched the Catholic Left drew from an extensive body of theological texts dating back to the late nineteenth century known as Catholic Social Teaching (CST). For years they had been adapting CST to the challenges they faced in the mission fields of Central America and Southeast Asia as well as the dispossessed neighborhoods of urban America. The theological basis for their action developed in a growing milieu of religious thinkers who elevated peace and economic justice as central concerns for the church of the twentieth century. When radical Catholics poured the blood on draft files for the first time in 1967, they invoked a set of traditions and body of theology developed around the common good and peace that was at least as deep as just war theory in the church's teachings.

Catholic Resistance drew heavily from the spiritual teachings of one figure in particular, the monk Thomas Merton. The British Merton had, by then, become a popular author who interpreted the church's social teaching within the context of Cold War threats to humanity. He was a convert to Catholicism who wrote voluminously from a remote religious community that he rarely left as his books drew acclaim across continents. The onetime bacchanalian first immersed himself in Catholic theology as World War II started ravaging the world around him. His dazzling personal journey to the faith captivated readers, Catholic and otherwise. Though he did not join or actively support the draft board raids conducted by his friends, as he feared they could catalyze violence, Merton articulated the arguments for peace that became the basis for these actions.[68]

Merton's journey into the peace movement started with an ill-spent youth. Young Thomas squandered a world-class education at Cambridge University provided by his affluent grandparents with a zealous consumption of alcohol and womanizing. But he found redemption after relocating to the United States, where he enrolled at Columbia University and converted to Catholicism. Trying and failing to become a priest with the Dominican order, Merton joined the Order of Cistercians of Strict Observance, otherwise known as the "Trappist" monks. By the end of the 1960s, Merton had become one of the most prolific and elegiac Catholic nonfiction writers of the twentieth century. He published more than fifty books before dying of an accidental electrocution in 1968.[69]

The peace activists who gravitated to Merton found themselves animated by his deeply personalist articulation of nonviolence. This vision touched the hearts of millions, who often found their anonymity in a world controlled by Washington elites to be crippling and isolating. Merton was a bard to activists seeking to understand their divine purpose. He wrote of a spiritual drive that originated within a person's core and spread outward, in a process that started with inner transformation and extended out to the community and out to the world.[70] Merton saw this development as an eschatological certainty, a sacramental gift from God bestowed through the incarnation. Peace came to humankind through the figure of Christ, which meant it could not be undone; it was already unfolding.[71] In "Peace: Christian Duties and Perspectives," he wrote in 1961 that "the Christian is and must be by his very adoption as the son

FIGURE 3. Thomas Merton at Gethsemani
The British-born Trappist monk Thomas Merton became a celebrated spiritual writer over the 1950s and 1960s. From his home at the Gethsemani Abbey in Kentucky, the Catholic convert penned numerous books and essays on prayer, solitude, and community. His works on Christian nonviolence made him one of the most influential voices of the Vietnam era. Photograph of Thomas Merton by Sibylle Akers; used with permission from the Thomas Merton Center at Bellarmine University.

of God, in Christ, a peacemaker (Matthew 5:9). . . . He is bound," continued Merton, "to imitate the Savior who, instead of defending Himself with twelve legions of angels (Matthew 26:53) allowed Himself to be nailed to the Cross and died Praying for His executioners."[72]

Five years later, Merton authored a chilling essay that juxtaposed the way in which Adolf Eichmann "sanely" dispatched orders to execute twenty million Jews with those he calls the "well-adapted ones." These apparatchiks, he writes, "can without qualms and without nausea aim the missiles and press the buttons that will initiate the great festival of destruction that they, the sane ones, have prepared." He concluded that sanity has as much value to modern human beings as "the huge bulk and muscles of the dinosaur."[73]

Merton corresponded with many influential Catholics of his day, including brothers Philip and Daniel Berrigan, who had been gaining notoriety for their outspoken opposition to the Vietnam War during the 1960s. These friendships started a few years before the Berrigans launched the draft board raids. The letters flying between these writer-activists also came to and from Dorothy Day, who cofounded the Catholic Worker movement with her friend Peter Maurin in 1933. Day had been incorporating pacifism into her sprawling economic-justice ministry since World War II. Decades older than Merton, the Berrigans, and other Catholic radicals of the 1960s, she became an influential elder and mentor to the emerging generation of activists.[74]

Merton became a formative influence for the Catholic Left when he organized a gathering of peace radicals in 1964, men whose ideas germinated into plans for draft board raids. The Abbey of Gethsemani hosted priests, Catholic laymen, and others from Protestant denominations over three days. The 120-year-old mother house of the Cistercian order sat on two hundred acres where monks carried on lives of quiet contemplation. In the bucolic, rolling landscape of Western Kentucky, where wooded hillsides gave way to sprawling meadows and tidy farm plots, the Presbyterian minister John Heidbrink joined Merton in hosting the event that presaged Catholic Resistance. Heidbrink was director of Interchurch Activities in the Fellowship of Reconciliation, a coalition of Christian clergy that had formed in 1915 to protest World War I.[75]

Though the dangers of nuclear arms proliferation had been the event's original focus, the participants turned much of their attention to Vietnam, where President Johnson had recently escalated the U.S. presence. Their retreat guests were, not coincidentally, all men, not only because the monastery prohibited women on its grounds at that time, but also because the press, their superiors, and the larger church community took seriously their power, as men, to upset the status quo. In short, these were men of note with track records of reform who arrived at Gethsemani eager to cultivate each other as leaders, spokespeople, and moral authorities.[76]

The thirteen guests assembled in late November 1964. They heard presentations from each other and talked about the Gospel-based solutions each was developing through their own writing and organizing. Putting their heads together, the men reckoned with the increasingly destructive, mechanistic, and totalizing warfare of their age. The Berrigans, along with fellow Catholics John Peter Grady, Tom Cornell, Jim

Forrest, Tony Walsh, and Robert Cunnane, thus exchanged ideas with Protestants A. J. Muste, John Oliver Nelson, John Howard Yoder, Elbert Jean, Wilbur ("Ping") Ferry, and Charles Ring. For three days, the group walked muddied paths between the monastery buildings and the hermitage to attend the loose programming developed by Merton. Though draft board raids were not on the schedule, six of the seven Catholics at this Gethsemani meeting later participated in at least one of these later actions. And three of the men—Philip Berrigan, Daniel Berrigan, and John Grady—served as its unofficial leaders.[77]

Already a noted public intellectual, Daniel Berrigan shared his latest reflections on the lessons of peace found in Scripture with the other retreatants. The Jesuit priest was becoming a controversial figure in the church for his public pronouncements and demonstrations. He and his brother Philip had come gradually to the work of peace. Like most Catholics, they learned the ways of the church through Mass, homelife rituals, and catechism rather than encyclicals. Phil and Dan had grown up the sons of a mercurial Irish American working man who occasionally participated in labor actions but did not immerse himself in theology the way his children later would. Their mother filled in the spiritual breach with a deep religious devotion and buffered her children from her husband's temper, but she was no radical herself. The Berrigan brothers carved their own path into the world of the Catholic Left. They were followed by many others.[78]

The story of the Berrigans maps directly over the church's development into a formidable institution of American life in the mid-twentieth century. Daniel Berrigan's political journey started in his early years of Jesuit formation, when a mission trip of the 1940s exposed him to the ecclesiology of French "worker priests." These brave and innovative clerics impressed the young American by immersing themselves in the lives of workers and the problems of capitalism. After Berrigan's return to the United States and his ordination, he started teaching theology and French at St. Peter's Preparatory School, a Jesuit high school in Jersey City, New Jersey, where he also began publishing his ideas on peace and economic justice. This writing habit never quit him, and it yielded volumes of books, articles, and essays in the coming decades as his appetite for spiritual action grew at the same pace. Berrigan also started to challenge entrenched Catholic practices that he and fellow priests came to recognize as barriers between clergy and laity. He joined the Walter Ferrell Guild, which gathered clergy and Catholic laymen over cocktails to discuss art and current events.[79]

Berrigan was in his early forties and working at Cornell University when he responded to Merton's invitation to take part in a 1964 retreat.[80]

Berrigan spoke about the universal presence of the "risen Christ" in the world, drawing from the work of French theologian and paleontologist Pierre Teilhard de Chardin.[81] These comments expanded on reflections Berrigan had published in two recent books. *The Bride: Essays in the Church* (1959), which addressed the relationship between life and action. In this text, Berrigan articulated visions for how "universal divinity" could be realized through the hope of "Church militant" and spiritually stimulated action. Berrigan built on these ideas in another book of essays two years later called *Bow in the Clouds: Man's Covenant with God.* Its chapter "Prophecy and Society" proved especially influential on the work of antiwar radicals by exploring the difficult life of the prophetic instigator who shepherded truth into the world even when the church stood in opposition to it. Prophets were not mere protesters, but "herald[s] of the golden age of man."[82] Both books underscored how people could and should use their power to bring grace into secular history.

Daniel Berrigan's and Thomas Merton's spiritual writing galvanized the sixties generation, but it drew from CST of the previous century. Once source proved especially foundational to the germination of their ideas. Released in 1891, the encyclical *Rerum novarum* (Rights and Duties of Capital and Labor) pivoted the church toward its new role of confronting problems of the modern world. *Rerum novarum* did not speak directly about warfare, but it did address problems of economic disparity in a way that later framed Catholic Left arguments for peace. This historic text, written by a Pope famous for his diplomatic and intellectual talents, stressed human dignity as a central right of all living people. The document identified a living wage and a healthy childhood free of work as necessary elements for securing that right. From the assertion that all people's lives have value emerged a moral vision for the common good and a focus on those who are economically marginalized, what the church eventually started to call the "option for the poor and vulnerable."[83]

Rerum novarum became a basis for Catholic Left radicalism even though Leo was no radical himself. The Pope aimed to staunch, not foment, revolution. In emphasizing humane working conditions and fair wages while supporting the right of workers to bargain collectively, the encyclical intentionally challenged socialism, which was gaining a foothold among working people and intellectuals in Europe. This rapidly expanding movement of economic reform and state centralization scared the Vatican both because it made no room for religion and also because it sought to involve the state in projects and roles that the church typically filled, like social welfare and education. Church teachings thus sought to keep Catholics out of socialist politics by addressing the stressful economic conditions that Marxism promised to ameliorate.[84]

The list of principles incorporated into CST grew as twentieth-century commercial and political life posited new challenges. The Catholic Left of the 1960s relied as much on these economic critiques of the state as it did on the Christian critiques of state-sponsored violence. Early twentieth-century texts addressed the growing alienation of people from each other, the degradation of work, the disintegration of community, and the disparities of wealth that accompanied the massive reorganization of life and institutions in modern capitalist society.[85]

Catholics also cultivated a school of thought popularized among continental philosophers that was known as "personalism." This system of ideas stressed the importance of people's direct connections and obligations to each other while emphasizing the value of these relationships over a person's individual rights within structures of government.[86] Although most Catholics did not debate the various "isms" and "ities" of social teaching, the theology of personalism found its way into their worship as well as home, school, and community interactions. Thomas Merton's writings represented an important vector of these ideas that broadcast his message about the inner spirit emanating out into the world among his admiring readers. Parish life promoted the localized face-to-face mechanics of care embodied in personalist thought.[87] The American system of courts, with its layers of bureaucracy, would be an unlikely place to find opportunities for personalism, but the Camden 28 tried as much as they could with their heartfelt pro se defense in 1971, when they spoke directly to the judge and jury.

Protestant theology intersected with CST in important ways for American Christians, including peace activists. The cross-fertilization of social justice theologies among different denominations of Christian institutions formed the basis of radical experimentation and action in the 1960s. CST flourished in the United States partly because its seeds dropped into a political and social context of progressive ferment that nurtured its growth—a context that was quite Protestant. Catholic social teachings of the early twentieth century developed as part of a larger reform movement dominated by ministers, church ladies, and other evangelicals bearing King James Bibles. As Baptist minister and scholar Walter Rauschenbusch exhorted his listeners, believers needed to witness Christ in the messiness of the world by taking Christianity off the "high shelf" where children could not reach it. "It has not evoked faith in the will and power of God to redeem the permanent institutions of human society from their inherited guilt of oppression and extortion," he wrote in his influential 1917 book, *A Theology for the Social Gospel*.[88]

Catholics and Protestants did not, as a rule, mix socially, but that rule could not prevent them from infecting each other with enthusiasm for social uplift. Protestant "Social Gospel" theology directed congregations to improve their communities, missionize, and proselytize. Christian reformers viewed the greed and harsh economic reality of the gilded age as a new millennium calling them to rebuild the Kingdom of God. The Social Gospel represented contemporary Protestant applications of the Gospel—the biblical renderings of Jesus's life and teachings. CST relied more on natural law theory rather than Scripture to assert the essential rights of all people to life's necessities.[89]

The unprecedented violence perpetrated by authoritarian regimes of the World War II era inspired a new wave of theological texts to address the dangers of totalitarianism. The writers producing this literature struggled with the complicity of their own church brethren in the vast humanitarian disaster. This complicity ranged from either enthusiastic endorsement for violence to passive tolerance. Catholics played a role in the genocide of the 1930s and 1940s by embracing fascist nationalists in Italy, Spain, Austria, and Vichy France. The Vatican, meanwhile, quickly appeased Hitler by signing the Reichskonkordat in 1933, which secured the rights and safety of Catholics in Germany by promising not to interfere with the chancellor's imperial agenda.[90] According to historian James Chappel, Catholic supporters of fascism saw themselves and their countrymen as "Defenders of the West" on whom God had bestowed the responsibility for upholding civilization against forces of modernization, including feminism, socialism, and sexual liberation.[91]

In opposition to this trend toward authoritarianism, French philosopher Jacques Maritain took the lead in articulating new Catholic arguments in support of democracy by wedding natural law and human rights doctrine. The Pope in Rome and Catholic scholars in America embraced Maritain, especially after he coordinated efforts to draft the document, "In the Face of the World's Crisis," in 1942. The manifesto, which he signed along with forty-two other European Catholics living in the United States, denounced totalitarianism as "absolutely incompatible with the message of the Gospel which made manifest to mankind the inalienable dignity of each human soul."[92] The problems in Europe also shaped the writing of John Courtney Murray, an American Jesuit intellectual who was deeply influenced by Maritain. Murray addressed the problems of Catholic fascism by developing a philosophy of church and state that recognized the religious liberty of all worshippers in the United States.[93]

Catholic Resistance represented the next stage of Catholic liberal thought, building as it did on the human rights theology of Maritain and Murray. The new movement broke away, however, from the previous generation's comfort with state solutions. Like the American "New Left," which split from the "Old Left" by jettisoning its reliance on the welfare state and the "Establishment," the Catholic Left of the 1960s took an antistatist turn away from the World War II–era efforts to elevate democratic institutions of government. Catholic radicals of the 1960s rebelled against their own religious orders and the hierarchy of the church. Like the New Left students who wanted to reform education on their university campuses, the priests, nuns, and missionaries of the Catholic Left wanted to loosen the tightly controlled structures that enfeebled relationships between clerics and laypeople. They seized the tools of civil disobedience and direct action popularized by the American civil rights movement, a movement that fueled their hopes and fired their visions of a peaceful and more equal society.

CHAPTER TWO

Civil Disobedience

"Martin Luther King died daily," wrote Dorothy Day in the April 1968 issue of the *Catholic Worker* newspaper. Grieving the civil rights leader just assassinated in Memphis, Day thus described King with the same words that St. Paul used to capture his own experience of living out the lessons of Jesus Christ. She reflected on King's powerful Christian witness, especially his fervid belief in the ability of people to transform into better versions of themselves.[1] Though she had been politically active since the 1920s, before Reverend King was born, Dorothy Day readily adopted him as a spiritual model when he entered the national political landscape in the 1950s. Day, who had been protesting racial violence and discriminations for decades, greeted the new postwar era of civil disobedience with excitement. As she spearheaded pacificist actions to protest the escalating militarization of American society, she readily acknowledged that the southern freedom struggle impacted her own understanding of God's project. The fight for racial justice in the United States did not emerge suddenly in the 1950s since activist predecessors had laid that foundation in previous decades. New campaigns launched in the post–World War II era nevertheless exerted a powerful force on American society that shaped the emerging Catholic Left along with the rest of the nation.

The Catholic Worker movement, established by Day and Peter Maurin in 1933, cultivated a spiritual basis for social protest that primed activists to receive and act on the messaging of King and other Black leaders. The cofounders shaped many aspects of this antistatist and anticapitalist Catholicism that the sixties generation rediscovered in the context of the Vietnam War and myriad campaigns for justice. In their lives of chosen poverty and Christian service, Day and Maurin drew a coterie of faithful who saw opportunities for following Christ's example in the most impoverished settings of urban America where they lived with each other in a new kind of family. The bare-bones Catholic Worker form of spiritual activism born in the 1930s captured a new wave of activists thirty years later with its nonhierarchical communal structure.

The American Day and Frenchman Maurin started the *Catholic Worker* as a newspaper in 1933 in the bleak atmosphere of economic collapse. Day came to the church over the 1920s and early 1930s through a slow but ardent conversion process. The radical journalist who once wrote for the *Masses* and went to jail as a suffragist adopted an austere and pious lifestyle. Day attracted young radicals who saw in her a model of real and unadorned Christianity. The spiritual metamorphosis that evolved into the Catholic Worker movement compelled followers as much as did Day's generosity, crisp prose, sharp wit, and sincerely expressed love for humankind. The newspaper, which cost one cent, brought readers together into a spiritual community that became the basis for its unique form of live-in ministry.[2]

The movement quickly grew into a loose network of autonomous houses and farms that had spread across the United States by 1940.[3] This prophetic tradition looked to Christ's disciples and Old Testament prophets as models for bearing the word of God, speaking bluntly about humanity's crimes against the oppressed and living on the margins of society with the poorest of the poor. A commitment to the common good that directed attention to the dispossessed drew Catholic Workers out of comfortable middle-class environs into struggling neighborhoods, where they lived in dilapidated houses and relied on donations to pay the bills. This movement also elevated peace as a Catholic Social Justice principle before the Pope addressed the problem of militarism in later decades.[4]

Day, Maurin, and other members of the Catholic Workers became recognizable by their threadbare clothing, which was a by-product of voluntary poverty. This lifestyle choice avoided the corrupting seductions of wealth and brought them closer to the impoverished communities they hoped to serve. By earning below the required minimum for paying income tax, Catholic Workers also avoided contributing to the American military-industrial complex and its growing nuclear arsenal.[5] Catholic Workers extended food, coffee, and shelter along with prayers. They aimed to provide the basics of sustenance to which, according to Catholic doctrine, every human was entitled. With bread and soup came the spiritual nourishment of smiles, company, and group worship. One of the earliest houses of hospitality, on Mott Street in Manhattan's Chinatown district, drew lines of people that wrapped around the corner when it opened in 1937.[6]

Day not only recognized the divine in the world around her but also observed the motions of the Holy Spirit in the people she served. She urged Catholic Workers to attend daily Mass and encouraged making regular times for prayer and the sacrament of confession. Day wanted to realize a transformation that went beyond the material improvement of her "guests"; she hoped for a deeper spiritual transformation in the lives of people who encountered the Catholic Worker. Maurin, whose contribution to this effort tended to be more intellectual, started a Friday evening tradition at Catholic Worker Houses called "clarification of thought." These presentations and discussions, often held over soup and bread, spanned a range of issues from racism in America and Thomist philosophy to the biographies of saints. Conversations often carried on long after the event in the dining room or neighborhood pub, getting more intense with alcohol and cigarettes.[7]

A pacifist since World War I, Dorothy Day opposed U.S. entry into World War II. She expressed her dissent forcefully and often in the pages of the flagship *Catholic Worker* newspaper, even though it alienated many of her readers and prompted more than a few volunteers to quit the movement. The subscription base, which reached 150,000 in 1936, declined as the Catholic population saw its sons and brothers march off to fight the Axis powers in Europe.[8] The war represented the lowest point for the Catholic Worker movement, which suffered a further blow when Peter Maurin died in 1949. Houses closed all over the country, and many people talked about the *Catholic Worker* in the past tense. Some local houses lived on but severed their relationship to Dorothy Day. The Chicago Catholic Worker House renounced her and distributed the Chicago *Catholic Worker* newspaper as an alternative voice (see figure 4).[9]

After the war, Day slowly gained followers again as she became outspoken against the threat of nuclear warfare. Civil defense drills created this opportunity for Day to revive the Catholic Worker movement by refusing to support the government in its campaigns to militarize American society. President Dwight D. Eisenhower's Federal Civil Defense Agency (FCDA) undertook the futile task of preparing citizens for a nuclear attack with a series of exercises in 1955. "Operation Alert" designated "target areas" in numerous cities that might sustain a hit. The government took these civil defense drills seriously, fining people who did not take cover up to $500, with possible time in jail. Protesters responded with visible and peaceful noncompliance.[10] Dorothy Day and fellow Catholic Workers sacramentalized the moment by doing public penance. In submitting themselves for arrest, they assumed responsibility for the bombings committed by others, notes scholar Mel Piehl, which they deemed "evil[s]" perpetrated by their fellow citizens.[11]

FIGURE 4. Dorothy Day
Dorothy Day at St. Joseph's House, New York City, 1955. Photo by Vivian Cherry, courtesy of the Department of Special Collections and University Archives, Raynor Memorial Libraries, Marquette University.

Like legions of civil rights protesters, Catholic activists repeated these demonstrations over the next several decades to protest the neverending wars perpetrated by the United States, obediently marching off to jail in handcuffs without offering struggle. Day became, over the 1950s, a new model of religiously inspired anarchy that pushed back against centralized government, but with prayers and alms instead of dynamite.[12]

The radical white-haired church lady of Mott Street, meanwhile, also started denouncing the war in Vietnam. As early as May 1954, a decade before the U.S. escalation of troops in the region, Day authored an essay characterizing the French occupation of Indochina as a form of imperialism.[13] In a piece for the *Catholic Worker*, she reflected on U.S. involvement in Vietnam, which was just starting with the Eisenhower administration's decision to send advisers in 1954. As was typical of Day, she made her point through storytelling, often by relating the lives of saints, martyrs, and historical figures she admired. Theophane Venard, she explained, had been martyred in the nineteenth-century French colonial project of extracting raw materials for its developing industrial economy. The young priest enthusiastically signed up to be part of the spiritual enterprise to convert souls to Christianity but eventually realized he was an instrument in their exploitation and demise. Venard observed the gushing Christian propaganda that promoted the church in Asia while sacrificing the livelihood of residents to profiteers. "Those who call themselves Christians," wrote Venard, "spoiled God's work wherever they went."[14]

Another reason why Day won supporters in the 1950s was because her message harmonized Catholic Social Justice with the racial justice teachings of the southern freedom struggle. Black spiritual leaders provided theological inspiration for these explorations in faith and action. While boycotters, marchers, and picketers executed successful nonviolent civil disobedience to protest segregation and white supremacy, Martin Luther King Jr., Fred Shuttlesworth, Fannie Lou Hamer, and other leaders from Black churches articulated compelling theological and intellectual arguments that moved Catholics. The florid evangelical language of the Reverend Shuttlesworth situated visions of civil rights within larger biblical narratives that intertwined the American and Israelite projects of freedom. The devout Hamer spearheaded a popular new genre of freedom songs that adapted the music of Black churches to the struggles of her day.[15]

King, Dorothy Day, Thomas Merton, A. J. Muste, and other influential Christians also animated the emerging generation by introducing them to the teachings of Mahatma Gandhi. Gandhi developed nonviolent strategies of resistance from Hinduism in the struggle to end British colonial rule in India in the 1930s and 1940s. He promoted the concept of Satyagraha, which in Sanskrit means "holding onto the truth." Satyagraha insisted that methods to victory were the means-to-the-means, in contrast to war's means-to-the-ends.[16] Drawing from his deep knowledge of Social Gospel theology and continental philosophy, King stated in 1956 that "Christ showed us the way and Gandhi in India showed it could work."[17] In 1967, Day described Catholic Workers as "followers of Gandhi in . . . [the] struggle to build a spirit of nonviolence."[18]

Many draft board raiders had spent formative time at the Catholic Worker and regarded Dorothy Day as an abiding influence on their commitment to nonviolence. With no central headquarters or leadership structure, the movement committed itself to a thoroughly decentralized form of organization long before any campus radical uttered the word "horizontalism." Daniel Berrigan, who brought his students to the Catholic Worker House in New York, regarded Day as an important mentor. "She became my friend and the friend of my family," he reflected in 1986, "and the friendship was to spur our moral and spiritual development."[19]

In his later years, Philip Berrigan declared that Dorothy Day influenced him "more than all the theologians" by teaching him how human suffering and poverty related to "war-making."[20]

Like Thomas Merton, Dorothy Day initially criticized the draft board raids and suggested that property destruction was, in fact, a form of violence. The broken filing cabinets reminded her of the years spent writing for a communist newspaper before she converted and denounced Marxism. When New York City police ransacked her offices back then, it felt like a form of assault. She sympathized with those draft board workers who had to deal with the blood and the mess. "These [draft board raids]," she wrote, "are not ours."[21] She remained a friend to the Berrigans, however, writing to them often when they were in jail. In later years, she praised the brothers for their creative witness, which she called "an act of prayer."[22]

If nonviolence pulled sympathizers into the Catholic Left, the increasing militarization of the New Left became the push factor leading them away from other organizations and to the priests and nuns. Secular radical groups of the late 1960s had started transitioning to what they regarded as "revolutionary" strategies designed to resist the brutality of white supremacy and the American military. While the war dragged on, demoralized activists came to feel it was their moral duty to escalate actions against the U.S. government, even if that risked violence. A splinter group that developed from SDS, the Weather Underground, formed in 1969 to bomb U.S. government sites that were responsible for implementing the war in Vietnam, while taking as much care as possible not to harm or kill people. Its members, the Weathermen, were inspired in part by civil rights activists in the Student Nonviolent Coordinating Committee (SNCC) who, having lost patience with the passive Gandhian traditions that had launched their organizations, shifted strategies. Rallying around "Black power," an ideology that championed Black Nationalism and self-determination as the means for realizing racial justice, the new Black Panther Party adopted a paramilitary style that foregrounded self-defense as a priority.[23]

Catholic nonviolence represented a peaceful alternative that men and women religious seemed to embody in their lifestyle. Philip Berrigan denounced the violent methods sanctioned by revolutionary groups, which he disparagingly described as "reactionary."[24] Although the Panthers also adopted draft resistance as one of their core platforms, the armed posture of the self-avowed Marxist-Leninist organization along with its separatist philosophy did not welcome white peace advocates, especially their interest in sacrificing their bodily freedom for the cause. Philip Berrigan accurately identified revolutionary and violent elements in the movement, but his comments also called attention to the advantaged position of relative safety that white Catholics could leverage.

In their opposition to the war, white protesters could fold their own racial justice goals into the larger objective of stopping the war machine. This made sense. Anti-"gook" propaganda dehumanized the Vietnamese people with racist characterizations while the white bureaucrats of the military-industrial complex in Washington, D.C., sent mostly working-class men, overrepresented by Black GIs, to fight in Indochina.

The discomfort with armed self-defense partly explains why Catholic Resistance, for all its interest in racial justice, remained overwhelmingly white. The risks its members took in goading law enforcement offers another explanation for why Black- and Brown-skinned activists did not raid draft boards with the white Catholics. By directing themselves to property destruction within draft boards, the Catholic Left adopted tactics that were far more dangerous for nonwhite activists than for whites. Catholic radicals sustained harassment and abuses at the hands of law enforcement, but none were shot, even when caught red-handed.

As *Washington Post* editor Christine Emba noted in a 2016 column on the privileges of white identity in political activism, "It represents an opportunity to speak out more loudly against injustice, knowing you're better protected from negative outcomes."[25] The privileges also included the ability to smoke pot or imbibe other illicit substances without much concern for how prosecutors would use these activities to impugn their character in front of juries. Nonwhite radicals also did these things, and often with white people, but at far greater jeopardy to their own personal safety.

The involvement of the church in this political equation added another level of security for the Catholic Leftists. Even as diocesan officials harshly rebuked and sanctioned radical priests and sisters, they also did everything possible to keep them safe. Religious orders were loyal to their members and stubbornly protective of them. It helped also that nuns and priests often enjoyed hands-off status in prison. The notorious gangster Jimmy Hoffa was a murderer but he was also a Catholic, and while serving a sentence in Lewisburg Federal Prison, he threatened retribution against anyone who harmed the famous draft board raider in his cell group, Father Philip Berrigan. One raider acknowledged the protections of racial status in recalling a police officer who threatened to beat her in the middle of an arrest. He stopped after his partner warned that she might be a nun. "If I was a Black girl," she thought, "I would be dead."[26]

Privilege offers some explanation for the chances Catholics took in these campaigns, but history offers a broader explanation. Since priests, nuns, and laypeople alike had been battling poverty, racism, and violence for decades, they were poised to take action when called on to step up in the 1960s. In addition to the Catholic Workers, Catholic Action and other groups that acted outside of the church's organizational structure, some communities of religious formed to tackle the problems of racial injustice. The Society of St. Joseph of the Sacred Heart, for example, focused on serving African Americans. Its members, called "Josephites," cultivated church and school environments that welcomed Black residents. They also addressed the specific needs of Black communities. Philip Berrigan joined this order when he entered the priesthood after fighting in World War II.[27]

The extent to which Catholics were already mobilized may explain why they responded in great numbers when Martin Luther King wired religious leaders across the country to join the 1965 voting rights demonstrations in Selma, Alabama (see figure 5). The march had already started on March 7 when several of the nonviolent protesters walking together across the Edmund Pettus Bridge were brutalized by state troopers as they made their way peacefully to Montgomery. Undaunted by this attack on "Bloody Sunday," as it became known, King reached out to religious supporters, asking them to join the march in Alabama. Many

FIGURE 5. Nuns at the Selma March
Mundelein College professor Sister Mary Griffin BVM arrives with her students at the Selma, Alabama, civil rights march of 1965. Photo courtesy of the Women and Leadership Archives, Loyola University Chicago.

of them had been eager to oblige the famous pastor after he published "Letter from a Birmingham Jail" in 1963, in which he chastised leaders of Christian churches, including Catholics, who prohibited their flocks from participating in desegregation efforts. He also addressed moderate white people who, "devoted more to 'order' than justice," would not condone the "methods" of the civil rights movement because of the attendant social unrest.[28]

Bloody Sunday represented an opportunity for religious Americans to rectify this problem, in King's words, of "a negative peace which is absence of tension" by offering affirmative solidarity. "Put on your clericals," the pastor urged. "If you don't wear them anymore, look under your bed." Catholics swarmed to Selma. The National Catholic Conference for Interracial Justice leaped to meet the challenge, drawing from their network of 112 councils around the country. "Priests, nuns and laypeople made the pilgrimage to Alabama in unprecedented numbers," notes a fifty-year retrospective of the event. They contributed, it continues, "a distinctive Catholic presence to the Selma protests." In fact, nine hundred Catholics participated in the protest.[29] When Congress passed the Voting Rights Act in 1965, it handed a victory to the Selma marchers and the broader civil rights movement. The Vietnam War escalated and segregation persisted, however, prompting activists to question the value of marching and propose other tactics for realizing their justice goals. The impatience for progress motivated the draft board raids three years later.

Most of the non-Catholics or former Catholics came gradually to the criminal operations, first dipping their toes into support work for the movement. The point of entrée for students tended to be campus vigils for the war dead, spring-break service projects, and demonstration caravans to the capital. Almost all the activists who participated in the Camden 28 action, including Cookie Ridolfi and Bob Williamson, first volunteered by helping with preparations for actions or tending to office duties. They sat in courtroom galleries, made phone calls, and canvassed passersby in public parks. They raised money, though never very much. Some adopted this work as a full-time job. Organizations called "defense committees" formed around each trial to coordinate these activities.

Several of the Camden 28 defendants, including Bob Good, came to the Catholic Left through a defense committee. The former seminarian had steadily immersed himself in the action community over the course of 1970 and 1971 through support work for the D.C. Nine. These defendants had decided to take the model of the draft board raid and apply it to the napalm manufacturer Dow Chemical to draw attention to the

Civil Disobedience

company's complicity in the burning of Vietnamese villages. In March 1969, they broke into Dow's Washington, D.C., offices and poured blood on the files.[30] Bob Good came to Washington to sit in on the trial. He had become interested in Catholic Left activity after he left the seminary and enrolled as a student at Xavier University, a Jesuit Catholic college in Cincinnati, Ohio, where he heard Art Melville, brother of Catonsville Nine defendant Thomas Melville and, like Thomas, a Maryknoll priest exiled from Guatemala. Melville and his wife, Cathy, who was a former nun, were traveling to college campuses to discuss the U.S.-sponsored violence that they witnessed as missionaries. Good was a farmer's son who had been raised in rural Pennsylvania. After attending a seminary high school in the early 1960s, he realized he did not want to be a priest. To the consternation of his parents, he dropped out of Xavier after conversations with the Melvilles made him more interested in the antiwar movement.[31]

The Catonsville defense committee, headed by Benedictine monk Paul Myer, organized a panoply of marches, rallies, and public-speaking events before and during that trial. The group aimed to maintain media attention and build solidarity in the activist community. The committee also coached and assisted the defendants themselves, pressing them, for example, to avoid confrontations with law enforcement and counter-demonstrators as they prepared their case.[32]

The Catonsville Nine defendants and their supporters hoped that the trial itself would also be an occasion for witness, whereby the defense team could bring its arguments against the war to the many observers who had started paying attention in the months leading up to the proceedings. Each defendant gave elaborate testimony that focused on their reasons for acting rather than the details of their crime at Catonsville draft board 33. From the nine protesters, jurors heard descriptions of poverty in Guatemala, the struggles of African Americans in Washington, D.C., the destructive capacity of napalm, and violent repression perpetrated by the Rafael Trujillo regime in the Dominican Republic. Having already settled into the reality that they were probably going to be convicted and sent to jail, they used their testimony to put U.S. imperialism on trial. When the jury found all the defendants guilty, their decision merely transitioned the Catonsville saga into its next stage.[33]

The judge, who noted that none of the protesters showed remorse or contrition for their crime, sentenced the nine harshly, giving each one anywhere from two to three and a half years. After all appeals were exhausted, four of them decided to disappear before being taken into custody: the Berrigans, Mary Moylan, and George Mische. Moylan went underground for a decade until she surrendered to law enforcement in

FIGURE 6. Daniel Berrigan
Jesuit Daniel Berrigan, one of the Catonsville Nine defendants, flashes a peace sign while in handcuffs. Photo courtesy of the Bob Fitch Photography Archive, Department of Special Collections, Stanford University Library.

1979. Federal agents apprehended Philip Berrigan and Mische within a couple of months of their flight. Daniel Berrigan traveled underground into fall 1970, before surrendering to agents who located him at the Block Island, Rhode Island, home of poet William Stringfellow. The fugitive occasionally surfaced for quick public appearances in these months, which is when Camden 28 defendant Bob Williamson first heard Berrigan give a talk that inspired him to join the movement (see figure 6).[34]

Over the next few years, activists executed scores of raids, most but not all targeted at draft boards. Before the Catonsville Nine went to trial, the Milwaukee 14 set ten thousand files ablaze with napalm while singing and reading the Gospels. In May 1969 the Chicago 15 broke into a South Side draft board, where they destroyed forty thousand files. Five months later, the Flower City Conspiracy destroyed FBI and U.S. attorney records as well as draft files in Rochester, New York. That same month, the Boston Eight broke into four different locations across the city in a twenty-four-hour period. They shredded some of the documents they stole from these offices and distributed others on the national mall in Washington, D.C.[35]

Dow Chemical continued to attract raiders in the capital and beyond. On the same day as the Boston action, a group of Midwesterners who called themselves the "Beaver 55" (despite their much lower numbers) raided a Dow Chemical office in Midland, Michigan, where they erased magnetic tapes reportedly containing biological and chemical research. As the media reported these successive actions, they discovered that some people had been attacking draft boards even before the Catholics poured their blood and made it into a movement. One draftee, who became known as the "Big Lake One," entered the draft board in Minneapolis that housed his and his brothers' records, walked right past the staff, and brazenly opened a drawer of files. He then poured in four buckets of manure from his hometown of Elk River, Minnesota. That was February 1966, two years before the Baltimore Customs House raid launched Catholic Resistance.[36]

As the actions continued from the late 1960s into the early 1970s, the Catholic Left overlapped with the feminist movement as well as the civil rights movement. The attacks on hierarchical structures made women attentive to their own secondary status in relationship to the men in their groups, especially in relation to the priests and other devout laymen, who tended to be older than the women. Women found ways to participate in raids while also bringing attention to the sex discrimination they faced in society. One group, called "Women against Daddy Warbucks," raided the downtown Manhattan draft board office. The activists absconded with and destroyed draft board files and removed the "1" and "A" keys on the typewriters before disappearing. Instead of waiting for arrest at the site, they resurfaced two days later, on the Fourth of July, at a rally in Rockefeller Plaza, where they threw torn pieces of the records among their hundreds of supporters before FBI agents started trying to grab the women.[37] The burglars made the action explicitly feminist as well as Catholic. The rich tuxedo-wearing Daddy Warbucks character from the musical Annie offered an apt symbol of the patriarchy undergirding the military-industrial complex, a system perpetuated by a socially implicit valorization of male strength, power, and wealth.[38] The participants also sent a message to their male cohorts in the Catholic Left. As Margaret Geddes explained, they wanted to challenge the assertion that this form of protest was "manly." "Some of us thought there must be a way to make a statement as women about women's opposition to the war that was more than the classic support role reflected by the poster."[39]

The Women against Daddy Warbucks action formally introduced feminism to the Catholic Left, though the sexism in the movement had activated the feminist consciousness of its women for some time. The men developed a masculine activist culture that marginalized their female cohorts, stepping forward as the spokespeople while leaving the secretarial and housekeeping work to their sisters in the movement. The women also typically procured supplies, transported people and materials, provided food, and maintained the apartments that housed everyone. They cased buildings, and many also broke into the draft board offices along with the men.

This sexism was not limited to the Catholic Left; it characterized the entire antiwar movement. The men leadings SDS and other groups, as historians have shown, relegated women to support roles and derided female reformers who brought attention to the gender hierarchy within their ranks.[40] Draft resistance was no less sexist, but it also promoted spiritually rooted patriarchal ideals about male character building. The Catholic model of manhood went beyond the patterns established by radicals. As historian Marian Mollin has demonstrated, Catholic Leftists were referred to as a "brotherhood of scholars, students, and clergy." The Berrigans, she observes, assumed the roles of modern prophet and apostle that the movement bestowed, mirroring the attitudes of "its religious base, where priests were valued above all others and where women, by definition of their sex, were excluded from authority." Mollin contrasts the Catholic way of peace with the Quaker egalitarianism that dominated American radicalism until that point.[41]

Radical priests also benefited from a decade of what historian Robert Orsi describes as "clerical noir," a genre of Catholic stories featuring fearless hero prelates who ventured into dangerous crime-ridden neighborhoods to save abused and disadvantaged populations. "The hardboiled priest combined the qualities of the martyr and the ward boss, the shamus and the desert father."[42] As biographers Murray Polner and Jim O'Grady describe Phil Berrigan's approach to organizing raiders: "If you're not doing this, you're not doing anything."[43] Male participants talked about draft resistance as formative to their development into manhood, and Daniel Berrigan described resistance as "man's movement toward himself" and as a way to remove the "bars to manhood."[44] The movement also celebrated the criminal work that men tended to do as sacrificial. The fugitives and outlaws called themselves "warriors for peace."[45] Hierarchies also developed around clerical status, age, and gender.[46] Middle-aged priests, professors, and devout male laymen positioned themselves as the strategists.

Philip, even more than Daniel, molded the movement's male bravado.

The intensity with which he mobilized resisters simultaneously motivated and intimidated the activists in his midst. An eighteen-year-old who had gone to prison for raiding a draft board in Chicago described Philip as forceful to the point of isolating. "If someone didn't participate, they were frozen out of his circle." Berrigan admitted this problem in the late 1970s, conceding that he was too "hard-nosed." Even later in life he elaborated, remembering how he would "lay a heavy rap on [activists] about the war, their Christian duty." He "never tried to ask anyone to do whatever [he] wasn't prepared to do himself [and he didn't] want to let others off the hook" any more than he would himself.[47]

Having immersed himself in civil rights and antiviolence work over the late 1950s and 1960s, Philip Berrigan developed an increasingly ascetic model for how to apply faith to justice work. Phil's drive, energy, and courage of conscience made him as magnetic as he was intimidating. "Handsome" and "strong" became common adjectives to describe him. Like his brother Daniel, he was seen by many as a saint and compared to Joan of Arc and Thomas Moore.[48] Though less pugnacious than his elder brother, Daniel Berrigan fortified the movement's masculinity with his spiritual and intellectual celebrity. Favoring black turtlenecks draped with a flashy medallion, sometimes wearing a beret and a soul patch, Dan charmed countercultural and mainstream followers alike. He even caught the attention of Peace Corps director Sargent Shriver, who brought him into the fashionable world of the Kennedys. For three years, Daniel Berrigan celebrated Mass for the family and visited them at their exclusive Hyannis Port, Massachusetts, compound. Berrigan described this time as "copacetic." He liked how the family drew in "talented" people, and "the more priests the better."[49]

The dominance of priests and other male spokespeople in the Catholic Left belied the contributions of women, who assumed every type of work in the movement. Starting with the Catonsville Nine raid of 1968, Mary Moylan and Marjorie Melville joined priests David Darst, Philip Berrigan, and Daniel Berrigan as well as the former priest John Hogan; Melville's husband, Thomas; Tom Lewis of the Baltimore Four; and layman George Mische. The Melvilles, Moylan, and Mische joined the action as the next logical step after their years abroad as missionaries in Latin America and Africa, where they had worked to promote peace and improve the living conditions of Indigenous people. The experience made them deeply skeptical of American Cold War projects in these regions, where their own government supported authoritarian regimes that were friendly to U.S. interests but abusive and violent toward their own people.[50]

Marjorie Melville grew up in Guanajuato, Mexico, in the 1930s in a Catholic family as the Institutional Revolutionary Party (PRI) became the dominant regime and cracked down on the role of the church in national life. She later moved to the United States to join the Maryknoll Sisters of St. Dominic, with whom she served for twenty years, mostly in Guatemala. Her order, along with the priestly and lay Maryknoll orders, became immersed in the struggles of Guatemalans suffering from the brutality of a dictator. She met her future husband, the Maryknoll priest Thomas Melville, in Guatemala, who was just as frustrated with the lack of church leadership in the region. The Melvilles actually joined the guerrilla movement that opposed its U.S.-backed president, Carlos Castillo Arnas. Expelled from Guatemala in 1967 along with all the others from Maryknoll, Marjorie and Tom returned to the United States, where they found solidarity in the coalescing Catholic Left.[51]

Mary Moylan came to Catholic Resistance with a similar background of experiences from a different part of the world. Raised by devoutly Catholic parents in Baltimore, Moylan trained as a nurse midwife before moving to Uganda in 1959 to work with the Missionary Sisters of Africa, where she provided medical services and taught English at a secondary school. "I was there when American planes were bombing the Congo and were very close to the border," she later recalled of accidental blasts that deepened her disillusionment with the Cold War projection of American power.[52] She identified these air raids as the "political turning point" of her life. After two tours as a medical missionary in Africa, she returned to the United States, first residing at a house owned by the Archdiocese of Washington, D.C., in which she lived with other activist Catholics. Rosemary Reuther, who later became a celebrated Catholic theologian, went to Moylan's house to be in the company of other Catholics who were driven by social justice concerns. It was a women-friendly space where they talked about liturgical and social reforms at meals with children underfoot.[53]

Moylan, Melville, and Reuther were part of a new generation of Catholic women who were animated by the potential for reform of Vatican II. Indeed, the Second Vatican Council had an ironically positive impact on female participation in public and religious life. The exclusively male gathering of pontiffs in Rome declared almost nothing about "women" as a distinct group, but female Catholics nevertheless embraced and carried out many of the decrees from Rome as if the Pope had been writing just for them. In church history, this period is called *aggiornamento*, or the era of modernization.[54] This emerging generation of women might best be represented with a new word. The expression "*aggiornamente*" does not exist in the Italian language, but adding the Italian feminine modifier captures how Catholic women, as historical actors, and *aggiornamento*, as a spirit of the times, mutually impacted each other.

The *aggiornamente* included Sister Mary Cain of Baltimore. Born in the late 1930s, Cain joined the Sisters of Notre Dame de Namur (SNDN) after receiving her BA and studying as a Fulbright scholar in France. She became a quintessential "new nun" of the postwar era by eschewing cloistered life to reside and work in a struggling urban neighborhood. New nuns lived in apartments rather than convents and chose not to wear the traditional habits as a means to be "in" the worlds they served.[55] Cain could acquire such training due in large part to the success of the mid-twentieth-century sister formation movement, which developed formal education and spiritual instruction for women religious who, until then, typically learned only "on the job."[56] The *aggiornamente* was a large, international, and politically diverse group of women that included civil rights marchers in Selma, Alabama, and Maryknoll missionaries in Latin America.

The Wales-born New Yorker Eileen Egan, who started Pax Christi USA in 1972, represents another important figure in the *aggiornamente*. Egan was part of an effort to expand the international reach of Pax Christi, which started in France at the end of World War II. The group's work in the United States launched as part of the civil rights movement of the mid-1960s. The American branch of Pax Christi represented the first Catholic organization to ignite the peace movement of the Vietnam War era. Pax welcomed pacifists and advocates of the just war tradition. It also published a magazine, *Peace*. The organization promoted the idea, according to Eileen Egan, "that by explaining the rational just-war formulations, and their contemporary inadequacy, we would help Catholics to question—and even reject—war, at least modern war."[57] More than any other group, Pax also pushed the Catholic hierarchy on matters of peace.

This spirit of modernization inspired women on the left and the right of the political spectrum, foreshadowing disputes that would divide the church in subsequent decades. Bolstered by the mandate of Vatican II, conservative Catholic women stood among the fervent opponents of the Equal Rights Amendment, formed Marianist anticommunist prayer groups, and organized as "pro-life" housewives.[58]

The most important *aggiornamente* of the 1960s came out of religious orders. On the East Coast, the SNDN, as well as the Religious of the Sacred Heart of Mary (RSHM) and the Sisters of St. Joseph (SSJ), became the origin points for many Catholic Left women activists. Pope John XXIII influenced them by advising all religious orders to renew the spiritual commitment of their communities and assess the needs of the modern world by going back to their biblical roots.[59] In the 1965 encyclical *Perfectae Caritatis*, he stated that "adaptation and renewal of the religious life includes both the constant return to the sources of all Christian life and to the original spirit of the institutes."[60] As one historian notes, the Sisters of Notre Dame de Namur responded to the Pope's directive by shifting their activities away from parochial school teaching "to direct work with the poor."[61]

SNDN Sister Mary Cain ultimately quit her teaching job at St. Maria Goretti in South Philadelphia to join the peace movement, bringing her former student, Cookie Ridolfi of the Camden 28, into the Catholic Left. The defense committee of the Catonsville Nine action served as Cain's entre into this world of activism, which she described as a "logical extension" of duties with the order. As she explained in a letter to her superior in the Maryland Province when she asked permission to work full time on the defense committee, the "ministry of reconciliation as Sisters of Notre Dame includes concrete efforts toward racial and social integration and promotion of a world vision on international peace and unity."[62]

Mary Cain was part of the Catholic Resistance vanguard, much of which tarried restlessly behind bars by the end of the 1960s. The arrest and incarceration of these original Catholic Leftists prevented them from organizing subsequent raids but galvanized other activists to assume these roles. This increasingly younger and less religious cohort transitioned the movement away from hit and stay to "hit and split" actions, whereby raiders burgled offices in the middle of the night to steal and destroy records. Some in the movement, especially the older and more religious generation, disdained this pivot as less brave and less Catholic since it eliminated the critical sacrifice of one's own freedom for the sake of the suffering world. But for college-age activists with more interest in momentum than Catholic martyrdom, going underground made more sense.

Tensions of all kinds mounted as 1970 approached—tensions between the women and men, the young and not-as-young, the religious and not-so-religious. Increased pressure from federal government and law enforcement officials compounded the stress, as it became more important for activists to keep secrets and stay out of sight. The mounting anxiety certainly led to bickering and strained friendships, but the raids continued, in part due to the web of close relationships that had deepened and drew more people in over a few short years. By the end of the 1960s, the Catholic Left had grown into a huge dysfunctional family, full of love, hurts, and resentments that fueled activist fervor.

CHAPTER THREE

One Big Catholic Movement Family

In his ethnographical work about Harlem Catholics, the scholar Robert Orsi describes what he calls the "domus-centered society." Through this understanding of community, the household represents more than a private site of family life. It is a holy place of prayer, ritual, and the transmission of values. Homelife, in many instances, shaped the piety of Italian Catholics even more than churches themselves.[1] Although Orsi's study focuses squarely on this one subculture in the earlier decades of the twentieth century, the centrality of and reverence for family life extended well beyond Italian enclaves. Much like Christians of other denominations, Catholics have historically drawn from the Commandments, Genesis, the Old Testament prophets, the Gospels, and other biblical stories to develop a theology and traditions that sanctify marriage, promote childbearing, and structure love relationships. But what about sexual relationships or family lives forged outside marriage?

In addition to activist work against the war, Catholic Leftists sought to reform the worlds of intimacy they inhabited. Coming into adulthood during the sexual revolution, many disobeyed the church teachings, which they regarded as outdated remnants of an old, hierarchical order. Living in a peaceful community required a break from their past. It often meant abandoning parents' homes to live with like-minded peers who devoted themselves collectively to promoting nonviolence. Some property-owning radical couples opened their own domus to less economically secure brothers and sisters in the movement. Catholic Leftists were by no means the only people radicalizing family life in the 1960s counterculture, but their experiences from seminaries, mission fields, convents, and Catholic Worker Houses brought spiritual dimensions to the intentional communities they established. Church officials rarely condoned such arrangements. Bishops shut down at least one communal house and oversaw the exit of many liberated religious from parishes and orders. The experiments in alternative lifestyles and sexual relationships did not reform the Catholic Church, as many radicals had hoped. They did, however, enable political activism.

The Catholic Left fell easily into communal living arrangements as a chance to apply traditions of communitarianism from their childhood upbringing and church teachings to the counterculture. Faith-based alternatives represented new iterations of utopian experiments that date back to the earliest days of the American Republic. Spiritual radicals had for centuries been forging communal living arrangements in the fields of American religious freedom to realize their visions of a perfect society. From Dutch Mennonites who arrived in 1663 to the nineteenth-century Shakers, every period of U.S. history produced communities seeking to eschew American social and economic relations by generating their own systems. The United States has also been home to other forms of religious communities, including Hasidic Jews, Amish, and Jehovah's Witnesses, whose members choose to live, work, and interact with nonmembers in some spheres of public life but observe strict codes within their flock.[2]

Catholics occupied this latter category of tight-knit closed communities for many decades. As a primarily immigrant and second-generation population for most of the nineteenth and early twentieth centuries, parochial schools and other parish institutions developed as forms of self-help and advancement.[3] The choice to live in their own neighborhoods, maintain old-world customs, and send children to Catholic schools earned disdain from nativist Christians of these decades. These critics judged Catholic habits as backward and cultish remnants of a medieval and autocratic church. But some Protestants admired the intractability of these practices, which continued to proliferate while their own institutions ossified. Distressed by the falling membership of urban churches in the 1930s, mainline denominations commissioned studies to track the relocation patterns of congregants, one of which negatively compared their "fragmentation" with that of the "splendidly organized" Catholic parishes."[4]

Though communitarian in theology and lifestyle, Catholics were rarely communards or communists. Church doctrine officially condemned Marxist socialism as atheistic and antithetical to natural law, but papal documents dating back to the sixteenth century had addressed the concept of the "common good." As one theologian notes in his systemic study of the encyclicals, "for all the popes, religious faith—whether nourished by custom, cosmos, or affection—is mediated by community. . . . [They] agree that human beings possess rights, but these are understood as grounded in God's will and linked to a moral requirement that their exercise not impair their common good."[5] This theology ultimately yielded the household-centered spirituality documented by Orsi, which was maintained "by the powerful demands of family loyalty . . . with the insistence on shared responsibility . . . and a concomitant insistence on self-sacrifice." "In all cases," he continues, "the individual was called upon to make important personal decisions with reference to the domus and not his or her wishes."[6]

The Catholic Left self-consciously adopted the church's communitarian traditions even as they challenged and pushed against its boundaries. By seizing on the church's fundamental organizing principle concerning community, Catholic Leftists sought to create a theological opportunity for prophetic intervention, for the Holy Spirit to move through its nonconformers as another means of realizing justice goals.

Some pointed to the example of Austrian martyr Franz Jägerstätter, the ultimate Catholic nonconformist of the World War II era. The deeply religious peasant refused to fight on behalf of the Axis powers. He was, in most respects, the model parish family man, who joyously but quietly observed the rituals of country life in the alpine Catholic world of mid-twentieth-century Austria. After the Anschluss forced him into military training, Jägerstätter decided his conscience, formed by the church's teachings, would not allow him to serve the Reich. With the tacit approval of Austria's cardinals and bishops, the Germans executed him by guillotine.[7]

Jägerstätter's story gained yet more power for Catholic nonconformists after the church censored attempts to broadcast it. When sociologist Gordon Zahn published *In Solitary Witness: The Life and Death of Jägerstätter* in 1965, the book contributed to the zeal of prophetic witness that drove the vanguard of Catholic Resistance.[8] Welcomed by activists but not by the mainstream church, Zahn's work exposed the rifts between prophetic and institutional Catholicism. Zahn brought unwanted attention to his employers at Loyola University Chicago when he published his research in the midst of the Second Vatican Council. Loyola's president prohibited a student organization from rewarding the professor its "Teacher-of-the-Year" award. As Zahn concluded that he was "persona non grata" at the Catholic university where he taught for fourteen years, the Fulbright scholar left for a position at the University of Massachusetts.[9] He also raided a Milwaukee draft board and napalmed ten thousand records with thirteen other raiders in September 1968.[10]

Those Catholic Leftists who took vows bore the brunt of admonishments from church officials for violating the rules. Sister Elizabeth

McAlister in New York became one of the most visible dissidents, and she was one among several to face excommunication by the authorities. Like many other religious, McAlister found herself tugged by the nurturing arms of her order on one side and the church's own moral teachings on the other. When she joined the RSHM in 1961, she entered into a French order more than one hundred years old. Within fifteen years, she was a wife and mother living in a faith-based community open to all denominations. McAlister's involvement in the Catholic Left started while she was working at the RSHM-run Marymount College in Tarrytown, New York, her alma mater. The daughter of Irish immigrants who was raised in New Jersey, McAlister started attending campus antiwar demonstrations where her fierce intellect and dynamic spirituality drew peers and youths into her orbit.[11]

Two of the Camden 28 found their way into the movement through McAlister's influence. Joan Reilly of Long Island burned with social justice fervor when she started at Marymount and was eager to make a difference in the world. She encountered McAlister on campus after taking a spring-break service trip to Appalachia. "She saw after my return from Kentucky," remembers Reilly, that "I became very involved on the campus in all the peace activities. So, she invited me into a smaller circle of folks to talk about our faith and our commitment to ending the war."[12] With her sister Rosemary ("Ro Ro"), who had been attending classes at another campus of Marymount in the city, Joan immersed herself in the antiwar movement.[13]

McAlister and the Reilly sisters joined Catholic Resistance when the draft board raids started to kindle interest in more actions—hit and stay or, later, hit and split burglaries in other cities. Like many of the Catholic Leftists, the Reilly sisters moved around to help with the planning and execution of these raids, but spent most of their time in New York, where operations revolved around "Iron Mountain," the East Bronx rectory that almost every draft board raider entered at some point. It was also where leader John Peter Grady, a sociologist and devout lay Catholic, lived with his family. "Belonging to such a community was like a prize," notes one historian, "a reward for risky action that gave activists a new 'family' and, just as importantly, provided them with the chance to have a great time."[14]

In addition to organizing actions, volunteers at Iron Mountain managed an economic operation to raise funds for the movement called Resistance Books. Through this small business, which was headed by Grady, professors at colleges and universities placed orders for course texts. Some proceeds of sales to students went into the movement overhead. Joan and Ro Ro Reilly reveled in the work of Iron Mountain, where they took the calls for Resistance Books and worked alongside others while groups like the Beatles and Crosby, Stills, Nash, and Young played in the background.[15]

About ten miles south of Iron Mountain bustled another cluster of radical activity around the residential facilities of the Woodstock Theological Seminary. Over one hundred years old, Woodstock had recently moved from a quiet and leafy Maryland campus to Morningside Heights on New York's Upper West Side. Its students went from occupying single rooms in residential halls to cohabiting in apartments, usually three in a single unit. The relocation was an experiment that aimed to develop a mutually beneficial relationship with the esteemed Jewish Theological Seminary and Union Theological Seminary, also located on Morningside Heights.[16]

The new Woodstock changed seminary life in unanticipated ways. It became a hotbed for liturgical and lifestyle experimentation. In Maryland, the Jesuit novitiates lived regimented lives with meals, prayer, and classes on fixed schedules that moved them uniformly through the campus and its rituals. In New York, Woodstock operated around different rented spaces rather than a centralized campus. The students lived more independent lives, with personal banking accounts and less oversight by superiors. Emboldened by the changing world around them, the seminarians experimented with new religious practices and relationships. They performed Mass in their unconsecrated home spaces, participated in political demonstrations, and socialized more freely with other youths of their generation, including women. Their quarters on Riverside Drive became gathering places for the Catholic Left.[17]

Overlapping friendship networks bound radicals at Iron Mountain and Woodstock College with other communities of Catholic radicals. After New York City, Washington, D.C., became the largest hub of these new families. Several activists lived and worked in the S Street home of Catonsville Nine defendant George Mische and his activist wife, Helene. In his mid-twenties, Mische had already served in the U.S. Army, labored among Catholic missionaries in Mexico, and attended the U.S. State Department's Service School. The Minnesota native had also worked for John F. Kennedy's Alianza para el Progreso (Alliance for Progress), which applied billions of dollars to fostering economic ties and supporting U.S.-friendly governments in Latin America. His tours in Mexico and Honduras cultivated in Mische a growing disillusionment with American government projects in the region. He also developed friendships with Maryknoll missionaries from the United States while he served there. The Maryknolls came honestly to their reputation as the

"Marines of the Catholic Church" by working in severely dispossessed communities across the globe. By the mid-1960s, Mische had returned to Washington, D.C., where he invited activists to live with him and Helene after the couple married. A community emerged as Maryknolls and other returning Catholic missionaries with fervid commitments to justice, but meager incomes, gladly welcomed the opportunity to cohabitate.[18]

Not far from the Misches' home, a Catholic Worker House attracted other radicals seeking spiritually driven activism. One navy veteran, John Swinglish, found his way into Catholic Resistance through this community, which ultimately led him to the Camden 28 action. Stationed in Oceanside, California, Swinglish had not served in Vietnam but his time in the military made him politically aware and ultimately skeptical of the war.[19] It was two years after his discharge, sometime in 1966 when he was working for a defense contractor in the capital, that his growing disillusionment with the U.S. military reached a breaking point. Swinglish's heavy conscience led him to a Catholic Worker House of Hospitality run by the Catholic Peace Fellowship. Though not especially religious, the veteran became so immersed in its activities that he quit his job to work there full time in 1969. The D.C. Nine Defense Committee became one of his projects.[20]

Communities in smaller cities attracted some activists, who soon moved to New York, Philadelphia, or Washington, D.C., to be part of the actions. Bob Good, the farmer's son and former seminarian who left Ohio to support the D.C. Nine during their trial, had not gone directly from Xavier University to the capital but rather spent several months at a Catholic communal house in Cleveland known as the "Thomas Merton Community." Founded by a cleric on suspension from the church, the community occupied a house on the west side of the city, where it aimed to serve the neighborhood's struggling inhabitants. The house, for example, sheltered local women dealing with domestic violence, like the one whose husband shot at its founder, Father Joe Begin.[21] Its inhabitants also organized protests against U.S.-backed atrocities in Latin America. Somewhat unmoored after ditching the seminary and then the university, Bob Good found a home in this place.[22]

Bigger cities with more universities and more problems generated larger activist networks. One community in Philadelphia developed around the work of the influential priest Joe Daoust. The thirty-year-old Jesuit was studying economics at the University of Pennsylvania and teaching at St. Joseph's University when he brought students together to live and work on the city's troubled Westside. Freshman Bob Williamson jumped at the opportunity. Williamson had been exhilarated by the brilliant people he met at St. Joseph's, including *The Feminine Mystique* author Betty Friedan and Dr. Martin Luther King, who both gave guest lectures while he was a student. "He [King] was easily the most charismatic person I have ever met, and his speech was devoted to explaining his opposition to the Vietnam War." "It affected me deeply," remembers Williamson. "It was the first time," he recalled, "I had heard someone make the case that this war was *morally* wrong."[23]

The summer project led by Daoust, remembers Williamson, sent students out to provide volunteer community services in the morning and talk about assigned texts in the evening. He and four other men received college credit for this work in what they called OPEN house (for Organization of People Engaged in the Neighborhood). Williamson met other community organizers, most of them about five years older and living in their own communal home, which they called Joseph House. Its inhabitants were ex-Catholics and non-Catholics who wanted to live in a community modeled on the Catholic Worker. "There was a social worker, a teacher, a lawyer, [and] Mike the housing inspector," remembers Williamson. A housemate brought him to a meeting with Daniel Berrigan and others at the movement's Iron Mountain headquarters in the Bronx. Bob participated in his first raid shortly thereafter.[24]

Williamson's path to the Camden 28 action overlapped with that of Terry Bucklew, another son of South Jersey who dropped out of college and landed in the Philadelphia resistance movement. Buckalew lived with his wife, Kathy, in a community called "Any Day Now" (a phrase from Bob Dylan's "I Shall Be Released"), which resided in a Quaker-owned property. The childhood sweethearts found themselves shunned by their families for their antiwar activism. "My parents disowned me," recalls Kathy, "changing their home phone number and the locks on their doors."[25]

Though not religious, Terry Buckalew reports a "coming to Jesus" moment that pushed him toward draft board raids. Looking for work, he signed up with Kelly Services, an agency that placed temporary office workers, who were known in the 1960s as "Kelly Girls." He landed a job at Philadelphia's Office of the Clerk of the Third Circuit Court of Appeals. While eating his lunch on the ninth floor one day, he observed a political demonstration on the street below. As Buckalew looked out the window, A. Leon Higginbotham, the first African American district judge of that circuit, approached from behind and asked what was going on. Buckalew responded that he was watching a protest. When Higginbotham asked about Terry's position on the war, the Kelly Girl temp responded that he supported the protesters. The judge then said, "Maybe you should be down there."[26] Buckalew, who had tremendous admiration for Higginbotham, started helping with an action in Philadelphia just a few weeks after that conversation.

Camden 28 defendant Keith Forsyth, who worked alongside Williamson and Buckalew in Philadelphia, came to Catholic Resistance with a similar ambivalence toward religion. Forsyth had been a history major at Wooster College in Ohio before his expulsion at age twenty-two. His relationship with his parents had been tense since his teenage years, especially with his father, a veteran of the U.S. navy whose politics leaned right. These tensions escalated into "open warfare" with his father, especially when Forsyth hitchhiked to Philadelphia, "crashing" with students there, and joining the resistance movement.[27] Forsyth was a nonbeliever by the time he was raiding for the Catholic Left. But like William Davidon, Cookie Ridolfi, Bob Williamson, and most of the other nonreligious resistors in the movement, he was at home in its spiritual milieu.[28]

Forsyth's parents raised him with no exposure to Catholicism except occasional references to "idol worshippers." Yet "these were people," he remembers, "who were into a religious tradition, and that was something I totally understood, and I totally appreciated." His upbringing as a Baptist in West Virginia and Ohio brought him close to his grandmother, a very religious woman. As someone who had given sermons as a youth and was, as a musician, moved by Gospel music, the religious context of the Catholic Left felt appropriate to Forsyth.[29]

Three hundred miles north of Philadelphia, a group of former nuns fed the political waters of Vietnam resistance from the intentional community they established in the Dorchester section of Boston. In 1968, after talking secretly among each other about withdrawing from their order to participate more vigorously in the social justice campaigns of their time, several Sisters of St. Joseph (SSJ) established what they called the "Bread Community" in St. Leo's parish. The parish pastor, Father Shawn Sheehan, supported their efforts to continue the commitment they made to each other and to the social justice charism they embraced as SSJs.[30]

The sisters, who had signed papers at the mother house in Milton, Massachusetts, asking to be excused from their vows, enthusiastically removed their habits, put on street clothes, and moved into apartments on Nightingale Street. While working menial summer jobs and teaching in the academic year, the women sought opportunities to continue their mission in poor communities. One of them, Andrea O'Mally, married a lead organizer for the United Farm Workers (UFM), Marcos Muñoz, and brought several of the other women into the boycott movement for migrant grape pickers. The sisters also brought friends and former students into the fold.[31]

Paul Couming grew up in St. Leo's Parish, which he remembers as "a hotbed of inner-city revolutionary activity for the Catholic church." Couming had already been protesting the war for a few years when he joined some of the women in the Bread Community for actions.[32] He had received a suspended sentence and probation for refusing to carry his draft card. To the consternation of his working-class parents, who lived in housing owned by St. Leo's, Couming raided draft boards starting in 1969 and continued until his arrest at the Camden Federal Building in 1971.[33]

The communal living of the Catholic Left forged more than spiritual and social connection. Sexual relationships abounded, especially where they were forbidden. The sexual revolution and radical movements did not merely converge in the 1960s; rather, they shaped and actuated each other. Hope in the collective power for change acted as a sexual elixir in settings where people fell in love with each other's political zeal. The popularity of "liberation," moreover, gave Leftists the green light to act on their longings for fellow activists. Parental, societal, and church approval lost their power to control relationships in movements based on the mistrust of authority. As one leader of the Weather Underground, Bill Ayers, remembered, "The movement swept us away completely because it demanded everything of us, and because it offered everything to us—high purpose, real work to do, love, dreams, hope."[34] Ayers readily admits, however, that his excitement and lust blinded him to the inequality of these relationships as women faced different consequences, such as pregnancy, than their sexual partners. As his friend Ruthie told him, "Free love only meant that movement men could screw any woman they could get, free of emotional encumbrances." The "problem of power," she added, was unavoidable.[35]

The erotics of activism shaped the Catholic Left as it did every other segment of the antiwar movement, resulting in the same spectrum of consequences, from lasting, meaningful relationships to unfortunate instances of sexual exploitation. Shared backgrounds in Catholicism, however, added a common ideological framework for understanding these bonds.

More than a few Catholic Leftists found their life partners in the movement. Anne Dunham, a student at New Rochelle College, met her husband, Frank Pommersheim of Queens, while she was preparing actions. Dunham had been working in the Resistance Books sales business that operated at Iron Mountain, which is where she first encountered Cookie Ridolfi, Bob Good, the Reilly sisters, and most of the other activists who worked on the Camden 28 action. Pommersheim, a recent graduate from Columbia Law School had just returned from completing a VISTA project in Alaska. He appeared one day in the midst of this activity. Dunham and Pommersheim fell in love while they were helping with the Camden action. The Reverend Michael Doyle married them after their 1971 arrests, in a low-budget wedding at the Woodstock Seminary.[36]

One hundred or so guests who had received handwritten invitations on construction paper gathered for a ceremony in the chapel, where a Navajo prayer rug served as an alter cloth. Dunham remembers it as "a kind of movement wedding, very impromptu." She made her own dress and Pommersheim wore a borrowed suit. The music was simple: Cookie Ridolfi and Lianne Moccia sang popular folk tunes, including Pete Seeger's "To Everything There Is a Season" (also known as "Turn! Turn! Turn!"). Festivities then moved to the Woodstock dining hall, where friends and family contributed to a pot-luck meal. The bride made the bread and Bob Good made a nutmeg feather cake for dessert. At one point, Pommersheim reached into his pocket and found a bag of marijuana. They never identified the gift giver, but they think it was Bob Williamson, who by then had changed his name to "Weed-Ex" in honor of his new, free-spirited identity (see figure 7).[37]

Bostonians Anne Walsh and Robert Cunnane had a similar story but had to deal with the complication of the vows they took to their orders before falling in love with each other.[38] Walsh and Cunnane were among several ex-priests and ex-nuns who married through the movement. The thirty-six-year-old Cunnane was one of the participants of the Gethsemani retreat. Educated in Rome, he was a Stigmatine priest when he participated in the Milwaukee 14 raid of 1968. He met Walsh, one of the former Sisters of St. Joseph, in the Dorchester Bread Community, shortly after the Milwaukee action. After leaving his order, the two wed in the presence of five hundred of their closest family members and friends. Both Reilly sisters married fellow activists as well. Rosemary wed Carl Brogue, a civil rights attorney who represented her and the other Camden 28 defendants, and soon they had a daughter. Joan raised four children with her husband, Philadelphia activist Michael DeBerardinis.[39]

For Catholics in religious orders, the choice to marry was not merely a matter of falling for someone and abandoning their vows. Many came to this decision after a significant period of discernment. For women,

FIGURE 7. Woodstock Wedding
Anne Dunham laying flowers on the altar for her wedding to fellow activist Frank Pommersheim on December 2, 1971. The nuptials took place at Woodstock Seminary in the Morningside Heights neighborhood of New York City. Photo courtesy of Anne Dunham and Frank Pommersheim.

leaving their sisters often felt like leaving their family and a way of life they loved. Anne Walsh of Boston left the Sisters of St. Joseph with a heavy heart. She was saying good-bye to an intellectual as well as a spiritual community, one that endowed her with the knowledge and critical capacity to recognize and tackle the problems of the modern world. She remembers one mentor, Sister Connolly, in particular. Connolly came to their convent after finishing her PhD at the University of Wisconsin. As their instructor of intellectual history, the accomplished academic taught them about the reforms of Vatican II. It was also from Sister Connolly that Walsh first learned about the Holocaust. "I think she enchanted those that wanted to be enchanted. And I was one of them."[40]

Sister Mary Cain similarly left her order and wed fellow activist and former priest Tony Scoblick, but she adamantly refuted rumors that the

66   CHAPTER THREE

marriage prompted her departure in 1970. Cain insisted, in fact, that she did not "leave" the order but that her status changed. "I never left. I just didn't. I am at present what we call an associate . . . someone who is familiar with the ideals of the commitment of Julie, the foundress, and carries that into their everyday life."[41] She even maintained her vow of poverty when supporters tried to raise bail for her after a criminal indictment in 1971. She refused to accept the funds.[42]

The most famous couple in the movement suffered an embarrassing and politically fraught exposure of their relationship, partly because they also refused to leave their orders when they married. Sister Elizabeth McAlister and Father Philip Berrigan carried on a clandestine love affair that mingled dangerously with secret plans of the movement. Officials charged eight activists, including McAlister and Berrigan, with conspiracy to overthrow the government, bringing them to court in what became known as the Harrisburg Seven trial. Prosecutors charged the activists with plotting to steal documents, bomb the heating tunnels underneath a federal building, and kidnap national security adviser Henry Kissinger. They based their case primarily on letters exchanged between the nun and the priest.[43]

Berrigan was in Lewisburg Federal Penitentiary in Pennsylvania. A fellow inmate, Boyd Douglas, who was out on furlough, facilitated the transfer of smuggled letters between Berrigan and Sister McAlister. Before delivering the correspondence to Berrigan, however, Douglas first shared the materials with the FBI. Those letters included musings by McAlister about the value of a citizens' arrest of Henry Kissinger, among many other random thoughts, including their feelings of deep affection for each other.[44]

To almost everyone's surprise, it was revealed that McAlister and Berrigan were married, at least in their own eyes. Though the state ultimately failed to convict any of the defendants, the Harrisburg Seven trial caused some chaos in the movement because it exposed a relationship the couple had deliberately hidden from everyone, including trusted fellow activists. They had been husband and wife for two years.[45]

Before the revelation, Berrigan had asserted the importance of celibacy for activism, arguing that romantic entanglements made it difficult for resisters to focus on political action. Now he was the one who was entangled. Once the district attorney's case exposed his relationship with McAlister, Berrigan not only reversed his position completely but revealed that the couple had been joined in a secret marriage of "mutual consent" since 1969. They had sealed the union through vows to each other, with no witnesses but each other, in an Episcopal church. Later, after their release on parole in 1973, the couple formalized their marriage, which ultimately led to their excommunication from the Catholic Church. This ceremony was blessed by their friend, another married priest, Paul Mayer, who faced the same consequence.[46] The Berrigan-McAlister relationship jarred some of the celibate activists in the movement, testing their commitment to the Catholic Left as well as to the priesthood and sisterhood.[47]

For many others, the McAlister-Berrigan marriage squared with the model of justice, resistance, and community that they believed were necessary to prepare the world for peace. The couple approached their marriage as a holy sacrament to be recognized in the eyes of God and a loving community only. The larger structures of Catholicism and the state mattered far less to them than the teachings of the church. They deliberately broadcast this choice into their community of faith as a way to evangelize their vision of a peaceful society. These radicals also sought to be deliberately prophetic, aiming to rattle mainstream Catholics into an awareness of how the complacent observance of rules and rituals lulled them. This avoidance of reality prevented people from perceiving how they perpetuated death and destruction.

In his prison journal, Berrigan described his wedding as "political" as well as "religious." Resistance was teaching them that love, fellowship, and faith were greater than the usual rules. "The issue is not marriage or celibacy," he wrote, "but mature fidelity to the Gospel, in contemplation and loving witness." In effect, married love allowed him and McAlister to nurture a broader ministry. Berrigan declared that they had no intention of giving up their vocations—marriage did not "nullify" their membership in the priesthood and sisterhood. Before marrying each other, they had married "all who suffer in consequence of war, poverty, racism."[48]

McAlister elaborated on these ideas in a 1971 interview with the Catholic periodical *Commonweal*, emphasizing that the movement sought to generate peace according to the Gospels. "I am part of a religious community," she explained, "but I think I grew to understand better what community was about by being part of a so-called peace community—for want of a better name. And both that peace community and my religious community have been enriched by one another."[49] Like Berrigan and others in the Catholic Left, she made frequent reference to the early Christians. Peace would emerge not only through civil disobedience, but also through real connections between people: "human relations, community, friendship which of course can only be preserved in the Lord." Jesus's disciples were threatening the governmental structures in their time, she said, and she herself was not interested in reforming the church or the government. She wanted to work on the level of community by developing an alternative model for relationships. "Bishops

68 CHAPTER THREE

and chancery officials will probably continue to act as bishop and chancery officials. Are they the people who will make a difference to the world? . . . I've never found administration on that level either interesting or—in Gospel senses—free."[50]

By casting their choice to marry in a wider theological framework, McAlister and Berrigan added their voices to recent Catholic debates about the importance of individual conscience in discerning moral choices. Developments of the post–World War II era, such as the Vietnam War and the sexual revolution, demanded that scholars of the church reckon with the role of individual subjective judgment in recognizing the mandates of natural law. Catholics sought answers to the questions about right and wrong in traditional teachings about conscience to help them understand how they should deal with pressing concerns such as how to respond to the draft or the church's ban on birth control. Priests in the United States, notes one historian, repeatedly defended the rights of laypeople to follow their conscience when it came to fighting in wars, planning their families, and in the case of the medical professional, performing procedures like abortion that violated their interpretation of natural law. When it came to militarism and sexuality, writes Peter Cajka, Catholics felt the "tensions" between the demands of the law (including church law) and their own moral judgment, with "both pulls congealing into one broader antiauthoritarian logic that led men and women to reach for conscience as a primary moral guide."[51]

As important as personal conscience became to mid-twentieth-century Catholics, this did not stop church authorities from harshly penalizing priests and nuns who openly violated their vows. The Pope excommunicated McAlister and Berrigan for wedding before church authorities could "laicize" them (bestow dispensation from the obligations of their orders).

Excommunication meant that the church no longer recognized McAlister and Berrigan as Christians. Nevertheless, they continued to earn wide respect in the Catholic Left, especially as both accumulated years behind bars, while taking turns raising their children. In 1973 they established a residential community in Baltimore called Jonah House, which exists to this day. Their vision of community also brought a theological edge to the late twentieth-century experiments with nontraditional lifestyles. Along with Paul Mayer, they spearheaded Catholic communal living and other post-1960 radical adaptations of the Catholic parish.[52]

Mayer, the celebrant of the official Berrigan-McAlister wedding, was a Jewish exile from Nazi Germany who converted to Catholicism and became a Benedictine monk. Liberation theology, the civil rights movement, and the writing of Thomas Merton radicalized him in the post–World War II era, landing him in Catholic Resistance. The full extent of his activist work remains unknown, but Mayer was also indicted as part of the Harrisburg Seven. He and his wife, Naomi Lambert, who was a nun in the order of the Medical Mission Sisters when they met, established Project Share in East Orange, New Jersey, whereby a group of families in two neighboring six-unit apartment buildings lived and supported each other communally.[53]

Movement romances did not all end so well. The tight-knit communal parish lives that characterized Catholic childhoods fostered an ignorance of the wide world of sexual opportunities that greeted women and men in the 1960s. Radicals often failed to consider the problematic outcomes that resulted when romantic partners with different stakes and unequal status jumped into bed together. In some instances, charismatic men of the older generation slept with younger, college-age women who reveled in the attention from their more worldly and experienced lovers. The men, however, did not enter into these relationships with the same interests or expectations, especially since some of them were priests. Others were even already married. The women grew up in Catholic communities where they had been gender-segregated in parochial schools that taught them to regard their bodies as holy vessels. Even as most of them happily shed these attitudes along with their plaid uniforms, the free love atmosphere posed dangers for them. They risked pregnancy from sex with men who had no interest in marrying them and who feared the consequences of broken vows.

Lianne Moccia developed a searing crush on John Peter Grady, the de facto leader of the movement after both Berrigan brothers landed behind bars. "I was completely under the sway of John Grady," she reflected; "I think I was totally in love with him, in my own 21-year-old way." She enjoyed flirting with this man of twice her age who, by all accounts, emerged as one of the bravest, most interesting, and most reckless personalities in the movement. But they never entered into a sexual relationship. Instead, Moccia distanced herself from him because it did not, in her words, feel "chaste" to the Catholic school girl in her.[54]

At forty-six, Grady was an established figure who had earned the nickname "Quicksilver" for his ability to slip through the fingers of law enforcement.[55] He had grown up in the Bronx in an Irish immigrant family before fighting in World War II and earning a BA at Manhattan College. He then started a PhD program in sociology at Fordham, where he earned a Fulbright scholarship to study at the London School of Economics. Grady was business manager at *Jubilee*, a popular Catholic magazine published between 1953 and 1967 that laid some of the foundations for the changes that Vatican II brought to American Catholicism. He and his wife, Teresa, raised five children in the Bronx, which is where the family became friends with the Berrigans.[56] With common, working-class Irish roots, John, Dan, and Phil shared lives infused with the daily rhythms of Catholic family life as well as a deep commitment to social justice. The Grady household became a welcoming home for the brother priests. A royalty check donated by Phil paid tuition for ten children at a Montessori school started by Teresa and John.[57] And when one of the Grady children was hit by a car and suffered a head injury, Dan conducted several private Masses at the home.[58]

Even as he emerged as one of the most galvanizing figures in the movement, it became apparent that Grady had serious problems with alcohol and women. Like her friend Lianne Moccia, Anne Walsh thrilled at the attention Grady paid her, and she did not put up the same boundaries to protect herself from his advances. Walsh, in fact, had sex with several men in the movement before starting a relationship with her future husband. These men, to her disappointment, did not see her the way she saw them. She beheld them as spiritual figures. Having spent five years literally behind the walls of a convent, she could not believe that these dashing, highly educated activists had their eyes on her. She slept with John Grady—once in the backseat of a car—which led to great disappointment when his amorous attention moved quickly to other women who were her close friends. Walsh then had a short sexual relationship with a Jesuit priest, Camden 28 defendant Ed McGowan. It came to an end when she thought she might be pregnant. She reported the news to her lover, thinking it would lead to their marriage. McGowan, who had no intention of joining Walsh in holy matrimony, responded that his mother "could count." A wedding would, in other words, never convince the elder Mrs. McGowan of their chastity before they wed.[59]

In hindsight, Walsh came to see Grady's and McGowan's behavior as exploitative. She had looked up to the men and found their interest in her to be intoxicating. "I thought I was Joan of Arc. I thought I was compelling, singularly compelling. And that was the reason that he was overcome with love or lust to me. I thought that. And so, I was naïve, and I was inexperienced."[60]

Walsh learned hard lessons from these relationships, which contributed to the feeling that she no longer wanted to participate in draft board raids. The Catholic Left by then had entered its final and riskiest phase. Chatter of a possible raid in Camden, New Jersey, quietly made its way through the movement grapevine. John Peter Grady, with help from

Cookie Ridolfi, would need to coordinate the planning since the other movement leaders were in jail. They had to find volunteers, establish a base of operations in the city, and work with the inexperienced locals who had initiated the idea for targeting the Camden Federal Building in the first place. By choosing to sit this one out, Anne Walsh set her life on a calmer course. She also dodged an elaborate trap by the federal government—a trap that ensnared many of her cohorts in the movement, kept them in legal limbo for two years, and diffused the momentum of the draft board raids. As a result, the Camden 28 raid marked the beginning of the end for the Catholic Left.

PART II

Exit 4 to Camden

The sound of strumming guitars filled the sanctuary at St. Vincent Pallotti Church. Located in the tiny suburb of Haddonfield, New Jersey, St. Vincent's had begun offering a new, folksy style of Sunday Mass that brought younger Catholics from far beyond its own parish. These Catholics sought a connection to God that the formal "smells and bells" liturgy of their childhoods had failed to awaken in their hearts. It was the 1960s and they were feeling the spirit of Vatican II. The new, simpler approach to the centuries-old ceremony filled the church with two hundred or more worshippers a month, including five from the region who became friends. Eugene Dixon, Martha Schemeley, Marnie O'Dell, Phil Madden, Joseph Kelly, and Michael Giocondo discovered that they shared not only this connection of their Catholicism, but also a common interest in the civil rights movement and opposition to the Vietnam War.[1]

As the group grew closer over shared meals and road trips to protests, they experienced the same frustration and fatigue affecting so many activists who were having to grapple with the realization that their time and efforts had not yielded results. The demonstrations were not working as everyone had hoped. Discussions about this problem revealed that the friends from St. Vincent's were only a degree or two removed from the central actors of the Catholic Left in friendship networks. This insight led to more discussion about Camden, New Jersey, where some of the group lived and others passed through on a regular basis. The city's problems made it an ideal location for a draft board raid. Before the end of 1970, the Catholic Left had started working with the friends from St. Vincent's to set up operations in the city.[2]

Camden not only gave up more than its share of men to the Vietnam War, it also sat at a crossroads. Almost every major South Jersey thruway led into Camden, which was the county seat and largest city in South Jersey. When the state built the turnpike in 1951 (at the time, one of the largest toll highways ever constructed), it marked its fourth exit "Camden" to direct traffic to this thriving center of industry. On Fourth and Market Streets, the federal building stood in the heart of a once-vibrant manufacturing center that had faced a steep decline after 1960. The neoclassical structure housed a federal courtroom, a post office branch, numerous government offices, and three draft boards.[3]

Even after the biggest employers moved to the southern cities over the 1960s, bureaucrats, clerks, lawyers, and judges continued to lug their briefcases around Camden's marbled halls of power. They still met each other in nearby diners or at the Plaza Hotel restaurant across the street. Just a few blocks north, on Cooper Street, hummed Rutgers University, where local and suburban students took classes in converted townhouses and studied in the library before returning to their parents' homes for dinner. Five blocks to the southeast, Cooper Hospital rose from the landscape almost as high as city hall. These buildings constituted an island of middle-class order around which the once thriving neighborhoods of the city crumbled.

Two overlapping political groups sought to tackle these problems. The Catholic Left and the Camden civil rights movement shared goals, ideals, and some—but only a few—activists with a foot in each world. The two movements grew out of geographical and cultural milieus that were racially divided from each other but both active in the common political landscape of the struggling city. At a crucial moment in the early 1970s, as class and political tensions in Camden reached a boiling point, the pressure pushed these two movements with shared interests into different directions. The Catholic Left was drawn to the troubles of Camden from origin points in other cities. The civil rights movement, on the other hand, was mostly homegrown. The close proximity within which these movements operated without fusing shows how class and racial differences made it difficult to work together over the color line, even though both sides shared basic ideals and many of the same end goals. To whom would you entrust your life when bullets flew and prison loomed? Only, it turned out, people who were kin.

CHAPTER FOUR

Camden Calls the Catholic Left

Camden came to the attention of the Catholic Left late into the movement, nearly four years after that first hit and stay action at the Baltimore Customs House in 1967. By that time, John Grady and Cookie Ridolfi had both become main organizers of raids, traveling from city to city to set up the actions. Anita Ricci of South Philadelphia often joined them in this work. Ridolfi and Ricci had been friends since they were teens at Maria Goretti High School. Now twenty-three years old, the two found that bond strained by John Grady, who became romantically involved with both women while still married to wife Teresa. This friction coincided with the greater mayhem the Camden 28 would encounter between 1971 and 1973.[1]

Participants in the movement did not know how to describe the connection between these three activists. Some called them "traveling companions," but that description inadequately captured the extent of the commitment they brought to the movement. It also glossed over the nature of their relationships. Ricci and Ridolfi had been friends for more than a decade. As these two brilliant women who met at Goretti High School grew closer to Grady, however, they found themselves in a problematic love triangle as they were organizing the raid in Camden. The planning for that operation started in fall 1970, when friends at St. Vincent's in Haddonfield proposed the Camden Federal Building as a target. Grady, Ridolfi, and Ricci agreed to this proposal because they could coordinate it with the other New Jersey actions that were already on the table.[2]

The trio had been deeply involved in casing sites in Princeton and Trenton when they arranged the first meeting to prepare for the Camden raid, which they put on the calendar for five months later, in summer 1971. It was no surprise that the first gathering of potential participants took the form of a retreat. It had, by then, become the preferred introductory setting for the movement, where people could start building relationships strong enough to hold its secrets. A small group, not more than a handful of interested parties, met at the El Centro Hispanic community center in Camden for that first local gathering. Michael Giocondo, a former Franciscan brother and one of the founders of El Centro, hosted this meeting and became a vital figure in the action at the federal building.[3]

Giocondo was one of the congregants at St. Vincent's in Haddonfield, where he and Franciscans Joe Madden and Phil Kelly met social worker Martha Schemeley, Schemeley's close friend Marnie O'Dell, and an automotive plant supervisor from Pennsylvania named Eugene Dixon. The five shared a common demographic among Catholics in South Jersey, where postwar economic development around Philadelphia had lifted them economically from the working-class, immigrant roots of their parents, grandparents, or great-grandparents. The folk Mass trend that brought them together had been a bohemian reach for church roots. Though it did not appeal to everyone in the Catholic Left, this liturgical turn of the Vatican II era represented another means of spiritual expression for a generation that was mistrustful of tradition.[4]

Like the formation of communes, the guitar Masses attracted Catholics seeking authenticity and intimacy. Newly written prayers and hymns became a means for liberal thinkers to claim Catholicism for themselves and the broader Left. The music also deliberately adopted what one scholar calls a "noncreedal universalism." "Whereas traditional Catholic liturgical music reminds people of the complexity and fanciness of Catholic ritual," he observes, "these folk songs could easily be sung in a Methodist, Lutheran, or Presbyterian church."[5] Gene Dixon remembers the fun of folk Masses but also the moment when he and his friends started feeling they were not enough.[6]

As the pared-down rituals led the friends into political protest, the Masses also made them aware of the cozy lifestyles and relative privilege they enjoyed in a world full of deep economic disparities and suffering. Concerning their eventual decision to raid a draft board, Dixon recalled that the group started talking about a spiritual emptiness that had befallen them. Since about 1963, when they carpooled to Washington, D.C., to hear Martin Luther King Jr. deliver his "I Have a Dream" speech on the national mall, a sense of futility had grown in fits and starts. It intensified after the Vietnam Moratorium demonstration six years later, where they joined a group of a half-million to protest the war.[7]

These South Jersey activists, who had either already graduated from or never started college, did not come from the common mold of sixties campus protesters. The church of St. Vincent Palotti, rather than classrooms and coffee shops, incubated their radicalism. They grew up in the homes of working people, origins quite different from the tidy two-story colonials they passed by on their way into leafy Haddonfield. They found themselves relaxing in the security that these new environs provided. Their economic fortunes had improved, but at a time when the inequalities in American society had become more visible. Dixon once described his circle of friends as "typical 'middle-class' Americans leading typical comfortable lives." After each journey to the capital, they drove back to their "middle class haven." It was easy. "You get on the train . . . get back to Woodbury," he recalled of patterns that came to feel increasingly meaningless.[8]

Dixon and the others came to believe that they had to do something that "cost" them if they were going to make an impact.[9] The city of Camden emerged from these conversations as the inverse of Haddonfield, as a place suffering from disinvestment while the surrounding suburbs drew affluence away into the expanding webs of subdivisions.

Camden had only recently landed in such terrible circumstances. The city was a thriving port until the mid-twentieth century, a place where people lived and worked in the nearby manufacturing plants or the businesses that served these larger companies. Directly across the Delaware River from the city of Philadelphia, in the early nineteenth century, its founders had created a harbor community that capitalized on ferrying people and goods from East Coast centers to its bigger neighbor across the river. Between 1880 and 1920, the city's population more than doubled, increasing from 41,659 to 116,309.[10] When what became known as the Benjamin Franklin Bridge finally opened in 1926 to join Camden and Philadelphia, the new artery accelerated the pace of Camden's development into an industrial center. Campbell's Soup Company, the radio maker RCA, and other businesses furnished thousands of jobs.[11] Parish-based neighborhoods developed to house the mostly Catholic newcomers as well as smaller populations of Black residents from the South.[12]

During the Great Depression, Camden suffered the same economic decline as every other U.S. city, but not for long. Its shipyard grew into one of the most productive in the world. The New York Shipbuilding Corporation employed thirty-three thousand workers during World War II, when it launched some of the best known naval vessels of the period, including the USS *Kitty Hawk* and USS *Idaho*.[13] The company grew into the nation's second-largest private shipbuilding manufacturer in these years.[14] Employees could boast of their battleship, the USS *South Dakota*, and eighty-six other land crafts they built, with which

U.S. troops stormed Utah Beach in Normandy in the historic D-Day invasion of 1944. By 1965, state and county thoroughfares such as Route 676, the White Horse Pike, and an elevated rail line known to locals as the PATCO High Speed Line connected residents across the metro region to each other and Philadelphia, through Camden.[15]

The city's Black residents, meanwhile, established a secure foothold even as discrimination blocked access to the best jobs and housing. They did not face the same level of threat as in the southern states they had left to relocate in Camden, but the Delaware Valley nevertheless became a segregated space like the rest of the industrialized North. Neighborhood boundaries in Camden mostly fell along the lines of its Irish, Polish, and Italian Catholic churches, where first-, second-, and third-generation residents did not welcome dark-skinned arrivals. Racial hierarchies moreover governed the distribution of opportunity favoring native-born whites at the top and non-whites at the bottom. The U.S. census of 1950 shows that Camden's Black residents earned a median income only 73 percent that of whites in the city.[16] But jobs were jobs, which is how Camden also became a destination for Puerto Rican migrants, who started trickling into the city in the 1940s to work in the food-processing sector, which thrived from war contracts.[17] By 1970, these Latino newcomers constituted a significant proportion of the city's overall population.[18] Black and Brown residents suffered far worse from whites, however, when this growth halted.

The process of deindustrialization that made the urban Northeast and Midwest into the "Rust Belt" hit Camden especially hard. Between 1948 and 1972 the city lost 27,567 manufacturing jobs.[19] RCA, which employed almost 10,000 people in the 1930s, opened plants in four other states following a 1936 strike in Camden. By 1952 only 770 RCA jobs remained in the port city. Other companies followed. As these better-paid industrial positions left Camden, so did the better-paid people, who moved their families to the suburban enclaves sprouting up in the rural outposts of South Jersey. Federal government policies aimed at improving economic circumstances during the Great Depression only worsened the problems of segregation.[20]

In 1933 Congress approved the Home Owners Loan Corporation (HOLC), which refinanced mortgages, and the next year it approved the Federal Housing Administration (FHA), which insured private mortgages. Both were aimed at helping Americans buy their own homes. The HOLC, however, created colored maps to designate worthiness for lending that favored areas dominated by white residents. The government thus redlined Black neighborhoods out of consideration for insured loans, making it difficult for African Americans to buy or improve properties while incentivizing white homeowners to keep their enclaves racially homogeneous.[21]

The city's population thus shrunk with deindustrialization, especially among white residents. Between 1960 and 1970, Camden's population decreased from 117,000 residents to 102,000. Of those 102,000 people, 6,500 were Puerto Rican and 35,000 were Black.[22] Nonwhites accounted for about 40 percent of the population by 1970. Professional offices and businesses opened across the city's border in Delaware Township, renamed "Cherry Hill" in 1961 after the shopping mall, which attracted shoppers from across the region.[23]

In contrast to the mixed housing stock of single-family homes, town houses, and apartments that characterized Camden, the new boroughs included very little in the way of affordable housing. Cherry Hill, Mt. Laurel, Moorestown, and other new communities drew residents and wealth from the region's urban centers. The lower-earning segment of the population, which tended to be Black and Puerto Rican, could not afford a mortgage in these places. Homes in Camden, meanwhile, lost value over the decade and succumbed to the ravages of neglect. Government-sponsored urban renewal programs and private development contributed to the economic woes by bulldozing Black neighborhoods to make room for transit and building projects. These new highways and the PATCO Speedline rails carried drivers and passengers over the decaying streets and dilapidated housing of Camden on their way into Philadelphia. No driver or passenger need set foot in Camden.[24]

A local civil rights movement was organized to address the problems of racial inequality that had been growing in proportion to white flight over the 1960s. With a branch of the National Association for the Advancement of Colored People (NAACP) dating back to the 1940s, Camden already had a decades-old history of activism that revolved around Black churches. The leaders of these institutions, however, shied away from tactics that might be construed as confrontational, especially as Black nationalists of the late 1960s made the civil rights movement more militant. The reticent older generation yielded to a younger generation of radicals who brought Black power to the city with protests that tended to focus on discrimination in housing and police violence against African Americans.[25]

This newer movement of the late 1960s coalesced around an organization called the Black People's Unity Movement (BPUM), which formed after the militant Black power activist Rap Brown delivered a rousing speech at the convention center in 1967. Brown's appearance drew four thousand people, 80 percent of them from outside the city.

Although its founders were Black men who had grown up in the city, BPUM expanded quickly to include women and youths. It soon enfolded Puerto Rican activists as well. Unlike many other Black power organizations, which distanced themselves from whites in the interests of self-empowerment, BPUM formed interracial coalitions. It allied itself with an organization called the Camden Civil Rights Ministerium (CCRM), which was made up of Protestant ministers, including white men of the cloth. It also worked with the Congress of Racial Equality (CORE) and the NAACP.[26] By the early 1970s, students from Rutgers University and Camden High School also became involved. Together, these different groups became a metropolitan-wide movement that attracted people beyond the city with roots or other ties, but not homes, in Camden.[27]

BPUM captured media attention in 1968 when it rallied behind the family of Clarence Shields, an African American construction worker. The city had forced the Shields family out of their home to make way for a high-rise luxury apartment complex called Northgate II. Civil rights advocates rallied around the Shields family because the first complex in the development, Northgate I, would not allow Black and Puerto Rican tenants. Black, white, and Puerto Rican protesters demonstrated at the Walt Whitman hotel, where the Shields family resided while waiting for a suitable apartment to become available. Members of BPUM and their supporters also stormed Northgate I, defacing its structures and triggering alarms. The actions succeeded in getting the Shields family a home in white East Camden, as well as payment of their expensive hotel bill. The family continued to struggle, however, after an arsonist set the new home on fire the night they moved in. Their plight drew widespread outrage, prompting the organization of white suburban supporters into "Friends of BPUM."[28]

Where were the Catholics in all this unrest? The story of Gualberto "Gil" Medina offers some insight into the parallel political tracks of the Catholic Left and local civil rights efforts. Medina straddled both movements, which did not intersect. The Rutgers student was active in a militant Puerto Rican organization modeled on the Black Panthers, called the Young Lords. "I was a very engaged activist in the region," remembers Medina. Referring to the Catholic Left, he explains, "You know our paths crossed." The Catholic Michael Giocondo at El Central was a friend, which is one reason why Medina participated in some of the raid preparations early on. Medina helped surveil the Camden Federal Building. He did not, however, maintain his involvement in the draft board action because, in his words, he could not do the work of the raids and also the work needed by his own community. "I wanted to be with them," he recalled in an interview, "but you know being with them meant that I had to sacrifice working with the Latino and Black community."[29]

Casing targets and planning a break-in required a huge investment of time. Advocating for the Black and Puerto Rican community required just as much time, especially as tensions with the police escalated in summer 1971. Medina said in one interview that he would have been the "Camden 29th" if not for the upheaval in his own community, which then demanded he work full time to broker a peace.[30] The youth, who later went on to have a successful career in public service, law, and real estate, remembers how the two movements sympathized with each other but remained separate:

> They [the Catholic radicals] were supporting us with what we were doing and this was something that they took leadership in; we took leadership in other areas. We were focused on things like education, equal employment, you know the things that really impacted the Hispanic and African-American community directly and this was an issue that was important to us too because you know we opposed the war in Vietnam. We opposed—our community was opposing the draft. You know, the left-wing community in the Hispanic and African-American community.[31]

Catholic radicals did not stand at the front lines of the Camden civil rights movement for two main reasons. Unlike the CCRM, which formed out of and focused on the region, the Catholic Left made its mark by launching draft board raids in multiple cities. Their actions, moreover, posed far greater risks for nonwhite activists. Burglarizing government buildings was not safe for anyone, but especially if that person was Black or Brown. Committing felony acts of trespassing and property destruction for political change meant potentially giving your life up for a cause. White radicals who raided draft boards could reasonably expect law enforcement officers to harass and manhandle them but probably not kill them, especially if they were priests or nuns.

As the 1971 death of Raphael Gonzales illustrates, nonwhites could expect different outcomes from these encounters. Police officers Gary Miller and Warren Worrell beat the Puerto Rican man into a coma after pulling him over on July 20. Some reports say it was a routine ticket violation; others say Gonzales was intoxicated. In any case, the patrolmen attacked him with excessive force. The beating prompted an explosive reaction in the Puerto Rican and Black communities that shut down Camden right before the draft board raid.[32] Gonzales died from his injuries in September.[33]

At the time of the Gonzales attack, the Catholic Left had been establishing operations in Camden for a few months. Activists busily prepared for a raid on the federal building as the city faced mounting protests by the interracial civil rights movement, which was pressing the mayor's office to take measures against Miller and Worrell. The draft board resisters quietly conceived and executed their plan, which started taking shape in February when the more experienced raiders, known in the movement as "old actors," began working with the locals to study the site.

The main old actor, at twenty-three years of age, was Cookie Ridolfi, who arrived that month to vet the group of friends from St. Vincent's. Ridolfi knew the area because Camden was her backyard. She had grown up on the other side of the Delaware River in South Philadelphia. As a student at Goretti High School she met the nun-turned-activist Mary Cain, who brought her into the Catholic Left. Goretti served the working-class families of the neighborhood, who could walk to its yellow brick campus on Moore and Ninth Streets.[34] Girls in plaid skirts and boys in black blazers passed each other in the early morning hustle before entering their different schools in time for morning prayers.

Goretti represented the expansive Catholic world of mid-twentieth-century America, when the church was reaching its peak size in the United States and generating the webs of parishes, schools, and other institutions from which the Catholic Left forged its networks. The Roman Catholic Archdiocese of Philadelphia grew with the city's post–World War II economic expansion. The high school, in fact, literally arose from the foundational work of the church in that period—it was built on the remains of a Catholic cemetery that was disinterred to make room for the new construction.[35] These baby-boomer children of Irish American and Italian American families stretched the church's capacity, including the geographical space it occupied, to serve the educational needs of a growing Catholic population. In less than a decade, many of the young men would grow out their hair in defiance of the rules imposed by parents, nuns, and priests. Boys and girls alike traded uniforms for the blue jeans they wore to march in civil rights and antiwar demonstrations.

Ridolfi eagerly joined this wave of activist ferment. She attended Goretti in the heyday of Catholic education in the United States after World War II, though she graduated with barely passing grades. Resentful of the nuns, who disciplined her often, she rebelled by skipping class and flouting other rules. Ridolfi paid little attention to her schoolwork, but she was smart and attuned to the volatility of the world within and beyond her enclave.[36]

Ridolfi followed the nightly news reports on her family's television set, which showed American GIs just a few years older than she was crawling through the jungles of Vietnam. These images made a huge impression on the teenager, especially as young men in her friendship circles started leaving the neighborhood to go fight in that war.[37] By the end of the decade, Ridolfi was deeply involved in Vietnam resistance. She dodged FBI agents, who monitored her every move until finally arresting her for raiding the Camden draft board offices in 1971. She could not have imagined, as a sixteen-year-old, how experiences at Goretti would profoundly shape her political attitudes and lead her to this activist life. Simultaneously acting on and rebelling against her Christian education, Ridolfi became one of the most effective draft board raiders in the Catholic Left movement.

Young Cookie Ridolfi might have seemed to epitomize these problems to the nuns who disciplined her. Smoking defiantly in her uniform, Ridolfi did not demonstrate the humble purity of her school's patron saint. Maria Goretti was an eleven-year-old Italian peasant who died in 1902 of stab wounds, reportedly from a man who was trying to rape her.[38] Goretti's statue commemorated a virgin ideal who favored death over deflowering. Memories of Catholic life in the twentieth century abound with rules such as no meat on Fridays, no birth control, no sex before marriage and no sex or marriage for clergy or nuns, and other strictures meant to keep the faithful observant of pious lifeways.[39] In rejecting these traditions, Cookie led her generation into a new era of secularization. She adopted the ideals of community and the Gospel examples of nonviolence but let go of the sacraments.

When she wasn't couch surfing in the apartments of friends, Ridolfi stayed with her mother, Kitty, near the Walt Whitman Bridge, on Ninth Street in South Philadelphia.[40] By then she had raided several draft boards. It had been a couple of years since Ridolfi's first "surfacing" event, at which she and other supporters of a Philadelphia raid circulated leaflets declaring their responsibility for the hit, which they did not actually perpetrate. The intent of these demonstrations was not only to cultivate new activists like Ridolfi, but to distribute culpability for the raids beyond the actual raiders themselves—to push law enforcement and the media to recognize every participant as part of a broader movement.[41] If FBI reports about the demonstrators and maneuverings are any indication, the surfacing strategy worked well. Local and national newspapers covered the event and officials in Washington, D.C.—who misidentified the perpetrators of the action—never successfully arrested anyone involved.

Ridolfi's experience shows that participation in surfacings came at considerable risk, however. When she pushed fliers into the hands of passersby at the demonstration, Ridolfi had not broken any laws, but she did make herself visible to the FBI. Soon, agents started tailing her. The petite twenty-year-old dropped out of college, became deeply enmeshed with Catholic Resistance, and worried her mother endlessly.

Ridolfi played a central role in planning and preparing for the Camden raid because she had managed to temporarily escape her FBI trackers. In winter 1971, Ridolfi noticed that agents were staking out her mother's house, so she told Kitty it was time to go underground. Despite the fright and anger triggered by this news, Kitty Ridolfi worked with her daughter to shake the FBI tail. They recruited help from the neighborhood as well. Ridolfi's brother had a friend named Blaze who drove a delivery truck with home heating oil and agreed to assist with the escape. He and a coworker came to the house one day and inserted the truck's hose in the family's tank as if it were a normal delivery. As Blaze handled the equipment, his partner knocked on the front door to consult with Kitty. After casually entering the house as he would during a normal delivery, he switched clothes with Ridolfi, who then walked out disguised as an oil guy.[42]

It worked. Ridolfi successfully left with Blaze in his truck under the nose of the watching agents. The men did this favor, according to Ridolfi, because their sense of community responsibility had been cultivated in the world of the local Italian mob. "There was a lot of mafia people," she remembered years later, "who were making money and sharing it with the community." Growing up in the territory of Salvatore Testa (a.k.a. "the Chicken man") conditioned Ridolfi and her childhood friends to protect each other from the G-men.[43]

Shortly after evading the FBI, Ridolfi turned her attention back to Camden. The depressed home values that BPUM had been protesting provided cheap apartments for the draft board raiders to rent. One of the rentals that became a temporary headquarters did not even include a bath or shower. John Peter Grady arrived for a second meeting at the community center a few weeks later in February. He was, by then, the most senior and experienced raider. With Philip Berrigan standing trial and Daniel Berrigan focused on his brother's defense, Grady was now the figure to whom people in the movement typically turned for leadership. He also captivated everyone involved with his outsized personality, which, after lots of alcohol, expressed itself in Irish songs. Grady was also somewhat unconventional in ways that interested the

Camden Calls the Catholic Left

younger folks. When he needed to shower, he dressed in white shorts and a white shirt, grabbed a tennis racket, and walked coolly into an athletic club, where he took full advantage of the locker room facilities as if he were a member.[44]

At the second Camden meeting, Grady gave plans for surveilling the draft boards, including the facilities in Trenton and Princeton. The Camden raid would involve many of the same activists hitting multiple sites. In addition to Grady, that second gathering included other old actors with previous experience in the work of casing and breaking into buildings.[45] A Wooster College dropout from Ohio, Keith Forsyth, was among them. By this time, Forsyth had trained himself with the help of a correspondence course to become an expert lock picker, whose skills were indispensable to raiding parties. The lanky twenty-two-year-old talked to the group about how to open doors without keys.[46] Grady walked the team through the work of using binoculars, walkie-talkies, maps, and other tools for surveillance of the draft boards. These tasks generally involved pairs or carloads of people staked out at a distance. For hours at a time, the patient casers watched buildings and noted the comings and goings of maintenance people, late-shift workers, guards, police, and all the other foot traffic. They combed through these reports for anything that established a discernible pattern that could be exploited for the purposes of entering without notice and without harm to anyone (see figure 8).[47]

At a third meeting, the group discussed plans for casing the federal building in particular. This gathering took place at St. Joseph's Rectory in East Camden, the home of a recent addition to the team who would become a central figure in the raid, Father Michel Doyle. Doyle (known to his friends as "Mick") brought a fervid spiritual commitment to social justice that had been hewn in the religious environment of his devout farm family in County Longford, Ireland. To the 1967 spiritual vanguard, Doyle represented a throwback.[48]

This recent transplant operated in a world suffused with sacramentalism, where he learned to see and bless the incarnation of Christ in the most mundane of things. God was everywhere in the world of his childhood; in his words, God was "completely integrated with everything in life." This was why his father threw blessed salt on his fields at the beginning of each growing season.[49] The thirty-six-year-old Mick Doyle then brought this religious worldview into the work of the movement. As a parish priest, Doyle did not enjoy the extensive education or deep theological training of priests in religious orders, like the Jesuits or Franciscans around him. He nevertheless exhibited a spiritually informed

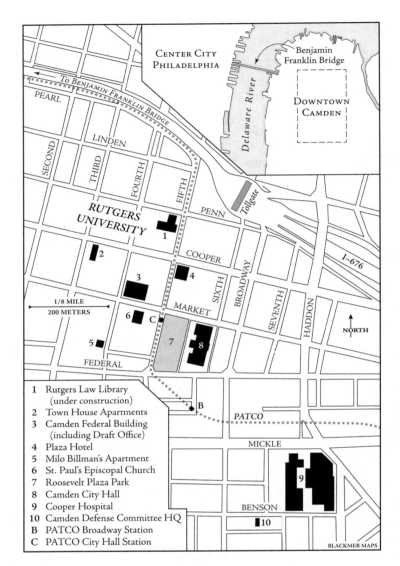

FIGURE 8. Map of Camden 28 and Puerto Rican Uprising Sites of Action, 1971

The events that roiled Camden, New Jersey, in August 1971 took place mainly within four blocks of the city's downtown, where the campuses of Rutgers University–Camden and Cooper Hospital bordered the city and county government buildings. Nearby structures, especially the construction site of a new law library at Rutgers and the roof of the Town House Apartment complex, offered elevated spaces from which activists could case the federal building in preparation for their raid of the draft board. On the night of the break-in, eight of the activists burglarized the draft board while others monitored the situation from the portico of St. Paul's Episcopal Church across the street and from the nearby home of Rev. Milo Billman. The federal building also housed the courtroom where the Camden 28 faced trial two years later. Trial participants dined and shared drinks at the Plaza Hotel across the street. Nearby Roosevelt Plaza contained the crowd of protesters who demanded answers from mayor Joseph Nardi after two patrolmen beat Raphael Gonzalez, a Puerto Rican motorist. Gonzalez lay in a coma at Cooper Hospital until his death weeks later. The August demonstration turned into a riot that shut the city down for days. Map by Kate Blackmer.

radicalism and a poetic way of expressing himself that made him popular among fellow activists and the media alike. Doyle's bare-bones agrarian background also gave him bona fide working-class credentials that the younger generation respected. Mick was as authentic as a person could be, and he applied a fierce commitment to the Gospels in his activism.

Doyle was teaching religion in the parochial school system when he first landed in trouble with his superiors. He took a public stance against the Vietnam War that generated press coverage and caught the attention of readers among the Catholic Left. The church fired Doyle from Holy Spirit High School in Atlantic City, New Jersey, after he criticized the school for allowing its band to perform in a rally for "Victory in Vietnam" at Bader field. Doyle declared that the bombing and the killing of innocents defied the lessons in peace and the common good that he and his fellow instructors taught as part of a Christian curriculum.[50] The outcry at Holy Spirit earned him a transfer to St. Joseph's parish in East Camden, where the bishop hoped the challenges of an underresourced and run-down urban parish would teach the outspoken cleric a lesson.[51] It did, but not the one the bishop had hoped for.

Instead, the assignment animated Doyle by bringing him into more intimate contact with Camden's poorest residents. He observed their struggles in parallel with the desperation of the Vietnamese people suffering from bombings, burnings, napalm, and Agent Orange. In response, Doyle started organizing youth Masses, for which he enlisted the help of South Jersey's newspaper, the *Courier-Post*, to provide the names and towns of people in the region who were killed in Vietnam. After the Gospel readings in his Sunday Masses, he made a regular practice of reciting the names of the dead.[52]

Mick Doyle also started calling Camden a "casualty of the war." His statements soon caught the attention of John Peter Grady, who reached out to the outspoken priest to ask if he was interested in helping with actions.[53]

Doyle's dive into the city's most vexing problems put him at the intersection of the church and the civil rights movement. Why did this activist priest not become more involved with BPUM? He could have joined fellow clergy, like the white Presbyterian pastor Sam Appel, in the CCRM. There is no evidence to suggest he was at odds with the local movement, and there were plenty of reasons—given his life choices up to that point—to expect that Doyle would ally himself with these organizations. The popular pastor was connected to the multiracial movement through friendships, like his ties with Gil Medina and Medina's parents, who came from Puerto Rico. Medina had, in fact, come to regard Doyle as a "brother," who bonded especially with Medina's father around a shared commitment to the self-determination of their respective island homes of Ireland and Puerto Rico.[54] Like the other priests in the Catholic Resistance, however, Doyle focused his attention on the draft, readying himself for a criminal act that might put him in jail or on a boat back to Ireland. He grew especially fearful about a possible arrest when he noticed two FBI agents watching his group during one of its meetings.

The preparations had been going well until a scare in early summer prompted the group to pause everything. The raiders gathered for a meeting in June at the home of Martha Schemeley, who lived in a suburb just south of Camden called Hi-Nella. Michael Doyle was walking to Schemeley's apartment at around six o'clock in the evening when he noticed two men in a car observing John Grady, who was standing in the main doorway of the building. The scene made Doyle nervous, so he walked around the corner and tossed a piece of paper into a dumpster before joining the others in Schemeley's apartment. When Doyle saw one of the men then leave his car and peer into the dumpster, he felt the cold realization of being watched. That feeling sunk deeper after the meeting dispersed at 10 p.m. The participants observed three cars following each of the caser's vehicles, confirming their suspicion that agents were tracking their movements. In response, the surveillance teams dispersed and canceled their plans to case the building.[55]

Michael Giocondo lived just two blocks from the draft boards. He hid in some bushes nearby and watched the agents in their vehicles on Cooper and Second Streets. Anita Ricci also watched them all night from the roof of Townhouse Apartments, diagonally across the street. Panicked, Mike Giocondo did not sleep that night or go to work the next day. Instead, he went to confide in Robert ("Bob") Hardy, a close friend in Doyle's parish whom he trusted.[56]

Hardy was an outsider who, at that point, had no knowledge of the planned raid, which meant that Giocondo took a huge risk in breaking the confidence of the larger group.[57] Giocondo went to Hardy as both someone he trusted and as a manager of construction projects whose expertise could benefit the action. The involvement of Hardy became a game changer. Over the next few weeks, Hardy provided critical knowledge on how to enter the draft boards unnoticed while also providing other forms of support, including financial help. As he developed his own friendships with various members of the group, he brought groceries, tools, and other items that were valuable to out-of-towners.

Bob Hardy was not a "cradle Catholic." The former Marine had converted to Catholicism under the influence of Michael Doyle, who became his pastor. Hardy's small business mostly serviced the construction needs of Black and Latino customers in Camden, which also brought him into contact with Mike Giocondo at El Centro. Hardy, who ran unsuccessfully for Camden City Council in 1968, was also a different kind of Democrat—not a radical. He was a moderate; in his own words, a "Kennedy" Democrat. Doyle and Hardy nevertheless became close, and the rapport spread quickly among the other raiders when Hardy joined the group. Fun times with each other's families hastened and solidified these bonds, especially since the children of Hardy and John Grady played well together. A Fourth of July celebration that summer in 1971 cemented the good feelings. Hardy reenergized the group, which had decided to lay low and see if the FBI continued to tail them.[58] They calculated that if agents did not see them continuing with preparations, the FBI would turn its attention to more pressing cases.[59]

Hardy became increasingly indispensable to the raid by virtue of his skills and equipment. These contributions from the newcomer prompted John Grady to talk with greater frequency about training his new friend for future actions. Hardy showed commitment and bravery by joining Gene Dixon in a reconnaissance visit to the boards during business hours. The two entered the Selective Service Office and claimed to be representatives of county prisoners checking the draft status of inmates. The ruse worked. Both men mentally mapped the room while waiting for staff to retrieve the records. Before departing the building, they stopped by the courtroom on the third floor, where they politely asked the maintenance crew if they, two tax-paying visitors, could take a brief self-tour. Their examination of the room and its view outside brought the fire escape to their attention—an external point of entry that the casers had identified as their main access to the fifth floor. For their last stop, they examined the post office loading platform on the way out (see figure 9).[60]

Hardy's bravery in the federal building impressed Dixon.[61] Not only was the man able to calculate detailed measurements in his head, but he also made the group aware of a major problem with the first-floor fire escape, which had a trip wire that would trigger an alarm when someone pulled the ladder down to the street. Hardy provided his own ladder as a work-around. It could be used to reach the second-floor fire escape, which did not have an alarm. He also taught the raiders how to penetrate the draft board office from its high windows by drilling around the handles and gently pushing them out with a block of wood and a mallet. The contractor provided the group with crowbars for the filing cabinets as well.[62] These insights and support so pleased John Grady that he told

FIGURE 9. Camden Federal Building
The federal building on Market and Fourth Streets in downtown Camden, New Jersey, housed the draft board that was raided by the Camden 28 in 1971. The burglars entered the fifth-floor offices through a window that they reached from the upper-story parapet. Their trial took place in the courtroom on the third floor. Photo courtesy of Todd Rengel, photographer, and the Historical Society of the United States District Court of the District of New Jersey.

Hardy his new friend possessed "the type of talent that was needed in the underground" and gave him the code name "Moses."[63]

"Moses" came to have even more value after two of the locals, Schemeley and Dixon, withdrew from the preparations. These friends, who were part of the St. Vincent's guitar Mass group that had developed the idea of the Camden raid in the first place, became convinced that the FBI was once again watching them after they saw two men in a car parked behind the federal building. When spotted, the passengers started to act like they were kissing, an embrace that did not convince Dixon or Schemeley. Spooked again by this discovery, the two locals stopped their participation. Neither wanted to continue when the action came to feel even more precarious, especially since both had children, who would suffer if they went to prison. John Grady, who had five children of his own, did not sympathize with the defectors. He told Schemeley and Dixon that the men were probably in a secret gay relationship and he did not want to stop or delay the action any longer. Edward McGowan remembers him as "livid" over the departure of Gene and Martha.[64]

The rest of the group stuck by John Grady, though evidence suggests that he had not been using good judgment. Though he was deep into an affair with Cookie Ridolfi, Grady also started a sexual relationship with her close friend, Anita Ricci. By two-timing with these women as a married man, Grady created tensions among the trio, which had been working closely together over months. Shortly before the raid Ricci decided to pull away from the action as well as from Ridolfi. Activists fell into and out of liaisons with each other just as friendships intensified and fell away—this was the nature of the emotionally intense relationships that made a movement. Perhaps it was time for everyone to cut their losses and move on to the next chapter of their lives.

Just as these associations started to fray, however, events in Camden offered an opportunity. A spontaneous racial uprising provided a distraction for law enforcement. The so-called Puerto Rican riot engulfed the city in violence and destruction over several days in August 1971, prompting the Catholic radicals to execute their planned action. As fellow raiders and helpers converged on Camden to fulfill their respective roles, John Grady seemed to grow more erratic.

What started as a peaceful protest on August 21 grew into a dangerous stand-off with the police. Youth activists had organized a gathering at city hall to pressure the mayor's office for answers regarding the death of Raphael Gonzales. They invited civic leaders from the Latino and African American community to speak. Poppy Sharpe, leader of the Black People's Unity Movement (BPUM), assured the Puerto Rican community that the city's Black residents were with them. Participants who were there that evening emphatically assert that the protest did not start out as a riot. Gil Medina, one of the organizers, remembers that the event began with a festive atmosphere. "The goal was to set up a protest in front of City Hall. . . . We struck a chord because it wasn't just students. . . . It was a cross section of Hispanics," he recalls; "It was a broad base, leaders of all sides of the spectrum, conservatives to the students. The whole mall was full of people." There was even a salsa band.[65] According to social worker Carmen Martinez, who also attended, it was "peaceful." "I mean, if it was going to be a riot people wouldn't have [brought] babies and carriages and all," she pointed out.[66]

Medina remembers that the atmosphere became uncomfortable when participants started seeing police with helmets and masks going into city hall from the back. Then word spread through the crowd that a Latino negotiator had been arrested, so some of the demonstrators

FIGURE 10. Joseph Rodriguez Walks through Riot Smoke
Attorney Joseph Rodriguez (center, in suit) walks through the smoking streets of Camden, New Jersey, in August 1971. Rodriguez played a key role in calming tensions between the mayor's office and locals after the eruption of a racial uprising known as the "Puerto Rican riot." August 20, 1971, photo courtesy of the *Camden Courier-Post* and Imagn Content Services LLC. © Camden Courier-Post—USA Today Network.

started rocking a police cruiser and others started smashing the windows of parked cars. Soon the police came out with tear gas, dogs, and clubs and were met with bottles and rocks from the crowd, which numbered about two thousand people. Angered and confused, the police lashed back with their batons. Over two days, seven major fires destroyed buildings. Medina and Joseph Rodriguez, a lawyer who had also been raised in Camden and had been working for Mayor Joseph Nardi at that time, served as the main conduits between city hall and the Puerto Rican community (see figure 10).[67]

The police commissioner put the city on lockdown, which meant that the draft board raiders had to pass through checkpoints as they drove through the city. Terry Buckalew, another experienced activist who lived in Philadelphia, had been assigned the job of driving John Grady around town in the midst of the unrest. Grady dazzled Buckalew with his fervid commitment to justice and exuberance for life. He also frightened the twenty-one-year-old with his unnecessary risk-taking.

On the night of August 21, the older radical convinced his chauffeur that they needed to go out and run errands for the raid. After some protest, Buckalew agreed and tried to steer them away from the police cruisers. As the two drove slowly through an alley, they passed a liquor store where men and women were walking out with stolen goods. John made Buckalew stop so he could jump out of the twenty-two-foot box truck and join in the looting. The shocked and nervous driver remembers looking straight through the front windows of the store onto the street, where he could see police officers. Before he could do anything, Grady ran out with three bottles of whiskey under his arms, followed by a group of young men.[68]

After they threw themselves into the back of the truck, Buckalew slammed the door, fastened the padlock, and drove out of the alley, but then a patrolman stopped him at a checkpoint. Frightened out of his wits, Buckalew told the officer he had made a wrong turn after crossing over the bridge. "I'm scared to fucking death," he remembers saying; "Get me the hell out of here." To his relief, the officer simply gave him directions, and after driving another half-mile, Buckalew dropped the youths off and brought John back to their headquarters with his whiskey.[69]

The raiders decided to go ahead with the break-in of the federal building the next night, despite the dangers posed by the unfolding riot. They also calculated that, as ubiquitous as the they were, the police might be too preoccupied with the burning buildings and sniper fire to detect the burglars. After the tools were readied and plans reviewed, the participants left to take their positions.

The operation started at about 2 a.m. on Sunday, August 22. Only eight men and women breached the building, representing about a quarter of the group: Cookie Ridolfi, Bob Good, Rosemary Reilly, Michael Doyle, Paul Coming, Bob Williamson, Michael Giocondo, and a Jesuit from New York by the name of Peter Fordi. The trespassers climbed the ladders and entered through an upper-story window facing the alley. Everyone else watched the site from three other locations. Milo Billman, John Grady, Terry Buckalew, Lianne Moccia, Sara Tosi, Keith Forsyth, Mel Madden, and John Swinglish waited in Billman's row house, where they nervously observed the draft board office from a window. Frank Pommersheim and Bob Hardy positioned themselves on the roof of the Town House Apartments, one of the favorite casing locations. And

CHAPTER FOUR

directly across the street from the federal building waited Joan Reilly, Barry Musi, Marge Inness, and Anne Dunham in their church courtyard observation point. The groups stayed in constant radio contact.

After reaching the parapets from their ladders, the eight raiders drilled around the window latches as Hardy had instructed them. The group then spent about two and a half hours vandalizing the office. While Bob Good slashed the sign-in register with a knife, Michael Doyle kept watch and Paul Couming maintained radio communication with the other groups standing by. Ridolfi, Reilly, Bob Williamson, Peter Fordi, and Mike Giocondo worked the filing cabinets. With their flashlights taped over to dampen the radiance, they crowbarred the drawers, tried to identify the 1-A files of the draftees most likely to be called up, and loaded these files into mail bags stolen from the post office.[70] At around 4 a.m. they were finishing and feeling good about the work they had accomplished. "There wasn't any thought," remembers Bob Good, "that there was anything going awry."[71] Couming announced that they were about twenty minutes away from departure, almost time for the drivers waiting at Billman's house to fetch them in cars (see figures 11 and 12).[72]

"Then all of a sudden there were these loud footsteps," recalls Good. The sound was like a "rumble." Couming radioed that a "guard" was coming. No one in the office could immediately identify who was about

FIGURE 11. FBI Surveillance Photo of Kathleen Ridolfi and Rosemary Reilly
Kathleen ("Cookie") Ridolfi (left) and Rosemary ("Ro Ro") Reilly (right) climb a fire escape ladder on the federal building in Camden, New Jersey, in the early hours of August 22, 1973. They were not aware that scores of FBI agents were waiting to arrest them after they committed the crime of stealing draft files. Photo courtesy of Anthony Giacchino.

FIGURE 12. Draft Board with Broken Filing Cabinets
The eight burglars who broke into the Camden Federal Building in 1971 pried open and emptied cabinets of draft files. This political action was one of more than forty such raids executed by the Catholic Left antiwar movement to protest the Vietnam-era process of induction. Photo courtesy of Anthony Giacchino.

to enter. From her position in the dark office, Ridolfi saw silhouettes on the parapet that were lit from the streetlights outside the windows.[73] FBI agents were on the raiders before they could make a move, rushing in from the door as was well as the windows. "The lights go on," remembers Ridolfi, "and we look around and there are FBI agents all around us with guns drawn."[74]

From the window of Milo Billman's house, John Swinglish saw the lights go on in the draft board office. He wondered, "Why are they turning the lights on? This is crazy." Couming then alerted everyone, announcing, "The party's over. The party's over." Swinglish responded, "That's okay. We all know there'll be other parties," just before agents kicked in both doors of Billman's house. One agent ripped the radio from Swinglish's hand and pushed him up against the wall before frisking the navy veteran and putting him in handcuffs.[75] Another group of agents swooped down on the four remaining activists standing lookout underneath the church portico. In those few minutes, the FBI seized twenty people among the three different parties. Frank Pommersheim, who was supposed to be waiting on the roof of the Town House Apartments, had fled to New York City.[76]

Scores of agents had been on the scene in Camden that night and early morning, where they waited patiently to proceed with arrests. Unlike previous captures, the bureau succeeded in apprehending many people involved in the crime beyond those eight in the draft board office. How did they manage to catch twenty-eight people? The answer to the question dawned on all the apprehended activists as they concluded, over the course of the day, that one of them was working for the FBI.

CHAPTER FIVE

Where's Bob?

As the eight burglars arrived with their FBI escorts at the local precinct, they, along with the now handcuffed getaway drivers and standby support teams, noticed that someone was missing from the room. A terrible realization started to make itself clear as they awaited booking: Bob Hardy had not merely escaped arrest. He was an informant.[1] Hardy had been spying on the raiders for weeks. He had volunteered for the job of infiltrator after his distraught friend Michael Giocondo unburdened himself of the group's secrets after discovering FBI agents watching their June meeting at Martha Schemeley's apartment in Hi-Nella. Upon winning their trust and gaining entrance into the action community, Hardy participated in the riskiest work of the raid preparations with the support of his FBI backers. Almost daily he fed the government reports about the action, and he broadcast conversations from a transmitter installed in his work van. He also funneled money from the bureau toward the action itself. These weeks of surveillance by the FBI and spying by Hardy ultimately helped agents cast a wide net that trapped accomplices as well as raiders, for a rock-solid conviction.

This is how the Camden 8 became the Camden 28. Everyone involved in the numerous draft board raids knew all along how easily an action could fail and result in a bleak future behind bars. Each had agreed to those stakes, and at the end of August 1971, it seemed that such a fate awaited them (see figures 13 and 14).

Strange and unpredictable events over the next few months carried these activists in a wildly different direction, however. A tragedy befell the Hardy family, one so shattering that it caused Hardy to rethink his cooperation with the FBI and to try and repair the damage he had done to the Camden 28. The Hardys suffered their most awful days, not from anyone's attempt to inflict retribution against the contractor. It was an

FIGURE 13. Arrest Photo of Sara Tosi

Sara Tosi (center with raised fist) of Boston, Anne Dunham (third from left) of New Rochelle, New York, and Marjorie Inness (behind and between Dunham and Tosi) were three of the twenty-eight activists arrested for the Camden draft board raid of 1971. Photo courtesy of Anthony Giacchino.

accident that resulted in the death of their son. This horrific mishap shook everyone in their community, ultimately finding FBI agents and defendants uncomfortably sharing space in hospital waiting areas and church pews. It also caused a shift within Hardy, who could never admit to anyone—especially himself—that he regretted taking advantage of Giocondo's confidence. To the frustration of the Camden 28, their defense in court hinged significantly on the decisions of a double-crosser who had deceived many of them into trusting him.

Hardy did not comprehend fully what he set in motion when he took Giocondo's secrets into the FBI's Camden field office that June in 1971. By initiating a relationship with the agents, he stepped into a swirling mess of bureau upheaval stretching from its regional operations to the highest levels in Washington, D.C. The FBI was in trouble, as news of its own secrets had recently trickled into public view.

Director J. Edgar Hoover targeted the Camden draft board raiders because some of them had stolen, and started leaking, files that revealed

FIGURE 14. Camden 28 Mugshots
On August 22, 1971, readers of newspapers across the country learned that twenty people had been arrested for the crime of raiding draft boards in the Camden Federal Building. The defendants became known as the "Camden 28" after law enforcement officials arrested eight more people who assisted with preparations for the burglary. August 23, 1971, photo courtesy of the *Camden Courier-Post* and Imagn Content Services LLC. © *Camden Courier-Post*—USA Today Network.

secret and illegal FBI activities. Hoover had to staunch the flow of this information, which was gradually leading journalists and government officials to the truth about systematic political harassment conducted by the FBI. Once celebrated as a lion of national security, the director now found himself severely criticized for harassing American citizens, controlling government officials with subtle threats of blackmail, and directly undermining the work of political organizations.

Instead of facing the music when the truth came out in April 1971, Hoover responded to the exposure by doubling down on the people who did the exposing. He surmised correctly that the activists who stole the files with damaging information were probably to be found in the Catholic Left. Since burglarizing government offices had been the movement's modus operandi for a few years by that point, the FBI focused its attention on draft board raiders operating in the greater Philadelphia region. Hoover thus moved swiftly to take advantage of the situation when Bob Hardy agreed to be a conduit between the bureau and the movement. As the successful culmination of these efforts, the August arrests at the Camden Federal Building led to much celebration in the FBI. But the events had an unexpected consequence: the ignominious downfall of J. Edgar Hoover.

The source of these troubles dated back to the burglary of an FBI satellite office on March 8, 1971. The war in Vietnam ground on while the nation voraciously consumed news about other events, including the trial of Charles Manson, the first live performance of "Stairway to Heaven" by Led Zeppelin, and another moon landing.[2] The Nitty Gritty Dirt Band singing "Mr. Bojangles" and Janis Joplin singing "Me and Bobby McGee" topped Billboard's chart of one hundred hits. One group of resistors realized that the distractions of American popular culture might help them execute a daring break-in while the nation's eyeballs, including those of law enforcement, focused on a highly anticipated sporting event. Due to the success of the burglary, this heavyweight boxing championship match had far more relevance to American history than anyone realized as "Smokin' Joe" Frazier defeated Mohammed Ali.[3]

Pacifist William Davidon was the main organizer of this planned attack on the bureau's satellite office in Media, Pennsylvania. The Haverford College mathematics professor had not raided any draft boards up to now, but he had become friends with Catholic Leftists who inspired him to coordinate his own action. It had been about five years (1966) since Davidon first traveled with the Protestant clergyman A. J. Muste to South Vietnam, where Muste's organization, the Committee for Non-Violent Action (CNVA), picketed the U.S. embassy in Hanoi.[4] Perhaps it was Muste, a celebrated liberal theologian and peace movement leader, who introduced Davidon to the Berrigans. Muste had attended Thomas Merton's 1964 Gethsemani retreat with them and John Grady.[5] A year after Davidon's Vietnam trip, Daniel Berrigan visited the Germantown section of Philadelphia to give a sermon at the First United Methodist Church. He was on the run, having fled authorities to evade his three-and-a-half-year sentence at a federal prison for the Catonsville Nine raid in 1968.[6] The scholar and activist Davidon hid Berrigan before and after his appearance at the church.[7]

Davidon helped the renegade priest because he admired the way Berrigan and other Catholic Leftists had resurrected nonviolent civil disobedience to protest the war. An atheist Jew, he befriended and worked with activists from many religious traditions over the course of his political career—Quaker, Buddhist, hippie, Baptist. Anxious about the revolutionary turn of the Weather Underground, which he perceived as a slippery slope into chaos and violence, Davidon saw the Catholic Left as a shelter from this combustion. The forty-four-year-old was not an ingenue caught up in the drama of the raids. Having already participated in different types of peace politics, he was drawn closer into the circle of the Berrigans as a stabilizing, moral, and effective flank of the antiwar movement. Davidon later described his Catholic colleagues as "grounded" and "disciplined."[8]

A few months after Berrigan's arrest in August 1970, Davidon assembled a team to investigate suspicions about FBI informants embedding themselves in peace organizations. He reasoned that his friends in the Catholic Left had pioneered the most effective way for finding the truth—raiding the source. Instead of breaking into a federal building to destroy documents, however, his team would steal files in order to disseminate whatever they discovered about the government.

Davidon ultimately recruited seven other people who kept the action a secret for decades, including a married couple with young children. The husband, John C. Raines, was the Methodist minister who hosted the fugitive Berrigan when he surfaced for a sermon in Germantown. Raines, a Freedom Rider in the civil rights movement, had met his wife and fellow activist, Bonnie, when both worked for a voter registration campaign in Georgia.[9] The Raines household became the primary meeting place for all the planning sessions.[10] Three college dropouts also joined the group: Keith Forsyth, Bob Williamson, and Judi Feingold. Forsyth and Williamson, who were deep into the Catholic Left, had already participated in draft board raids by the time Davidon recruited them (see figure 15).[11]

The burglars timed the raid to unfold simultaneously with the "Fight

FIGURE 15. William Davidon and Bob Williamson at a Rally
Haverford professor William Davidon (third from left) and St. Joseph University student Bob Williamson (fourth from left) at a political rally in the Philadelphia region circa 1971. Davidon, Williamson, and four other activists exposed secret and illegal FBI programs when they burglarized and stole files from an FBI satellite office in March 1971. Though federal prosecutors never succeeded in identifying the perpetrators of that crime, agents arrested Williamson six months later when he broke into the Camden Federal Building. Photo courtesy of photographer Greg Moore.

of the Century," when the nation's two undefeated heavyweight champions faced each other at Madison Square Garden. The activists correctly anticipated that viewers would turn up the volume on their television sets just as the raiders were picking locks, prying open doors, and crowbarring metal drawers. This FBI office occupied a unit on the second floor of an apartment building. The residents of the apartments worried the raiders, especially since the building manager lived directly below the FBI office. There was also a courthouse across the street. To conceal their activities, the burglars "dressed up" for the occasion to blend in with other middle-class people who came and went from the building.[12] The intruders then made quick work of their burglary once they penetrated the office, swiping the documents they found in filing cabinets.[13]

The uniformed guard at the courthouse watched the nicely clothed raiders without interest as they nonchalantly exited the building and placed the luggage full of paper into waiting cars, like residents or visitors leaving for a trip. The security officer suspected nothing.[14] The burglars then took the files immediately to a Quaker conference center in a rural area near Pottstown, Pennsylvania, about an hour away from Philadelphia. This out-of-the-way spot, which was often used for retreats, became the group's new meeting place, where they did the work of reading documents, destroying irrelevant files, copying important materials, doing analysis, and mailing packages. In order to feign normalcy, they continued to work at their day jobs even after staying up all night with the project. Knowing that law enforcement would soon be asking questions, the burglars tried to avoid any change in their daily patterns that might cause suspicion among the people around them.

The sleepless nights proved worth the results. After mailing cover letters and copies of explosive reports to legislators and newspapers under the name, "Citizens' Commission for the Exposure of the FBI," the members quickly disbanded the group and dissociated from each other. From their separate residences, they nervously read news reports of the break-in while waiting for the damning information they had discovered to surface. Historian Beverly Gage notes that "it was the first time since the Coplon case . . . that raw files had slipped out of Hoover's control."[15] That was in 1949, when a judge had forced the FBI to turn over confidential documents relating to accused spy Judith Coplon.[16] Now, Hoover could only wait for someone, somewhere to report on the missing documents. After two weeks, senator George McGovern (D-S.D.) reported that a mysterious envelope with photocopies of files had arrived at his office. McGovern, senator Parren Mitchell (D-Md.), and the *Los Angeles Times* turned everything mailed to them from the group over to the FBI instead of disseminating the information revealed in the files, as the burglars had asked.[17]

Other reporters chose to break the story. Journalists revealed information that, within a few years, would lead to congressional investigations of the FBI. These secrets included the Security Index, a list of alleged subversives started by J. Edgar Hoover in 1939. By 1971, this list included twenty-six thousand names of people who, according to Hoover, should be arrested in the case of a national emergency. The director made sure that agents kept the index confidential because it was not authorized by law. He used illegal wiretaps and raids on homes to collect damaging information on people he targeted as state enemies, knowing that his bosses in the executive branch would not fire him because he had incriminating information on them as well.[18]

Hoover had been collecting information to wield as a political weapon for years. What started as campaigns against suspected mobsters, terrorists, and communists in the earlier days of Hoover's career transformed into illegal investigations of activists in the civil rights, free speech, antiwar, and other movements. Hoover had monitored Martin Luther King Jr. since 1955, and he started targeting the Freedom Movement leader more aggressively in the 1960s. By bugging his home, office, and hotel rooms, the agency recorded proof of King's extramarital affairs but never found evidence of subversive activity. In 1964, the pastor received a package in the mail with tapes of this sexual misconduct and a typewritten letter denouncing him as a fraud and suggesting that he commit suicide.[19] The effort to discredit and harass King intensified in the final months of his life.[20] The Media, Pennsylvania, burglary also revealed that the FBI had furnished the Chicago police department with a diagram of the apartment belonging to Black Panther Fred Hampton, which had guided the officer who assassinated him in his bed.[21]

As the Raineses, Davidon, and the other burglars combed through the stolen documents, they kept finding a word they could not identify—COINTELPRO. It would take a few more years of investigation by government officials and journalists to learn that the term referred to a highly developed and unlawful FBI operation known as the "Counterintelligence Program."[22] The operation reflected Hoover's belief that it was his duty not merely to investigate and arrest people who threatened the status quo, but to quash efforts before they even started.

The director launched this program in 1956 after the Supreme Court ruled that the government could no longer prosecute activists for radical political speech. By creating a secret program that circumvented court oversight, Hoover determined on his own what constituted dangerous political activity. This category came to include the work of Dr. Martin Luther King Jr. After listening to his "I Have a Dream" speech on the steps of the Lincoln Memorial in 1963, agents judged King to be a dangerous demagogue who needed to be stopped by the bureau. To that purpose, agents harassed the civil rights leader through COINTELPRO illegal operations. The Media files also revealed that, while the FBI had monitored the activities of professors and students who spoke out politically, it targeted Black students more than whites as suspected threats.[23]

Hoover felt justified in undertaking this unscrupulous activity, notes Betty Medsger, one of the journalists who helped publicize the Media files, because he believed that "all dissent and all movements for basic rights flowed from communism."[24] Many Americans shared his conspiratorial thinking, which cast any form of political unrest as "subversive" and "pro-communist."[25] This belief also drove his swift response to cover up COINTELPRO after Medsger first printed that term in one of her articles about the Media files on April 6, 1971. Though she knew she was handling explosive information, the reporter did not know she had triggered an alert in the bureau when she published this story. When the

Where's Bob? 105

news hit, Hoover immediately released a flurry of memos to stop internal communications about COINTELPRO cases. This order was just the beginning of a cover-up effort that would unfold over the next year.

Hoover had to move fast because even before journalists revealed the damning information, critics had started to post stories that damaged the director's legacy. The breach of the satellite office in Media drew reprimands, but so did other recent decisions by Hoover. Even *Time* and *Life*, which had celebrated the head G-man throughout his long career, started criticizing the director. A *Time* magazine story detailed in-house feuds and deliberate isolation that hampered the bureau's ability to effectively protect national security. The story blamed Hoover's own dictatorial behavior for bringing down the FBI with his own mistakes and secrets.[26] Tom Wicker at the *New York Times* declared that month to be "the worst period of controversy in Mr. Hoover's career." The director was rightly concerned that the Media raid had put his career in jeopardy.[27]

The public attacks vexed Hoover and his many supporters in the FBI. At a dinner in April hosted by the Society of Former Agents, an organization uniformly loyal to Hoover, attendees gave their hero a standing ovation. From his podium, Hoover ranted against the "few journalistic prostitutes" disparaging the FBI. In other venues, President Nixon as well as his attorney general, John Mitchell, effusively praised the director, both because they wanted to defend the reputation of the FBI and because they hoped the accolades could usher Hoover into a celebratory retirement. The number one G-man had become a problem for them. White House tapes reveal that in private conversations among administration officials, Nixon and other higher-ups at the White House thought Hoover's advanced age caused him to make mistakes. "He should get out of there," said the president in October 1971.[28] Noting the decline of Hoover's approval ratings, speechwriter Pat Buchanan recommended pushing the director to retire for the sake of his legacy.[29]

All the scrutiny aside, Hoover knew that his critics in the press did not yet possess the worst details of his crimes, so he escalated efforts to suppress the information. In addition to stifling interbureau communications about COINTELPRO, Hoover canceled COINTELPRO operations on April 28—on paper, at least. The Media burglary investigation, titled MEDBURG, was well underway at that point.

The director circulated a memo to the field offices ordering the immediate discontinuation of the illegal countersurveillance program. "This would appear to have been a profoundly significant decision," observes Betty Medsger, "one that would be disruptive to some of the major operations of the bureau."[30] As with the Security Index, how-

106 CHAPTER FIVE

ever, COINTELPRO continued to operate under other names. In the words of Hoover, new operations would be approved by him on an "ad hoc" basis.[31] That change was really no change at all, notes Medsger, because Hoover had always approved COINTELPRO operations in that way. The scrutinizing eyes of the press, the public, and Congress necessitated great care in hiding the deep history of this malfeasance. As Hoover wrote explicitly in that April 28 memo: "In exceptional instances where . . . counterintelligence action is warranted, recommendations should be submitted to the Bureau under the individual case to which it pertains. These recommendations will be considered on an individual basis."[32]

The informant Robert Hardy thus entered the FBI's field of vision at the perfect moment. Amid the harsh criticism, Hardy extended an exhilarating opportunity when the building contractor walked into the Camden field office that summer in 1971. Though he did not know it, the contractor was offering to help stop people who possessed damaging information against Hoover—offering to help the bureau keep its fingers in the dam holding back its worst secrets, so to speak. The FBI had suspected correctly that Catholic Left draft board raiders had committed the Media burglary but had no proof. Robert Hardy appeared to be the person who could deliver this most cherished evidence. To signal their belief that the Camden draft board raiders would lead them to the Media office burglars, the bureau renamed the MEDBURG investigation "MEDBURG-CAMDEN."[33]

Hoover had put a seasoned and well-regarded agent in charge of the MEDBURG investigation as soon as it launched that spring and a few months before Robert Hardy entered the picture. Roy K. Moore had earned widespread respect in federal law enforcement circles for the work he performed in investigating the murder of three civil rights activists in Mississippi: James Chaney, Michael Schwerner, and Andrew Goodman. Moore had developed a reputation for the methodical nose-to-the-ground approach he and his agents adopted while under the threat of intimidation by white supremacists. They secured nineteen arrests and seven convictions in 1964.[34] Americans eventually came to know him through the Oscar-nominated film of 1988 *Mississippi Burning*, decades after his work in Mississippi, Pennsylvania, and Camden.[35]

Moore arrived in Philadelphia on April 7, 1971, to serve as "special agent in charge" (SAC) of MEDBURG. After reviewing the investigations of suspects, he immediately expanded the team of agents working the case and appointed local bureau leaders to supervise different

Where's Bob? 107

parts of it. The titles of Moore's reassigned supervisors betray the extent to which the Philadelphia bureau had fulfilled Hoover's mandate to infiltrate radical groups. One agent, W. B. Anderson, was head of the region's "New Left squad," and his colleague, Terence Dinan, supervised the "racial squad." Within four days, SAC Moore had assembled a special MEDBURG squad of one hundred agents that proceeded to carry out over four hundred different investigations of New Left activities throughout the northeastern United States.[36] Working seven days a week, the special squad narrowed in on four principal subjects whom it identified as the perpetrators of the Media office break-in. Those round-the-clock investigations, it turns out, led them *close* to the right people.[37]

The misplaced focus on John Grady also explains why the bureau mobilized so quickly around the information provided by Bob Hardy. The third-generation Marine first talked to agent Terry Neist in the Camden office, with whom he shared a background in the Marine Corps. Hardy told Neist he did not approve of the raid that his friend Michael Giocondo and others were planning. At the same time, he was uncomfortable about informing on his friends. Neist responded by urging Hardy to join the group, collect information, and report it back to the bureau. It took a matter of minutes for Hardy to accept the offer.[38] As useful as this break in the case seemed to be for the Camden field office, revelations over the next few days generated far more enthusiasm in the bureau for Bob Hardy, attracting attention to Camden from top officials at the FBI.

Bob Hardy gave Neist some exciting information—he had identified a leader of the group. At a fundraising carnival to benefit Michael Doyle's parish, Hardy took a break from his volunteer duties to meet secretly with Neist, to whom he slipped a piece of paper with two words that screamed off the page—words that ultimately lead to the arrest of the pastor who organized that fund-raiser. Those words were "John Grady."[39]

This news set several efforts in motion. With Hardy's identification of Grady, agents realized they now had access to the inner circle of the Catholic Left, which was led by the man they suspected of breaking into their own office. If they could arrest Grady and those associates closest to him, they reasoned, they could stop the people who were leaking the explosive information about illegal FBI activities.[40] Shortly after the disclosure at the church carnival, Hardy successfully embedded himself in the preparation for the Camden actions with the support of his bureau handlers. He attended a meeting of the group at the home of Dr. William Anderson, a local supporter of the Catholic Left who lived with his family in nearby Collingswood, New Jersey, and operated his medical practice in Camden. Hardy learned that Grady often stayed with the

Andersons when he was in town and that other raiders used a payphone in a park about a block from the Anderson residence to communicate with each other.[41]

Starting with this first vetting event at the home of "Doc" Anderson, as the group called the thirty-six-year-old osteopath, John Grady made one of several dangerous errors by bonding with Hardy so quickly. Perhaps Grady was worn down by all the raids as well as the drinking and drama. His simultaneous relationships with three different women also suggest an emotional neediness or desire for connection, which the FBI exploited through their friendly informant. In any case, Grady was making bad decisions that put everyone at risk. Quicksilver had not been home much over the previous year. Though his wife and children valiantly visited him in the various places where he headquartered planning operations, the sociologist was deeply involved in an affair with Ridolfi when Bob Hardy entered the picture. He was also about to start a sexual liaison with Ridolfi's best friend, Anita Ricci. Now he welcomed the newcomer, Hardy, into his confidence with no hesitation.[42]

After only one hour of assessing Hardy's reliability, Grady assigned him the task of visiting the federal building offices in daytime business hours to get the lay of the land. Hardy complied enthusiastically, completing the much-celebrated reconnaissance mission with Eugene Dixon. That operation brought them into conversation with office personnel while Hardy eyeballed the dimensions of the room. It was this June 30, 1971, floor-plan inspection that reenergized the Camden action after the frightening discovery of agents at Martha Schemeley's apartment complex, which had spooked them into putting plans for the raid on ice for a few weeks. The night after his draft board visit with Dixon, Hardy also gathered valuable information from a long truth-telling conversation with Grady. Many boring hours spent casing a building together prompted the Irishman to open up. While sitting in a car, Grady regaled the informant with stories about some of his many draft board raids.[43]

Over the next month, Hardy reported on the nightly meetings, street surveillance activities, and dry runs of the raid. He also furnished agents with copies of notes and building floor plans. The FBI learned who would do the break-in and how they would enter the building as well as their plans to bundle the stolen materials for transportation off site. Agents knew, from Hardy, that the group was rehearsing in a nearby vacant building, where they practiced climbing ladders quietly and cutting glass with a battery-operated drill. They also knew from their informant that the out-of-towners tended to convene in Camden on the weekends for preparations, gathering for meals at Giocondo's, Dixon's, or Anderson's residence before returning to their homes in other cities.[44] Hardy informed agents that, in addition to the eight raiders, a group of four would stand across the street at St. Paul's church to observe the scene outside as the action unfolded. Grady, meanwhile, roved around in a truck and seven others stayed on alert at the home of the Reverend Milo Billman.

In the meantime, agents used this information to arrange additional surveillance of the casing and planning operations. They installed a low-wattage transmitter in Bob Hardy's van that enabled listeners to hear discussions between Hardy and the raiders in the cab of his vehicle. Starting on July 18, they also established a post for visual observation of the building casers by occupying an office in the federal building itself. While Mitchell H. Cohen, chief judge for the U.S. District Court for New Jersey, left town on vacation, agents set up shop in his third-floor chambers. They monitored the movements of activists on the roof of the Town House Apartments, in the Rutgers Law School construction site, and in an alley behind the federal building. Looking through binoculars, Giocondo, Dunham, and Ridolfi had no idea that FBI agents were looking right back at them with sophisticated navy binoculars and a starlight scope, which electronically intensified light to capture images at night.[45] Agents entered the building in the light of day, then closed themselves in Judge Cohen's office between 8 p.m. and 7:30 a.m. the next morning. Agents also eavesdropped on the plotters' communications. They used cassette tapes to record chatter among the casers on citizens band (CB) radio walkie-talkies, then studied the tapes to determine which code names, like "Filmore" and "Portico," stood for which persons standing by on stakeout.[46]

The Philadelphia field office struggled mightily in these weeks to determine who, among these suspects in the Catholic Left, participated in the March 7 break-in of its Media office. The FBI poured resources into overtime hours, technology, informant expenses, and other costs associated with the MEDBURG investigation. Hoover and SAC Moore grew stronger in their conviction that John Peter Grady and his associates had engineered the burglary and still held documents that could further damage the bureau's reputation. Agents had cataloged the missing files and now carefully monitored which documents appeared in national media venues. Alex Rosen, who headed the bureau's General Investigative Division, reported on July 7 that 77 of the 1,013 stolen items had found mention in news reports. Unlike the draft board files targeted by war resistors, the FBI made copies of these intelligence documents, which it now maintained in a bound volume.[47]

The FBI also sought to find its perpetrators amid the densest concentration of pot-smoking hippies in Philadelphia—Powelton Village.[48] This on-the-street "physical surveillance" (also known as FISUR in FBI memos) dispersed agents across this twenty-four-block neighborhood in West Philadelphia, near the University of Pennsylvania and Drexel University. In bell-bottoms and headbands, and with newly sprouted beards, agents wore disguises that mainly served to make them more visible. Their shiny cars with government plates emitting chirps from two-way radios did not help them blend in either. The operation failed to reveal the raiders, but they did create an opportunity for neighbors to "bring all of us in Powelton Village together" in opposition against the FBI's invasion of their privacy, according to one resident interviewed by a *New York Times* reporter.[49]

After agents wielding a warrant broke down the door of a twenty-two-year-old who worked for the American Friends Service Committee on May 16, residents gathered in a demonstration outside her home. Other residents, noted reporter Donald M. Janson, "photograph[ed] the agents, follow[ed] them in cars and generally [sought] to make life miserable for them." This mounting esprit de corps directed against the FBI reached its apex at a street fair organized by residents to focus on the snooping FISUR operations, where they hosted a public auction to sell copies of the burgled files. Visitors could pose next to a life-size photo of J. Edgar Hoover for a picture with the director, and some residents acted in skits that satirically reenacted scenes based on information from the released Media documents.[50]

Agents also turned their attention to the movements of the principal suspects in the Media raid, whom they identified by looking at the circle of people in closest proximity to John Peter Grady. The group included the Jesuits Edward McGowan, Peter Fordi, and Joseph O'Rourke, as well as Bob Williamson, Paul Couming, and Cookie Ridolfi.[51] The FBI took particular interest in the relationship between Grady, Ridolfi, and Anita Ricci. Ridolfi "was a constant companion of John Peter Grady in the planning of the Camden, N.J. draft board break-in," noted one MEDBURG memo. Since she, Grady, and Ricci lived together during the month of July 1971, SAC Moore concluded that both women must have been part of the FBI office burglary if Grady was involved.[52]

So convinced was the FBI of John Peter Grady's involvement that officials diverted significant manpower toward tracking him and investigating his past. The activist's drinking habit and family life won special attention from the agents put on Quicksilver's case. Having learned from Hardy's infiltration of the Camden group that "subjects supported themselves by theft and shoplifting," including stealing "Grady's liquor supply," agents got to work canvassing the state liquor stores in Pennsylvania around Media and nearby Wilmington, Delaware, to see if Grady or any of the others had made an appearance in these establishments.[53] Agents in New York City talked to Grady's coworkers and neighbors, who confirmed that the father of five was a "heavy drinker." A neighbor who clearly disliked the Gradys said that John was a "scotch drinker" who kept irregular hours and whose children were "not well behaved."[54]

None of this intelligence on Grady helped build a case to prove his participation in the Media raid—because he did not participate. Internal communications indicate that higher-ups seriously considered arresting Grady nevertheless and charging him for crimes they felt confident prosecutors could bring before a judge or grand jury. Since they had no evidence with which to accuse him of burgling the Media office, however, they decided to wait. The Camden action would give them the opportunity to arrest this suspect and subject him to intense questioning. Informant Bob Hardy indicated that the Camden "rip-off" would take place at the end of July. Caught red-handed, Grady and his associates would face severe felony charges that interviewers could leverage for information about Media. Resources thus shifted to the big upcoming "hit" on the Camden Federal Building. In a July 19 memo, Alex Rosen expressed hope that "Fordi, and McGowan will participate in the Camden break-in as well as others involved in the Media burglary."[55] He had the wrong people.

It took four more weeks than anticipated, but the FBI were ready when the Camden action finally happened. On the night of August 22, the raiders executed their meticulously laid plans while the FBI agents assembled in a handful of locations around the city to prepare. As was typical before a draft board raid, everyone taking part gathered for a shared meal. This particular enactment of that ritual left a strong imprint on the memory of several people who were present for the dinner since, in retrospect, it foretold the betrayal that was about to happen. Ro Ro Reilly, Joan Reilly, and some of the other women who prepared the food watched the men (they thought there were thirteen at the table but could not recall for sure). The friends ate, drank, and readied themselves for the grave work of that night, a night they had discussed and rehearsed for weeks. The iconic symbolism of this tableau seemed to beg for a witty remark to break the tension. Ro Ro Reilly turned to her sister and said, "I wonder which one is Judas," in reference to the last supper before Christ was betrayed by his disciple. The sisters laughed about this in later years, especially because Hardy gave Joan a big hug before the group left the dinner gathering and told her that everything would be okay.[56]

The FBI, meanwhile, braced themselves for the roundup. About eighty agents divided into eight or nine teams fanning out across the city on foot, in buildings, or on wheels. While the raiders sorted and bagged documents in the draft boards, agents waited in silence on almost every floor of the building for the signal to capture the raiders. Some managed to photograph Ridolfi and Reilly on a fire escape outside the upper stories. Twenty agents stood ready in a nearby funeral home for orders to seize the standby activists, who watched from across the street and from Billman's apartment.[57] When the eight raiders inside the building heard "Freeze, FBI," the bureau sprung this trap it had also spent weeks setting.[58]

Agents waited until the very last moment of the crime to catch the raiders red-handed, after they had done as much damage as possible. They wanted to furnish prosecutors with the evidence necessary to convict the defendants and put them away for a long time. FBI memos from that night suggest the top officials deemed the operation a huge success in that regard. As news of the arrests hit the newspapers, supervisors in the bureau were already typing up their commendations to celebrate and reward the agents who contributed to the heroic capture of the radicals.[59] Hoover, who was still smarting from the break-in at the Media satellite office, must certainly have felt validated, especially since Moore and others believed that John Grady was the leader of the FBI break-in. The relieved FBI director sent Robert Hardy a handwritten thank-you note and five thousand dollars in cash.[60]

The federal government did not wait a minute in launching the full force of its prosecutorial powers against the Camden 28 through the Office of the Attorney General (AG). It used information collected through grand jury examinations of witnesses shortly after the arrests. Under the leadership of Nixon appointee John Mitchell, the AG's Office had already transformed the process of seeking indictments for federal crimes into a mechanism for harassing radicals and pressuring subpoenaed witnesses. Grand jury investigations allowed prosecutors to dig into the personal lives of activists and collect information by calling them in to testify, even if their connection to the crime was tangential. If agents arrested someone for a federal crime, such as tax fraud, the AG's Office liberally defined "witnesses" so that it could question, in a secret grand jury hearing, people who might live in the vicinity or cross paths with the indicted person. They could thus question people they suspected of other sinister activities by naming them as witnesses. Prosecutors from the federal Internal Security Division based in Washington, D.C., flew around the country to question these so-called witnesses to bolster the government's collection of intelligence on radicals, incriminating material that it could later use to charge them with crimes.[61]

While preparing for the Camden 28 trial, the Attorney General's Office utilized another common abuse of the grand jury system—jailing witnesses. By putting people who refused to testify behind bars, lawyers for the government pressured defendants to plea, confess, or give evidence. Federal prosecutors thus questioned a married couple who were active in the Catholic Left, Patricia and Donald Grumbles. The court granted them immunity, which it has the power to do in grand jury hearings at a prosecutor's request.[62] While this might seem like an advantage for the witnesses as protection from self-incrimination, the government used this tool to force them to give testimony that would incriminate their friends (and, without immunity, would have incriminated they themselves).[63] After the Grumbles refused to testify against the Camden 28 defendants, the court found both husband and wife in contempt and ordered them into the custody of the United States Marshals Service. The married activists then went to jail for fourteen months for refusing to testify. Convicted of nothing, Bruce and Pat Grumble nevertheless served more time behind bars than most of the radicals who were arrested for draft board raids.[64]

This abuse of the indictment process was as old as the Justice Department itself. Recent political trends of the Cold War, however, prompted officials to misuse these powers in new ways. The Internal Security Division, established in 1954, hunted communists with grand jury indictments until senator Joseph McCarthy's downfall in 1956 brought scrutiny to such practices. Attorney General Mitchell resurrected the Internal Security Division in the late 1960s, after it lay dormant for more than ten years and created a Special Litigation Section to reinvigorate the aggressive application of indictments. Between 1971 and 1973, Mitchell's office presented evidence before more than one hundred grand juries in thirty-six states and eighty-four cities. It subpoenaed more than one thousand witnesses, about thirty of whom faced contempt of court citations for not giving testimony.[65]

Even before the Camden 28 arrests and incarceration of the Grumbles, federal officials had been collecting information on the defendants through these exploratory examinations of grand jury witnesses. In 1971 and 1972, government prosecutors convened more than twenty grand juries to investigate political radicals and antiwar activists.[66] Guy Goodwin, leader of the Special Litigation Section of the Internal Security Division, had a mixed reputation among fellow prosecutors and lawyers. Impeccably dressed in fine tailored suits, Goodwin made federal prosecutors mutter over the drama he brought to courtrooms. Some said he lacked the litigation skills to match the bluster. Goodwin also developed a reputation for lying. In one of his most famous indictments against

Vietnam Veterans against the War, Goodwin planted an informant among the defendants and went so far as to subpoena him along with two others. About a year after the Camden 28 arrest, Goodwin lied to a judge who asked him "if any of these witnesses represented by counsel are agents or informants of the United States of America." Under oath, he replied, "No."[67]

Many colleagues nevertheless admired Goodwin for his ability to remember and deploy a multitude of facts from his "computer mind," as some called it.[68] The Kansas-born lawyer especially relished the minute biographical details that he possessed from all his grand jury investigations. In the early morning hours of August 22, Goodwin surely delighted in being the person to turn on the lights of the draft board office as the FBI swooped down to make the arrests in Camden. He greeted the burglars with his intimate knowledge about their backgrounds—using their nicknames and talking about their families while handing them their indictments on the spot. He then turned to one of the FBI agents, who had been carrying a radio in a suitcase. Goodwin grabbed the receiver and spoke directly to J. Edgar Hoover. Ridolfi remembers hearing him greet the FBI director with the report, "We got them. We got them all."[69]

At first paralyzed by the feet pressed in their backs, Ridolfi, Good, Couming, Doyle, Fordi, Giocondo, Reilly, and Williamson lay still with their faces to the floor. Agents eventually pulled them to their feet, giving the friends an opportunity to check on each other's well-being. They were relieved to find that every one of them was okay, although Bob Good had fallen into his nervous habit of chewing on his lip. Among the many thoughts running through Cookie Ridolfi's mind in that moment flitted the concern that Good was going to start bleeding.

The other Bob, Weed-Ex Williamson, surprised the group by starting a chant. He aimed to lift their spirits with a silly call-and-response while they stood there with their hands pinned uncomfortably behind their backs, using a cheer that they all knew from Paul Couming's stories about high school. Bob started softly asking: "What do we eat?" The others responded in whispers: "Eagle meat." They did this several more times, getting louder and louder until the final question: "What do *they* eat?" In response to this he received a resounding, "Shit!" Ridolfi remembers a flickering exuberance passing through her from this final expression of solidarity as the friends shared one last laugh before agents separated them for individual interrogations.[70]

After the FBI announced the arrests, newspapers leaped on the story, especially as reporters gathered knowledge about the informant. To the chagrin of the Hardy family, much of the media coverage criticized Bob's part in the operations. South Jersey's *Courier-Post* interviewed Hardy as well as the defendants. When asked why he volunteered to infiltrate the group, he responded, "I don't think anybody has the right to break the law." Did he get paid? the reporter asked. And if so, how much and for what purposes? The *Courier-Post* profiled Hardy the next day in an article headlined, "The Man Robert W. Hardy: Good Friend, or a Fink?" It reported that Camden's Junior Chamber of Commerce, to which Hardy belonged, gave him a "voluminous round of applause in a show of confidence" in one of the informant's few endorsements.[71]

The defendants, meanwhile, refused to condemn him. Father Joe Daoust, a Jesuit priest close to Bob Williamson and active in the Catholic Left, served as a spokesperson for the those in the men's prison. He told the *Courier-Post* they had decided not to name the informant.[72] They used the occasion, instead, to broadcast their reasons for executing the raid in Camden, a city that represented the "major evils" confronting society. In their joint statement, which they had put in the hands of Father Daoust, the defendants noted an ironic inscription on the city hall building that read, "Where there is no vision the people perish," and added, "The people are perishing; there is no vision."[73] The women deflected by stating their joint expression of "solidarity with the Puerto Rican and Black communities in Camden, with our sisters and brothers in jail, and with the resistance everywhere."[74] In a public letter, Hardy's pastor, the defendant Michael Doyle, told his congregant that he did not blame him, and that Doyle had "no ill will or bad feeling" toward him. Speaking on behalf of the other defendants, Doyle said the government was at fault, and that they wished Hardy "the best of everything" (see figure 16).[75]

Journalists also explored the beguiling ways by which Bob Hardy poured praise on the Camden 28 after delivering them to the FBI with so much evidence. The *Philadelphia Bulletin*'s prize-winning reporter, Sandy Grady, zeroed in on this tension between Hardy's earlier behavior and his later feelings in an interview about three weeks after the arrest. Grady visited the family's home in Camden and spoke directly with Bob and his wife, Peg. Hardy bizarrely "lit up" when he spoke about the defendants, calling them "the greatest Christians I have ever known." He then told his interviewer that he "loved" them but "disagreed with their methods," and he described them as "beautiful people." Hardy also aligned himself with the Catholic Left's criticism of the "stupid, tragic" war in Vietnam. Peg Hardy told the reporter she really hoped that their "friends [would] eventually understand." Hardy was, perhaps, missing the warmth he felt in the sun of movement sociability, gatherings that brought his five kids together with the John and Teresa Grady clan for

The Man Robert W. Hardy: Good Friend, or a Fink?

Some say Robert William Hardy of South 29th Street, Camden, is a great man to have around.

"He's just a wonderful neighbor, a wonderful friend and a good family man," said Mrs. Martin Melincavage, a next-door neighbor of two years.

Others say Hardy is the informant who tipped the FBI to a Sunday morning raid on Camden's draft boards. Hardy, who has not been charged but is named several times in the FBI complaint, appeared before a grand jury today in the Federal Building where the raid occurred. The grand jury is studying the FBI complaint which charges 21 persons in connection with the raid.

Mixed Beliefs

Hardy's avowed political beliefs are a mixture on anti-war liberalism and Marine Corps conservatism. He claims he is opposed to the war in Vietnam, but he says he believes in working within the system to bring about change.

So far, though, Hardy has been saying little about his involvement — or lack of it — in the draft raid matter.

But last night 35 or 40 of his fellow Camden Jaycees gave Hardy a voluminous round of applause in a show of confidence. And Hardy later was willing to discuss his views on almost anything but the raid.

Informers, Hardy says, are not necessarily bad. "I have to go to Shakespeare to answer that. 'Unto your own self be true.' You needn't look at it as an informer as generally thought of. I think you're obligated. If I saw a man taking poison, I'd try to stop him."

Working within "the system" Continued on Page 8—Col. 2

ROBERT WILLIAM HARDY
In 1969 *In 1971*

FIGURE 16. Robert Hardy

The Camden 28 defendants were shocked to learn that one of their coconspirators, Robert Hardy, was an informant for the FBI. The intelligence gathered by Hardy over many weeks assisted the bureau in capturing the draft board raiders red-handed. August 26, 1971, photo courtesy of the *Camden Courier-Post* and Imagn Content Services LLC. © *Camden Courier-Post*—USA Today Network.

cookouts. Those days were over and the Hardys now found themselves isolated. Bob suggested that his predominantly nonwhite neighbors in Camden had been shunning him for what he did to the 28. "The Black and Puerto Ricans won't understand this," he told Sandy Grady, adding, "Nobody comes around."[76]

The official statements by the Camden 28 insisting that they held only the government responsible belied the deep anger simmering beneath their printed words. Many in the group felt irredeemably betrayed, especially Michael Giocondo, since he and Hardy had been close for several years. Giocondo had arrived in Camden after completing a mission in Costa Rica, where he was training as a Franciscan brother. He did not continue into the priesthood but did remain interested in Latino ministry, which is how he got to know Bob Hardy, who was a volunteer at El Centro. Hardy's duplicity shocked Giocondo, keeping him up many nights in jail while the group awaited bail. Described as sensitive and soft-spoken by his friends, Giocondo experienced nightmarish thoughts about what he would do if he met Hardy on the street by chance.[77] The news that Hardy had betrayed them also surprised Bob Good, who had warmed to Hardy and his family over the weeks of planning the raid. Good felt conned. And unlike Giocondo, he did encounter Hardy in Camden shortly after release from jail. The now familiar work van pulled alongside Good, and to the young resister's amazement, the man most responsible for the forty-seven-year prison sentence looming over his head offered him a ride. Good cannot remember whether he "flipped him the bird" or simply waved him off.[78]

Keith Forsyth, who disliked Hardy from the start, had told Bob Williamson before the action that he thought the newcomer might be an informant, but Williamson had replied that Forsyth was being paranoid. However, a conversation two weeks prior to the raid had put Forsyth on the alert. The two men were sitting in Hardy's van talking about the spike in police presence around the federal building, which was making many of the group's members nervous. Forsyth said he thought they should probably call the action off but Hardy told him not to be afraid, that he had something for Forsyth if he got caught in the building. He instructed Forsyth to open the glove compartment, which he did, revealing a loaded .38 revolver. Forsyth responded by castigating Hardy, telling him there was no way he was going to shoot anyone.[79]

Then came the awful events of September and October. In early September, in the midst of the media storm surrounding the Camden 28 arrests, Peg Hardy's father, John Gross, was struck by a car and killed.[80] Sandy Grady of the *Philadelphia Bulletin* wanted to talk to Hardy again shortly after the awful accident. He drove over the bridge to Bob's house, as he had in the past, to catch him at home. Bob Hardy was already in his car, on his way out to get a bite to eat and possibly buy shoes with his son Billy. But father and son were happy to oblige the reporter, so Billy played in the yard while the two men sat inside to talk further about the action and the case, which was now in the pretrial stages.

Then there was a knock on the door and the world of the Hardy family changed forever: "Mr. Hardy, Billy's been hurt. They are taking him to the hospital." It was Billy's friend George, who had seen Billy Hardy fall out of a tree. He landed on a fence with six-inch spikes, which impaled him in three places, including his stomach. A neighbor had to lift the boy off the fence before putting him into his car. The man took Billy to the hospital immediately, where the child was conscious enough to apologize for his blood spilling on the car seat. Hardy instructed his wife to stay in the house, assuring her, "It's going to be okay." She sat pale and wordless with the reporter, as the minutes slowly passed without news—five, then fifteen, and then thirty. "There's been so much trouble lately," she finally said, adding, "He has to be alright [sic]."[81]

But Billy was not all right. He seemed to be improving at one point, which lifted everyone's spirits, but then someone at the hospital accidentally gave him milk, which his healing organs could not process. Billy Hardy lingered for three excruciating weeks at Cooper Hospital in Camden before dying of a pancreatic infection.[82]

The hallway outside the Intensive Care Unit (ICU) where doctors treated Billy Hardy brought a weird mix of enemies together in surreal encounters. Michael Doyle remembers that the resistors came to the Hardy family with "unreserved" support. According to Gene Dixon, Michael Giocondo was crushed by Billy's death. He had been close to Peg and the children as well as Bob Hardy. Not yet prepared to forgive and forget, Giocondo still came to the hospital to check in on the boy. He tried, in fact, to carry out a stealth visit with Dixon, aiming to come and go quickly so as to avoid any contact with Hardy. Not only did Giocondo and Dixon cross paths with the informant, however, they found him standing with Terry Neist and other agents from the local FBI field office. The meeting was awkward. But in direct contrast to Giocondo's disturbing fantasies about meeting Hardy on the street, he instead took his former friend's hand, looked him in the eye, and expressed his sympathy with, "I'm sorry." Hardy responded with, "I'm sorry, too," though he never expressed public regret for the betrayal.[83]

Michael Doyle performed the funeral Mass at St. Joseph's parish after Billy died on October 3, 1971. He also said the Mass for Peg's father.[84] He had pastored the family throughout those trying days in the ICU and had known Billy well.[85] FBI agents and the defendants occupied pews on opposite sides of the church's aisle, avoiding each other out of respect to the grieving family and the memory of Billy Hardy. Michael Giocondo joined fellow mourners that day but did not approach Hardy at all as he could not muster the compassion he expressed at the hospital.[86]

To his dying day, Bob Hardy stood by his decision to deliver his friends to the FBI, but something changed after his son Billy's death. In public statements, he always coupled a defense of his actions with effusive praise for the Camden 28, the "good Christians" whose faith and courage he seemed to admire even as he rationalized his duplicity toward them. However, guilt might have been lurking somewhere deeper inside him, acting on him in the weeks after his son's funeral. Was he seeking to make amends? The voice of his conscience was Michael Doyle, Hardy's friend and pastor and the man who buried his son. As the Camden 28 sought counsel and started preparing for trial, Doyle operated quietly behind the scenes to work on Bob Hardy, gently pressing on a sense of remorse that he suspected Hardy harbored.

Meanwhile, the defendants started building their case with the knowledge it was likely to fail. The government had charged them with felony offenses that could land them in prison for decades. "Forty-seven years," John Swinglish thought to himself as he stared at the ceiling of his cell in the Mays Landing jail.[87]

Audaciously, they decided to build a risky defense that was actually no defense at all. The defendants decided to honestly tell the jury that they did, in fact, commit the crime and were proud of it. They would use their last breaths in the courtroom to denounce the war and expose the unscrupulous methods of America's highest law enforcement officials. The defendants had drawn out the heavy-handed tactics of the FBI and the Attorney General's Office, which they intended to lay bare in their arguments, examinations, and testimony. Given how hard other radicals had tried and failed to navigate the tight management of their trials by unsympathetic judges, the Camden 28 knew this strategy represented a long shot. Given that they had already grossly miscalculated the movements of FBI agents who were eager to shut down the Catholic Left, they probably should have faced their charges conservatively to avoid the maximum sentence.

Fortunately for them and their anxious loved ones, the Camden 28 instead followed their idealistic instincts through to the end.

PART III

Putting the Vietnam War and the FBI on Trial

The activists arrested for the Camden Federal Building raid of August 22, 1971, became known as the "Camden 28" after the charges filed by federal prosecutors officially made them defendants. They were not a unified group, however. With overlapping friendship circles, the 28 contributed to the raid in different ways and at different times. Some of the defendants, like local Gene Dixon and college student Jayma Abdoo, did not even know each other until after the arrests: Abdoo only entered the raid preparations in the final weeks after Dixon had dropped out of the action.

The large size of the group and differences among group members posed problems. The twenty-eight activists had trouble agreeing on decisions, such as how they wanted counsel to defend them. Even the desired verdict could not be settled on at first. Some of the defendants wanted to focus on acquittal to avoid prison and get back to their lives, while others wanted to use their time before the jury to double down on protests against the war. Over the year and a half between their arrests and the trial, the group sorted through these issues well enough to at least launch their opening statements as a unified front even while quiet disputes simmered in the background.

"Political trials" had become a recognizable feature of movement politics by the 1970s. From the trial of the Boston Five to that of the Chicago Nine, defense teams pursued acquittals with less urgency than they pursued their objective of broadcasting U.S. atrocities in Vietnam from the witness stand. In some instances, like the case of Black Panther Angela Davis, volunteers made preparations, fundraising, publicity, and litigation into full-blown activist projects in and of themselves.

The Camden 28 were not the first defendants to turn the tables on their government adversaries, but they were the most effective. They followed the playbooks of earlier trials but managed to transform the courtroom far more extensively than their predecessors had. The trial lasted from February to May 1973. In that time, the Camden 28 successfully unleashed a three-month-long fusillade of testimony against the government that was attempting to prosecute them.

The Camden 28 trial also stands out because the defendants succeeded in making the courtroom atmosphere so intimate it was almost spiritual. Earlier political trials in California, Chicago, and elsewhere, with movement lawyers representing activist clients, had created a carnival setting or a pageant of protest politics in their courtrooms. But the trial of the Camden 28 was different. In keeping with the Catholic Left's principles of communitarianism, peace, and personalism, the 28 crafted their statements and testimony to promote familiarity even as they argued their points fiercely.

In his opening statement and testimony, Michael Doyle invoked God and laid the theological groundwork for the draft board actions. He explained how he and the others had acted according to Catholic Social Teaching to promote "life" when they targeted the U.S. draft system. The defendants called everyone but the judge by their first name. They referred to each other as "brother" and "sister," welcomed school groups in the gallery, and honored people in the courtroom on their birthdays. As one legal scholar observed, "The Camden draft board break-in trial became one of the most intriguing and interesting judicial proceedings in American history."[1] Over the course of three months, the walls between people on opposite sides crumbled. Tired courtroom rituals and processes became new and transformative—more shared than adversarial. The trial became at once intimate and transcendent. Indeed, it became sacramental.

CHAPTER SIX

Research, Preparations, and Communion

After the chaos of arrest, booking, and lockup, the Camden 28 faced numerous challenges. Cash bail presented the most immediate concern, with amounts ranging from $5,000 to $25,000 (roughly $36,320 to $181,600 in 2023).[1] As worries go, however, the bail problem was minimal compared to the potential prison time of forty-seven years, especially considering the mountain of evidence the government had accumulated over the summer for the purposes of imposing a harsh sentence. In addition to the intelligence gathered by Bob Hardy, agents also intercepted and transcribed the raiders' walkie-talkie chatter during the night of the action. Though grainy, photographs of the ladder entry into the federal building showed the slim figures of Cookie Ridolfi and Ro Ro Reilly ascending to the scene of the crime clearly enough. Sheathed in black from sock hats to shoes, their appearance screamed "guilty." With or without bail, the case would go to trial, which created the necessity for representation.

Or did it? Several antiwar defendants had declined to hire lawyers in their recent trials, opting instead to appear pro se, or "for oneself." By 1971, defense teams without lawyers had become a common (although hardly universal) feature of political trials, or "movement trials" as they became known.[2]

The Camden 28 had an added problem with which their predecessors had never reckoned: that of having so many people charged together. Twenty-eight defendants arrested for the same action had to make at least some decisions as a group while government adversaries did everything in their power to divide them against each other. Federal prosecutors targeted some, by virtue of their age, family status, or profession, as potential outliers who might give evidence against the others to secure acquittals for themselves.[3] Exacerbating the risk of multiple plea deals, a variety of perspectives and interests among the 28 complicated decision-making. Some of the more radical defendants had already resigned themselves to a prison sentence as an act of defiance. Others wanted to do everything possible to reduce sentences or beat the charges. Disharmony loomed at every moment from start to finish, but the Camden 28 ultimately found just enough consensus to proceed in what seemed to outsiders like a unified way.

The bail proceedings introduced the first test of group solidarity. Family and friends scrambled in those hot weeks of August 1971 to get representation for their loved ones. The defendants acquired several different lawyers, but those who were sitting in jail decided that none would leave until all could raise enough money for bail. Supporters watched anxiously alongside journalists at the August 30, 1971, hearings to learn the amounts, which might require that homes be put up as collateral or donations be solicited.

The archdiocese sent an attorney who successfully secured the release of Father Michael Doyle, but the stubborn priest refused to leave the jail.[4] The resilience of Jayma Abdoo dazzled everyone when her father, a successful New York City lawyer, entered a not-guilty plea for his daughter in a bench conference with the judge, Mitchell Cohen. When Cohen then announced the plea, the young woman stood and declared that she was, in fact, not pleading. "Don't you speak to your father?" asked the annoyed judge. After a brief discussion between father and daughter in the corridor, Abdoo returned and announced that her father would not be acting as her attorney.[5]

To everyone's relief, the court released all the defendants that day with the agreement that the group would raise tens of thousands of dollars over September. Cookie Ridolfi remembered how her South Philadelphia neighborhood rallied around her by putting money in a jar labeled "Free Cookie," which her aunt put on a counter at Pinto's, a small watering hole on the corner of Ninth and Cross Streets. Those coins did little to make a dent in the thirty-five thousand dollars needed to keep Ridolfi out of jail, but they felt to her like another set of arms in the embrace carrying her through those difficult months.

The support enjoyed by Ridolfi from her family and neighborhood contrasted sharply with that received by Bob Williamson, who grew farther from, rather than closer to, his parents in this period. Mr. and Mrs. Williamson, in their shock over Bob's arrest, could not bring themselves to visit him in jail, so they asked their pastor to do so instead. The monsignor obliged, but Williamson remembers him "oozing with disapproval" during that one visit. After communicating how much Williamson had disappointed his mother, the priest asked him if he needed anything. Williamson responded, "Cigarettes." After the priest dropped them off, Williamson swapped this gift for extra coffee and other goods through the jail's barter system.[6]

Shortly after their release, the group met for the first time since the action at a storefront office owned by Glassboro State College in Camden. As they bandied about ideas for how to move forward, tensions arose over the question of hiring legal representation. The varying stakes faced by different defendants made it difficult to settle on a common strategy, at least in the early stages of preparations. In addition to the costly lawyer fees, some of the activists opposed the idea of legal counsel because they wanted to represent themselves. Like many radicals of their day, some of the defendants viewed lawyers as the embodiment of the establishment—mere tacticians, tricksters, and technicality talkers. This contingent within the Camden 28, represented most forcefully by Jesuit Ed McGowan, wanted a more authentic, truthful defense of their principles, one only they could mount. Others favored legal representation to help them win acquittal. Father Michael Doyle, for example, wanted an attorney because he faced the possibility of deportation back to Ireland with a conviction. The concerned parents who worried for the futures of young Joan and Rosemary Reilly were also interested in hiring lawyers for their daughters. Afraid of losing their jobs, locals Michael Giocondo, Eugene Dixon, and Martha Schemeley came down on the side of professional representation as well.[7]

To add to the awkwardness, the early deliberations included attorneys who had shepherded them through the bail reduction phase. These advisers, according to defendant Ed McGowan, "made the point that [our] collective heads were on the block, with big-time charges against [us], complex legal doctrines, and maneuvers beyond their capacity to learn by on-the-job training."[8] As a result, Dixon, Schemeley, Doyle, Giocondo, and the Reilly sisters chose to proceed with counsel. This decision ultimately helped all twenty-eight because their attorneys advised every defendant throughout the trial.[9] The team of talented young lawyers—none more than three years out of law school—included E. Carl Broege from Newark, New Jersey (who had helped represent Bobby Seale in the Chicago trial), Martin "Marty" R. Stolar from New York City (another veteran, already, of representing antiwar protesters and Black Panthers), and David Kairys from Philadelphia (who was more a civil rights lawyer than a criminal defense lawyer).[10] As recent graduates, Broege, Stolar, and Kairys offered strong and idealistic representation with a lower price tag than fees charged by more established attorneys. Once these professionals came on board, they worked with the defendants on a strategy that took advantage of the rapidly changing political circumstances roiling the nation.

In the eighteen months between the Camden 28's arrest and their trial, Americans turned steadily against the war and against President Nixon. Shifting attitudes about the government contributed to the bold strategy of the lawyers, their clients, and the other defendants. They sought jury nullification: a not-guilty verdict rooted in the jurors' own sense of justice that overrode the overwhelming evidence of legal guilt. The defense would also aim to prove that the FBI set a trap by contributing significantly to the crime with its own resources. This risky approach demanded that the 28 embark on an ambitious jury selection process requiring hours of group research to assist counsel in the voir dire phase, when lawyers question prospective jurors. The two linked objectives of the defense, achieving jury nullification and revealing outrageous government conduct, leveraged a growing public mistrust of the federal government in the wake of the Pentagon Papers scandal. The steady trickle of evidence showing that the White House had long been lying about developments in the Vietnam War also helped the Camden 28 win sympathy.

Acquittal remained such a long shot, however, that the defendants tried to begin settling into their projected futures behind bars. As Bob Williamson remembers, "From my perspective, the end result was a *fait accompli* . . . we were going to prison."[11] Williamson made this prediction based on national attitudes about the war. Although the peace movement had been vigorous since the 1964 troop escalation, the national mainstream tended to either support the troops in Vietnam, criticize the protesters, or both.

More Americans started experiencing disillusionment with the war beginning in about 1968, mostly due to revelations in the press about U.S. failures in Indochina as well as the government's efforts to conceal them. Americans had to face the reality that families had already sacrificed tens of thousands of sons, brothers, and fathers to a war they were losing. Having been gulled by the rosy reports of military successes in the news—reports based on the misrepresentations of events by the presidential administrations of Lyndon Johnson and his successor, Richard Nixon—the 1968 Tet Offensive shocked most Americans. North Vietnamese forces launched a string of attacks on scores of cities and villages, including Saigon and the provincial capitals. The National Liberation Front (also known as the Viet Cong) blew a hole in a wall at the U.S. embassy and waged a six-hour battle with Marines before U.S. forces defeated them. Although the NLF's main objective of triggering a popular uprising in the South failed, its massacre and occupation of the city Hue, its steady barrage against the U.S. base at Khe Sanh, and its attack on the U.S. embassy disturbed once-supportive Americans.[12]

Outrage grew in 1971 with the leak of a secret study titled, "Report of the Office of the Secretary of Defense Vietnam Task Force," which quickly became known as the "Pentagon Papers." Daniel Ellsberg was one of thirty-six analysts who worked on the project, which compiled thousands of pages of historical investigation and related government documents into forty-seven volumes. Over the years, however, Ellsberg had turned against the war. This change of heart inspired him to secretly photocopy the report, which took weeks, and then send it to national newspapers. The *New York Times* published the first excerpts in June.

The exposé revealed that the United States had started to intervene in Indochina in the mid-1950s, essentially creating the nation of South Vietnam by investing millions of dollars in training its civil guard and assisting with the military coup of 1963. "In October we cut off aid to [Ngo Dinh] Diem in a direct rebuff," it revealed, "giving a green light to the generals. We maintained clandestine contact with them throughout the planning and execution of the coup and sought to review their operational plans and proposed new government."[13] The United States thus assisted in the overthrow of the anticommunist President Diem, an ally of the United States, because American officials feared that his weak and corrupt regime could not repel the communist North Vietnamese. The coup led to Diem's assassination.

Amid national shock at the discovery of American involvement in these events, which discredited the Kennedy and Johnson administrations, John Mitchell, Nixon's attorney general, secured a court injunction against the *New York Times* and sought to prosecute Ellsberg for releasing highly classified government documents. National security adviser Henry Kissinger convinced Nixon that the Pentagon Papers set a bad precedent for the handling of future state secrets. As the *Times* appealed its injunction, the *Washington Post* released another series of articles based on parts of the study given to its editors by Ellsberg. When the administration sought an injunction in that case, fifteen other newspapers responded by printing more of the leaked materials. Rival newspapers thus rallied to support each other in an effort to protect the First Amendment.[14]

The Supreme Court decided 6–3 in favor of the press in its historic ruling *New York Times Co. v. United States* on June 30, 1971, just four days after hearing arguments in the case. Seven weeks before the Camden 28 arrest, Justice Hugo Black wrote that "every moment's continuance of the injunctions against these newspapers amounted to a flagrant, indefensible, and continuing violation of the First Amendment."[15] The victory for independent journalism further eroded public trust in the federal government.

The Camden 28 defense team worked to take advantage of the growing disapproval by seeking to demonstrate that the Federal Bureau of Investigation had lured the raiders into a crime they otherwise would not have committed, a defense known as entrapment. Since the early 1930s, Supreme Court rulings affirmed that U.S. prosecutors could not convict on the basis of evidence that investigators had obtained by coaxing, or "entrapping," defendants into committing a crime. In a series of cases over the next forty years, justices sustained appeals against prosecutions that used "overzealous law enforcement," as described in the 1932 ruling *Sorrells v. United States*.[16] In 1973, however, lawyers prepared to once against test the definition and scope of "entrapment" with an upcoming case, *United States v. Russell*. Criminal defense attorneys monitored *Russell* closely because the ruling threatened to narrow how the Court defined unlawful overreach by the government.[17] In short, it threatened to make the "entrapment" defense harder to execute.

Catholic Church leaders in the United States meanwhile started taking positions against the war. Peace activists noticed a shift in attitudes at the 1968 meeting of the National Council of Catholic Bishops (NCCB), which had been silent about Vietnam up to that point. It had already been five years since Pope John XXIII had released his monumental declaration on peace, *Pacem in Terris* (Peace on Earth), and the NCCB (later called the United States Conference of Catholic Bishops) had still not released a statement or pastoral letter condemning the war.

In November 1968, just days after the election of Richard Nixon, members of the organization Pax Christi withstood cold temperatures to greet bishops one-on-one as they came out of their meetings at the semiannual organizational gathering in Washington, D.C. The Catholic peace group had, for weeks, already been sending the pontiffs letters asking them to address the problem of war: "We strongly recommend that our bishops act to make the Vatican Council statement on conscientious objection a reality for American Catholics," they wrote in a statement.[18]

Maybe this worked. Several bishops came over to talk to them. One even gave the shivering protesters a key to his room with the instructions, "Someone has given me a bottle of whiskey. . . . Go to my room, get dried off. Take a drink if you like." That invitation was accepted. Four days later, the NCCB released a pastoral letter, "Human Life in Our Day," that affirmed the tenable position of nonviolence, condemned the arms race and indiscriminate warfare, and updated the Catholic position on conscription to "make it possible, although not easy, for so-called selective conscientious objectors to refuse—without fear of imprisonment or loss of citizenship—to serve in wars which they consider unjust."[19] The bishops finally asserted, in November 1971, that the United States should cease hostilities in Vietnam with the "Resolution on Southeast Asia,"

Research, Preparations, and Communion

where they argued, based on the just war principle of proportionality, that "whatever good we hope to achieve" in Vietnam could not justify the level of devastation.[20]

As support for the war eroded, the Camden 28 defendants and lawyers worked diligently to develop a strategy. One of the three attorneys representing the 28, David Kairys, decided he could do more to lay the groundwork for an entrapment defense. Fearing that the *Russell* decision might undermine that aspect of their defense, Kairys prepared an amicus curiae, or friend of the court, brief for the *Russell* appeal. The American Civil Liberties Union (ACLU) and the National Emergency Civil Liberties Committee (NECLC) filed the document, arguing that the "courts have found it permissible for an official to offer an opportunity for crime; more creative activity than that is not justified by a legitimate state interest." The brief further asserted that "supplying an element of the crime implies that that element was available only from the government, and creates a correspondingly great risk of convicting the innocent."[21] The *Russell* defendants ultimately lost this battle when the Supreme Court decided in favor of law enforcement 5–4. The ruling constricted the latitude of the defense attempt to prove entrapment. Moving forward, prosecutors could remove entrapment from consideration if they could prove that defendants were "predisposed" to the crime. Since the Camden 28 could not deny, and did not want to deny, that they were predisposed to executing the raid, they could not pursue an entrapment defense.

The ruling came late in the Camden 28 trial schedule, however. The prosecution and defense had already presented arguments when the *Russell* decision came down in spring 1973. The Camden defense team had already proceeded with an entrapment defense but operated under the assumption that the judge hearing their case might, at any point, block them from pursuing this defense. But fortunately, the jury was another matter.

In the United States as in England, the law does not prevent a jury from disobeying the judge's instructions. Defying those instructions is not legal, however. Jurors have the power, but not the right, to rule as they choose. This tradition in Anglo-American jurisprudence known as "jury nullification" was carried over from common law after the colonies freed themselves in the eighteenth century. Jury nullification is rare, however. Judges can hold lawyers in contempt for seeking such a verdict. In this strange paradox, which the legal system has left unresolved, jurors necessarily violate their oath to "uphold the law" when they nullify those laws. Most Americans fail to realize that juries have an absolute

130   CHAPTER SIX

power to hand down not-guilty verdicts no matter the circumstances. As with the fugitive slave cases in the 1850s, juries have occasionally been known to acquit when they deem the laws broken by the defendants to be unjust. The refusal of antebellum juries to convict Americans who harbored escaped slaves underscores an important way jurors can use their independence to challenge unjust laws.

These powers cut both ways through American democracy. All-white Jim Crow jurors used the same prerogative to acquit perpetrators of lynchings despite the overwhelming evidence of murder, as was the case with the Emmet Till trial in 1955.[22] Although the power to nullify has withstood more than two hundred years of case law (and has done so in a real sense because it is a lawless power, no matter how just—or unjust—in a given case), Supreme Court rulings have sought to impose limits. A 1969 federal appellate court decision in *U.S. v. Moylan* ruled against the Catonsville Nine and upheld the right of courts to refuse to instruct juries on jury nullification as an option for fear that "the rule of lawlessness" would overcome the "rule of law."[23] Since judges could thus forbid attorneys from mentioning jury nullification in the courtroom, Kairys, Broege, and Stolar proceeded carefully with their strategy when the trial commenced.

The seventeen months between the arrest and opening arguments were an ordeal, during which plans for the future had to wait until the defendants knew if, and for how long, they would go to prison. The 28 put varying amounts of effort into preparations for the trial. Bob Williamson did not want to stay in the Northeast any longer. He quit his job as a social worker for the state of Pennsylvania and went to New Mexico. He remembers some initial discussions about how the defendants should make their case, but 1971 ended without any agreement. Williamson packed his bags and drove his Volkswagen around the country, over-nighting at KOA campgrounds and visiting the places he wanted to see before starting a life behind bars. Driving west on I-40, he fell in love with the Sandia Mountains as he passed through Tijeras Canyon. He rented a cabin not far from Albuquerque in winter 1972, where he stayed until someone notified him to come back to Camden to prepare for the trial.[24]

The other defendants stayed close by. Keith Forsyth worked at an automotive plant in Philadelphia stamping sheet metal into car parts. Anne Dunham and Frank Pommersheim settled in New York City. Nine months after the arrests, though, Dunham landed in the hospital. Guillain-Barre syndrome had paralyzed her almost completely, after taking one muscle at a time. She could move her eyes but needed a tracheotomy to breathe. Slowly regaining her strength, Dunham recovered on another floor of the hospital before her discharge in September.

Other defendants split their energies between antiwar work, trial preparations, and odd jobs. After Michael Doyle purchased a dilapidated house on Sixth Street in Camden, Cookie Ridolfi and some of the others moved in. Cookie, Ro Ro Reilly, and Lianne Moccia continued to move between the New York, Philadelphia, and Washington, D.C., regions to demonstrate. In 1972, they participated in a hunger strike to protest the war's atrocities. Dunham remembers them visiting her in the hospital, chugging water from plastic milk jugs while they tried to cheer her up.[25]

Ridolfi had also been working with volunteers in South Jersey and Philadelphia who helped the lawyers prepare the defense. Starting in the latter part of 1971, the Camden 28 made jury research and analysis into a group project involving at least fifteen main volunteers and an extended network of supporters who also helped in various ways. This 1970s version of crowdsourcing used phones, cars, pen on paper, and typewriters instead of the internet. Many of the participants in this process, including some of the defendants, had been close friends. Others joined on their own out of interest in the case. They all acted under the direction of an organization called the Camden 28 Defense Committee (CDC). The CDC did everything from raising bail funds and finding lodging for the 28 to organizing public events in their support and assisting with legal research. Drawing from Burlington, Camden, and Gloucester Counties in South Jersey as well as Philadelphia, the committee operated from a bare-bones headquarters at 574 Benson Street in Camden, a few blocks southeast of the federal building.

The CDC, which formed shortly after the August 1971 arrests, asked supporters to recommend local churches, schools, and clubs that might want to join in the effort. The organization wanted to know who they knew—names and addresses of individuals, newspapers, and magazines, as well as radio and television stations that should be contacted. One of its flyers asked readers to tear off the attached "coupon" and check the boxes that applied:

I can give myself (time) ____ Needed supplies ____ Funds (amount) ____ Contacts for a job ____ A house in Camden ____ Sleeping facilities ____ Mailing lists ____ Media contacts ____ [26]

Within weeks, the defense committee was regularly sending its newsletter to seven hundred people. One full-time and three part-time workers staffed the office, which had an automatic folding machine, an electric stapler, and a telephone. The committee generated mailings with

132   CHAPTER SIX

the help of some mid-twentieth-century technology rarely used since the rise of Xerox. An addressograph machine, which printed addresses mechanically from inked embossed plates, made it easier and quicker to send out mailings. And a Gestetner machine duplicated flyers speedily through two stenciled ink drums that squeezed and pushed copies along, much like an old-fashioned mechanical laundry wringer.[27]

Between the 1971 raid and the trial two years later, few months would go by without a CDC rally or gathering in support of the defendants. Less than a month after the action, the defense committee circulated a flyer inviting people to "Come to a Gathering for Peace" at the First Baptist Church in Moorestown, New Jersey, an affluent suburb near Camden and Philadelphia. Defendants gave remarks and led informal discussions about who they were, the purpose of the raid, and how they should respond. With music and free babysitting, the CDC urged people to bring all their family members and friends for a spirited get-to-know-you event. These relatively small gatherings proved instrumental in making the Camden 28 defense a community project that drew people together toward a shared future objective.

Some of the defendants helped substantially with the defense committee work while others needed a break from the drama. Jayma Abdoo had grown up in nearby Washington Township, a rural and working-class suburb of Philadelphia. She had been attending Trinity College in Washington, D.C., for a year and a half before she dropped out to work full time on the draft board raids. At twenty, she was the youngest of the Camden 28. Like Cookie Ridolfi and Bob Williamson, Abdoo hailed from the region but did not represent the locals. By the time she joined the federal building action in Camden, she had been operating through the underground and assisting with raids in different places. Abdoo did essential legal research in the preparations for the trial. Her studies of the law and the history of political trials eventually landed her a paid job in the office of David Kairys and his partner.

An enthusiastic researcher, Abdoo focused much of her attention on the history of jury nullification cases in the United States. She assembled files of decisions, showing numerous defendants over the centuries who had successfully urged jurors to act on their conscience and disregard the instructions of the judge. She typed up eighty double-spaced pages of notes about why Vietnam War draft resisters were increasingly turning to the "time-honored" tradition of jury nullification in their defense. "Their argument," she wrote, "is a simple one." If the jury represents a cross section of the community, and the defendant is willing to admit he is indeed guilty of the acts in question, why, then, may he not be acquitted if the community, represented by the panel, approves of the crime? "The problem," she continued, "is that jurors almost never know that they have this power—to ignore the judge. And the law made it exceedingly difficult to inform them of their power to nullify."[28]

Abdoo's brief circulated only among the defendants and attorneys, more like a white paper than a published article or brief. Her volumes of notes and typed statements, however, reveal that this bright college dropout was developing an interest in the law. Like her codefendants, she was facing a prison sentence that could have put her behind bars for most of her adult life. In October, two months after the raid, she published an article in her college newspaper that betrayed the youthful exuberance powering her through the nerve-racking months of trial preparation. The government, she argued, did not understand its adversaries at all. "What J. Edgar Hoover, John Mitchell, and our other government officials fail repeatedly to comprehend," she asserted in the *Trinity Times*, "is that they cannot arrest our spirit—we will not be stopped. . . . We are twenty-eight men and women who, together with other resisters across the country, are trying with our lives to say 'no' to the madness we see."[29]

Trial preparations included several events that helped to raise money, draw press attention, and bolster support for the Camden 28. Some drew protesters as well. In January 1972, less than five months after the arrests, a sixteen-member cast performed *The Trial of the Catonsville Nine*, a play written by Daniel Berrigan, which was based on the 1968 trial. The students from Delaware County College in Media, Pennsylvania, came to Haddonfield, New Jersey, to stage their production at St. Mary of the Angels Academy. They hoped to raise money for the Camden 28 defense fund. The 250 people who attended walked past thirty-five protesters, who were disgruntled that the school would allow its facilities to be used for the raiders. One of the women who stood by the entrance wielding a sign to express her disapproval told a journalist from the *Courier-Post* that she had asked the school principal if "she would lend a group of women's libbers promoting birth control use of it." The principal, Sister Maureen, replied, "No." In this second of two performances, attendees had to evacuate the auditorium for thirty minutes so police could investigate a bomb scare. One audience member told the reporter that this threat did not frighten her. She was prepared to wait it out in the below-freezing temperatures. "If it blows up," she said, "we'll have an idea of what it's like to be in Vietnam." But the school did not blow up, and the students performed to a standing-room only crowd.[30]

Two months later, the defense committee raised the spirits of the action community with a dramatic religious observance to launch the Christian liturgical season of Lent. As the days grew brighter and crocuses started pushing shoots through the cold ground, preparations for Easter commenced. Catholics typically observe the season by leaving work, school, or home to attend a special midweek Mass for the application of ashes on their foreheads, reminding them that "to dust they shall return."[31] This blessing of the ashes at the altar also symbolizes the death of Christ on the cross and his rising, looking forward to the celebration six and a half weeks later, on Easter. Lent serves as a period in the liturgical cycle for repentance and fasting, a time when Christians ponder their transgressions and pray for pardon as preparation for Christ's forgiveness of sin.

Churches typically make ashes by burning palm leaves blessed in the previous year on the Palm Sunday of Lent, a Mass during which parishioners wave palm fronds to reenact the warm greeting received by Jesus from his followers as he arrived in Jerusalem. Though the burning of palm fronds into ashes represents a nearly universal process in church tradition, no church texts actually codify the practice. Some celebrants have used the Ash Wednesday tradition to burn other materials with symbolic importance.[32]

Michael Doyle of the Camden 28 made ashes in 1972 by burning a copy of the Pentagon Papers. It had been eight months since Daniel Ellsberg had released the classified documents. The Camden 28 Defense Committee hosted their event to launch a program called Project Life, a series of projects and demonstrations that used the upcoming trial as an opportunity to offer meaningful ceremonies that would maintain the momentum of protesters and pressure against the war. Sixty supporters joined the celebration, including other Camden 28 defendants. While Michael Giocondo made an audiocassette recording of the sermon, the worshippers huddled together as Doyle guided them through a dark and chilly service. With gloved fingers gripping flickering candles, "the flame," noted *Courier-Post* reporter Craig Waters, "was passed like a gift of light and of warmth between friends" (see figure 17).[33]

Doyle told the participants who joined him that evening that it was important to "wear the Pentagon Papers" as penance for the violence in Vietnam. He emphasized a sacred mandate to welcome the presence of the Holy Spirit through the eyes, nose, fingers, and tongue. The priest brought to the moment an understanding of the incarnation shared by many Catholics, especially the middle-aged generation of radicals. Doyle, however, possessed a unique ability to envelope listeners into the Mystical Body of Christ. It made no difference to him if those whom he addressed were Catholic or not, religious or not. He knew how to bring the spirit directly to the senses in a material way. As the adults listened quietly and children murmured in the usual background chatter, Doyle

FIGURE 17. Father Michael Doyle Preparing for Ash Wednesday Service
Father Michael Doyle, an immigrant from County Longford, Ireland, burns a copy of the Pentagon Papers in an army helmet to prepare for a 1972 Ash Wednesday ceremony he celebrated at Johnson Cemetery in Camden, New Jersey. Photo courtesy of Anthony Giacchino.

urged the gatherers not only to receive the ashes on their foreheads, but also to "lick" them, to "taste" them—"to taste the death they symbolize and take upon ourselves the burden of the guilt and do penance the rest of our lives for the destruction."[34]

Organizers had planned every aspect of the ritual with care to symbolically invoke the collective loss of life to warfare. Doyle asked the "Almighty God, who looks down upon the dead and upon the ashes of dead men everywhere, the dead, who had been killed and are being killed, . . . to bless this ash into something purposeful, that we might wear it and remember it, but it would sink into our hearts and we would be compassionate." With the assistance of fellow Camden 28 defendant

136 CHAPTER SIX

Eugene Dixon, Doyle burned the ashes in a soldier's helmet to "focus . . . minds on the ashes of Hiroshima, on the ashes in the ovens of Germany, the ashes in concentration camps, and the mountains of ashes in Southeast Asia that have been created by our bombs and our destructive forces." In essence, Doyle equated the destruction in Vietnam with the crime of the crucifixion.[35]

The liturgy unfolded on the hallowed ground of Johnson Cemetery, where generations of African American residents of Camden lay buried. The location underscored the heavy toll suffered by America's working-class and nonwhite communities in Vietnam. At the intersection of Federal and 38th Streets, the cemetery held an estimated 250 to 300 graves, including those of 123 Black civil war veterans. The city had seized the land in 1953 as a penalty for unpaid taxes, ushering in a decades-long period of neglect that would invite foot traffic to trample the garbage-strewn grounds.[36] "It is sad," noted Doyle in his sermon, "when the dead must pay taxes. . . . If they cannot rest in peace," he continued, "we should think hard about our condition and ask God to have mercy upon us and to free us from this terrible burden that's upon our hearts."[37]

Father Doyle committed an audacious breach of tradition by performing this ceremony in order to attract attention, which it did. Resisters across the river at LaSalle University in Philadelphia held a similar ceremony by burning draft cards for ashes in a chapel basement. Their special guest Dorothy Day found the liturgy, not insolent, but rather "very beautiful."[38]

Doyle's superiors in the archdiocese swiftly rebuked him. Within three days, bishop George J. Guilfoyle called the defiant priest into his office for an explanation of the unconventional service. He also told the press that he "regret[ed] and disapprov[ed] of the religious ceremony conducted by Father Doyle at Johnson Cemetery on Ash Wednesday." He also removed Doyle from his post as assistant pastor of St. Joseph's parish in Camden and assigned him to duties at a home for sick and dying priests.[39]

Autumn 1972 brought Jane Fonda to South Jersey in support of the Camden 28. Five months before the trial, Fonda spoke at community centers and universities in the region, including Rutgers University–Camden, as part of the Indochina Peace Campaign. Defendant Michael Giocondo, representing the Camden 28 Defense Committee, served as one of Fonda's hosts and drivers. Giocondo alarmed the actor when he got them temporarily lost and accidentally drove them onto the Fort Dix Army Base in Burlington County, New Jersey. "Let's get out of here," she reportedly roared, adding, "I don't want to end up in their clutches."[40]

The jury research performed by the defense committee proved at least as important as these other activities before the trial. This investigative work helped attorneys select jurors who would be most favorable to the defense. The project dispersed volunteers across South Jersey to scour three counties for demographic data and investigate the personal lives of potential jurors. It was only the third application of this new process, which came to be known as systematic jury selection or scientific jury selection (SJS). New York University sociologist Jay Schulman first introduced the methods of SJS in the 1971 Harrisburg Seven and Angela Davis trials. The goal was to provide defendants with access to personal jury information that would at least approximate the data advantage prosecutors enjoyed through the work of FBI investigators. It involved the statistical analysis of attitudes, behaviors, and living environments for the purposes of developing juror profiles. Over the next thirty years, these techniques grew into a lucrative industry as demand from law firms spawned jury-consulting businesses.

Information gathered via SJS helped defendants go further than the theories of lawyers to discern who would ultimately be a desirable or an undesirable juror. Family status, occupation, race, age, gender, level of education, relation to a law enforcement official, military status, religious affiliation, organization memberships, hobbies, and other characteristics served as factors for consideration.[41] After the Camden 28 verdict, Schulman applied his social science–based method of jury selection to the famous Attica trials. In 1975, he formed a nonprofit called the National Jury Project, which provided low-cost jury research assistance to defendants in civil rights and other political trials. The National Jury Project continued to offer its services to clients who lacked the financial resources to pay for this intense labor.[42]

The Camden 28 jury project employed a survey with about fifteen questions that volunteers asked over the phone to residents in communities from which the jury pool would be assembled. They called about sixteen hundred people and asked questions like, "Should Daniel Ellsberg be punished or praised for publishing the Pentagon Papers?"[43] It is ironic, given the hefty price tags it would eventually command, that systematic jury selection first appeared at movement trials. The anticapitalist clients served by SJS had no clue that they were launching a niche industry for wealthy clients like O. J. Simpson because in the early 1970s, it was activists providing free labor—not highly paid professional consultants—who performed this work.[44] Resisters, in fact, rallied to the task as a form of solidarity. They operated like close kin, united behind the goal of realizing a bolder vision of community.

Jayma Abdoo was one of many who put their college degree or career on hold to do this work, which proved instrumental in helping to build a stellar defense.

The Camden 28 Defense Committee distributed a list of more than 160 potential jurors to a team of about fifteen volunteers who organized the job by county. Attorney David Kairys found himself galvanized by the collective energy. Like many other activists in the antiwar movement, Kairys was not Catholic, but the sacramental aspects of Catholic Resistance aligned seamlessly with his own devotion to peace and social justice. As a young lawyer with a fledging practice operating out of the back office of another firm, Kairys was equal parts smart, ambitious, and radical. When the Camden 28 reached out to him for assistance, they presented him with an exciting and life-changing opportunity to contribute his talents to the movement while developing new aspects of trial law. In this respect, he represented an emergent cadre of former student radicals who were eager to flex their degrees to fight the war in the courts. Not only lawyers, but newly minted psychologists and sociologists like Jay Schulman, the architect of SJS, jumped in to provide their professional services to aid in Vietnam resistance. Kairys, a son of Baltimore, had completed his JD degree at the University of Pennsylvania three years earlier.

Though not profitable for Kairys in the financial sense of the word, the trial launched what became a successful career in the legal and teaching profession. He published articles in law journals while preparing for the Camden 28 defense and other cases, cultivating a specialization in jury selection. In a 1972 issue of the *American Criminal Law Review*, he wrote about new "mathematical methods" and applications of census data offering trial lawyers the ability to improve on the faulty process of picking juries of real peers. "Black, young, and poor" defendants were disadvantaged by a system that relied mainly on voter registration lists, "which automatically excludes everyone under 21 years old and [others] who, for ideological or other reasons, do not vote."[45] Statistical data, he argued, with the help of mathematical equations, yielded more accurate maps than the voting wards' boundaries, which favored white, middle-class suburbanites by mischaracterizing population densities.[46]

Kairys was a lawyer and scholar for the movement, but he was also *of* the movement. He could take a case like the Camden 28 because he did not live a lawyer's lifestyle. When he started his practice, in contrast to his affluent colleagues, he was part of a collective of six people residing in a three-story Philadelphia Victorian. Like many of his clients, Kairys and his housemates split the expenses and ate together in their common first-floor kitchen. When the firm of Kairys and Rudovsky opened its doors, David and Rudy welcomed clients into a small room they rented from the criminal law firm of Seagal, Appel & Natali. The new practice had been taking cases for less than six months when the FBI arrested the Camden 28. Outfitted with a hodge-podge of equipment provided by movement friends, the lawyers hunched over desks from someone's attic, prepared briefs on an IBM typewriter provided by Kairys's parents, and sat in two donated swivel chairs.[47]

As critical as Kairys became to the defense, he could not have done his job without the SJS workers. Defendants living together on Sixth Street in Camden, including Cookie Ridolfi, Sarah Tosi, and Anita Ricci, did much of this research to prepare for jury selection in the voir dire phase of trial.

The team also included a young mother by the name of Mary Schmelzer, an activist who wanted to be part of Catholic Resistance but did not want to assume the risks associated with the draft board raids. Schmelzer, who was born Mary Murphy, brought the world of Philadelphia Irish Catholicism into the resistance movement. Raised within blocks of her aunts, uncles, cousins, and grandparents, Schmelzer's childhood in the Juniata Park section of Philadelphia revolved, in her words, around a "simple, uncomplicated, unsophisticated" Catholicism.[48] This religious upbringing fueled her commitment to social justice when she entered adulthood. Though steeped in habits of prayer and ceremony, including daily Mass and weekly confession, Schmelzer's family had not been especially strict or orthodox in their devotion. This spirituality was, in Schmelzer's memory, more ritual than fire-and-brimstone holiness— there was "no piety."

Schmelzer was in her twenties when the Vietnam War started, having recently graduated from college and already married with two children. She and her husband, John Schmelzer (another Catholic), were radicalized by the civil rights and antiwar movements. This put them at odds with her family, whose attitude on Vietnam was, in Schmelzer's words, "Oh hell no, we should all go." The young mother was reading Dorothy Day, Thomas Merton, and Daniel Berrigan. She became involved in the peace movement through a cousin a priest who had recently joined Clergy and Laity Concerned about Vietnam (CALCAV), which was led by Daniel Berrigan, A. J. Muste, and Martin Luther King Jr., among other prominent men of the cloth.[49]

Though she was already busy raising children, Schmelzer also taught classes part time at the Philadelphia College of Textiles and Science, a job that would in later decades grow into a full-time academic career. It was in the classroom that she first met Cookie Ridolfi, who was briefly her student and then became a lifelong friend. Ridolfi called Schmelzer after the arrest and told her friend she should join the Camden 28 Defense Committee, which Schmelzer did enthusiastically.[50] The new volunteer assumed a variety of tasks for the CDC. She took care of the house on Sixth Street, helping with daily cooking and cleaning chores. She lent her professional wardrobe of "adult clothes," as she called them, to the young women resisters for their court and speaking appearances. She even housed defendants and supporters in her family's home.

Schmelzer remembers the jury project as having vividly taken over her life. The Schmelzers' dining room became a clearing house of data, a "vast pile" of information on potential jurors. The effective choreography of the operation left a lasting imprint on Mary's mind. "Everybody played her or his part. I was so edified [by] how good of a job everybody did and with great integrity." It was thrilling but serious, "no kumbaya," since the future of the defendants was on the line and the war was dragging on.[51]

The work required hours on the phone and in the car sleuthing. Put in charge of Burlington County, Schmelzer and her phone tree of volunteers combed through fat voter registration books and made random phone calls to collect the coveted demographic information for developing profiles of the jury pool. Schmelzer had friends on the committee, but many of the volunteers remained unknown to her. There was a culture in the resistance, she remembers, of keeping your head down and avoiding other people's business for security reasons.

Once the list of potential jurors had been furnished, she drove to the neighborhoods of the names assigned to her, noting bumper stickers and yard signs and checking out prospects' homes. Schmelzer and the other volunteers filled out intake forms, typed up statements about their charges, and made recommendations based on their assessments. One woman, a last-minute alternate added to the list, could not be easily profiled in time for the selection process. In a last-ditch effort to learn something about her, Schmelzer recruited her own sister, who actually sat to have her hair done in the Maple Shade, New Jersey, salon where the woman worked. Fortunately, there was a lot of chatter about the upcoming trial among the staff and clients in the establishment. This high level of interest landed the stylist in the desirable juror category. The defense team identified her as someone who wanted to do the job as a learning experience, or "educational event." They regarded this attitude favorably, though the hair stylist did not ultimately serve.

The SJS team applied what they saw as systematic judgments in their assessment of jurors. This work sometimes included racial profiling. Schmelzer, for example, tracked down information about another prospect, a young Black man, by going into his Camden neighborhood and joining some people playing basketball on a court across from his home. She recommended that the defense team not choose this man because of his poverty, as she believed the paltry five-dollar-a-day jury stipend for a long trial would make him possibly resent the defendants for taking him away from better-paid work.[52]

Defendant Jayma Abdoo also factored racial identity into her profiles. Abdoo wrote up short and roughly jotted, eight-line descriptions of her assigned juror prospects. One person was, in her words, a "black, very fair, level-headed, male Democrat" who "lived in a small town, population 6,000, with racial problems." She recommended that the defense team "take him." A Cherry Hill woman proved less appealing, however. She was so devout in her Catholicism, noted Abdoo, that she "thr[ew] Jehovah's Witnesses of[f] steps." Describing the woman as rigid and "opinionated," Abdoo added that she "doesn't do anything with neighbors." As a result, she removed this church lady from consideration (see figure 18).[53]

The project continued even as the trial started. Sitting in the courtroom and observing potential jurors as they answered questions, volunteers checked boxes and circled numbers on a scale of one to seven on their "Voir Dire Rating." What was the level of deference to the judge? What was the level of interest displayed? Did the volunteer's "gut judgment" tell them that this person was rigid (1), loose (7), or somewhere in between? Was initiative low (1) or high (7)?[54] All this information was collected and given to David Kairys and the other "generals," in Schmelzer's words, who made the decisions about how to construct the defense.[55]

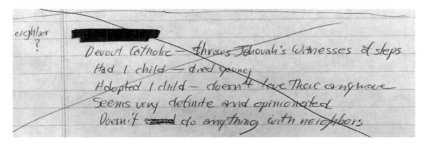

FIGURE 18. Handwritten Jury Research Note
In 1972 a group of supporters assisted the Camden 28 defense team by researching the jury pool. Defendant Jayma Abdoo was one of these volunteers. The group kept detailed notes to help attorneys assess how favorable prospective jurors might be to the draft board raiders who were on trial. Image reproduced from the Jayma Abdoo Papers, courtesy of the Swarthmore College Peace Collection.

142   CHAPTER SIX

As Schmelzer did her research, the generals of the team developed another important element of the case, FBI informant Bob Hardy. The quest to secure Hardy's signed affidavit testifying to his entanglements with the FBI required feats of secrecy and subterfuge that David Kairys had not learned from his professors in law school. In fall 1971, the attorney spent hours in his car to dodge FBI tails and avoid having conversations on his tapped phone. One of these journeys led him through side streets, highways, and boulevards to a modest residence in Philadelphia, the home of a couple who attended Father Michael Doyle's church in Camden before the archdiocese moved him. The O'Donnells left that day so Doyle could host a private meeting in a location unknown to and unwatched by the bureau.[56]

After greeting the priest at the door, Kairys walked to the den, where Robert Hardy was waiting. The three men discussed what kind of role Hardy would play in the trial. Would he be friendly or hostile to the defense? Was he ready to reveal everything? The grieving father had many regrets and wanted to make things right for the defendants, his former friends. Though he felt no shame for his decision to inform on them to the FBI, the consequences troubled him. He told Doyle and Kairys that he never thought he was setting up his friends to go to prison for decades. When he cooperated with the FBI, it was in the belief that the agents would make arrests ahead of the break-in and stop the raid before anyone could commit crimes such as theirs, which might now land them in prison for forty-seven years. He said he never really supported the raid, which is why he wanted it stopped before it began—so his friends would not go to jail. As Kairys wrote later, the attorney judged him to be "deluded" but "sincere." This man who had willingly deceived his friends over the course of weeks wanted to talk about how the FBI had not only used him, but deceived him. Because this meeting created an opening for Bob Hardy to share his testimony, it was critically important to the trial, which was then still several months away.[57]

Earlier conversations with his pastor and friend Michael Doyle had led Hardy to the point of speaking out. As Hardy recalled twenty years later, "I don't think the Camden 28 would've turned out anyway different whether Billy [his son] died or didn't die. I still was gonna do what I knew would be the truth. That's how I am."[58] At the same time, he admitted that maybe he was in "denial." In any case, he was eager to "heal" his relationship with Doyle. So, in a church confession, he related the whole story about how the FBI helped the raid become a reality. The revelation stunned Doyle, but the priest honored the confidentiality of Hardy, who was his parishioner. The Catholic Seal of Confession dictated that any information gained during penitence must

Research, Preparations, and Communion   143

remain secret.[55] After a couple of weeks, Hardy recommended that they get it all in writing. "I suggested that we make it a legal document using his lawyer," he recalled later.[60] David Kairys was also bound to keep the discovery confidential as Doyle's attorney.

Doyle and Kairys moved quickly to secure the statement, arranging for a court stenographer to record and type Hardy's spoken words. The process of discussing the document, recording it, and signing the finished text required significant caution and effort since they had to complete these tasks in person. The defense did not want to tip agents off to this maneuver lest they use it as an opportunity to change Hardy's mind again. As Hardy described the process, "We kept going from place to place because we were looking for a so-called, as the Irish say, a safe house."[61]

The finalization took place under a bridge in South Philadelphia after much driving around by the parties involved to avoid FBI tails. When it was completed, Kairys gave Hardy three copies, two of which promptly went to trusted people—a sister-in-law and a brother—who knew to show it to the press should something happen to him. Then Hardy updated the FBI on his change of allegiance. He would not show the agents his statement, but he wanted them to know it existed. At that point, he saw the affidavit as a way of keeping himself safe from government agents who, having now caught wind of his defection, might choose to intimidate or even kill him to suppress his testimony. In interviews decades after the trial, Hardy revealed that agents had warned, "Someday you might be hit by a truck." He remembers telling special agents Terry Neist and Michael Ryman, "If I get hit by a truck you guys are in serious trouble, because it's going through [the] *Washington Post*."[62]

Hardy then waited two weeks before actually giving Kairys permission to finally release the document to the court. He was nervous. Lead assistant U.S. attorney John Barry had called him into his office and said Hardy had put himself in serious trouble. It angered but also scared the former Marine. He was concerned about the publicity that would ensue since the affidavit would certainly stir up a hornets' nest when it hit the headlines. But a deadline for filing the affidavit loomed. They had to submit the document to the court within two weeks or it could be excluded from trial. Hardy waited a little longer, consulted his wife, and talked to the Lord. "I went home and told Peg and we just prayed about it for two days." Finally, he called Doyle and gave his permission. On March 15, 1972, David Kairys filed a motion asking to dismiss the trial based on the new testimony, which showed that the FBI had brazenly set up the defendants for arrest by enabling the crime.[63]

It was national news the next morning. Readers learned that Hardy admitted to not merely to spying for the bureau, but acting as a "provocateur." The defendants, he stated, did not have the necessary skills or tools, which Hardy provided with financial assistance from the bureau. The raid would not have happened, moreover, if he had not convinced the resisters to proceed, as the FBI had urged him to do. They paid him $60 a day for this work. Agents stayed in constant touch with him throughout the planning stages of the raid and paid for tools, vehicles, fuel, and even the groceries the defendants ate while they were preparing—all of which he described as "indispensable" to the crime.[64] As expected, when Kairys filed the affidavit, it dropped like a bomb on the government's case against the Camden 28. By flipping Hardy into a witness hostile to the FBI's activities, the defense locked into place its government overreach strategy.[65]

The lawyers feared, however, that the Camden 28 might not be ready to assume their own place at the defense table. As David Kairys and Carl Brogue wrote to their clients in a group letter on December 22, 1972, "We are concerned about the apparent lack of realization that in less than six weeks the government of the United States of America is going to begin its attempt to imprison you." Before outlining four different matters that the defendants needed to resolve before trial, they stated that, "If you think we can show up at the trial or shortly before and things will just fall together, we think you are wrong."[66]

Would the 28 cohere around a theory for their defense, one that could capture the complicated aspects of their case in a clear-cut way that jurors could digest? Could the defendants, who argued over the very goals of the trial, find enough agreement to rally around a successful strategy? They had less than two months to decide.

CHAPTER SEVEN

A Prosecution Disarmed by Loving Kindness

What do you do when a child is on fire?
Father Michael Doyle, opening statement[1]

Father Michael Doyle tried to explain why he, a man of the cloth, broke in and laid waste to a government office in August 1971. When the thirty-three-year-old immigrant from County Longford, Ireland, respectfully addressed the judge, jury, and onlookers, he was speaking in the same federal building he had burglarized almost two years earlier. Doyle was among the first Camden 28 defendants to give opening statements in a trial that would last three months. What started in the deepest of winter, February 1973, ended on a mild rainy day in May. Defendant Anne Dunham, still recovering from Guillain-Barre syndrome, started the trial wearing leg braces and finished it with enough muscle strength to walk on her own.[2]

Those sixty days mixed arguments about evidence with animated and emotional testimony. Family, friends, supporters, journalists, and other observers filled the room daily. Over the course of those weeks they developed an uncommon esprit de corps. Participants and onlookers packed the windowless, wood-paneled space lit by stately chandeliers, which was located on the third floor of the federal building on State Street in Camden, two flights below the draft boards. The defendants, meanwhile, rallied together in a new way.

Almost all of them lived in or around Camden during the trial. The defendants awoke, dressed, and made their way to the courthouse together every day. "It was like your job," remembers Frank Pommersheim.[3] While Doyle stayed at the rectory, Milo Billman lived on his own property nearby. Terry Buckalew and lawyer David Kairys continued to live in Philadelphia. The rest of the group occupied three different dwellings nearby. Ro Ro Reilly and lawyer Carl Broege, who were soon to be married, stayed in a duplex owned by a friend of a friend, along with lawyer Marty Stolar, Jesuits Peter Fordi and Ned Murphy, the now married Anne Dunham and Frank Pommersheim, and Bob Good. In another house operated by the defense committee lived Mike Giocondo, Ro Ro's sister Joan Reilly, Keith Forsyth, Marge Inness, Jayma Abdoo, and Barry Musi. Ridolfi continued to reside at the Sixth Street house, where John Grady, Ed McGowan, Lee Ann Moccia, Sarah Tosi, and Paul Couming joined her. Except for Couming and Fordi, the men mostly left the "shitwork," in Ridolfi's words, to the women. "A bunch of us . . . went upstairs. . . . We were talking about the problem of the men not doing their share of things. . . . It was almost like we were having our own little feminist movement . . . [that] evolved within the house."[4]

The parents who came to Camden for the trial supported each other as well as their children. Ro Ro Reilly remembers waking up to the voice of Estelle Fordi, who drove ninety miles down from Jersey City each morning with her husband to get Peter out of bed. Every morning, recalls Reilly, she walked into the house yelling, "Peetah! Are you out of bed yet Peetah?"[5]

Ro Ro and Joan's mother also commuted every day from her home in Long Island, driving over 150 miles each way, often with her husband. Mrs. Reilly made a point of taking anyone to lunch who was willing, usually at the Plaza Hotel. "You would walk in the dining room," recalls Ro Ro, "and the judge and his clerks would be seated in one area. The prosecution over here; defense attorneys there. And Dr. Reilly and Mrs. Reilly and whoever they brought down with them, and whoever wanted to join them for lunch."[6]

Kitty Ridolfi, Cookie's mother, was the other person whom the defendants and families leaned on. "She was there for all of us," remembers Joan Reilly.[7] The trial was hard on the South Philadelphia legal secretary, who left the courtroom in tears when FBI agents described the evidence implicating her daughter. "My fingerprints were on everything," recalls Ridolfi, "and I had drawn the maps."[8] Ro Ro Reilly remembers that her father "worshipped" Kitty for her strength.[9]

By the time of opening arguments in February, all parties knew that the trial would be an ordeal, but none could have known it would be epic. The case of the Camden 28 was historic for a host of reasons. In addition to the systematic jury research, the trial also incorporated questions directly from the jurors themselves. Cutting edge in 1971, these scribbled notes traveled hand-to-hand from the jury box to the judge, who decided if they were proper and, if so, read them out loud. The slips of paper typically communicated requests for clarification or explanations of the law.

The word that stands out in most recollections of this trial, though, is "latitude." The judge, Clarkson Fisher, gave the defendants remarkable liberty to protest the war alongside the arguments of their case. Some defendants, moreover, amplified these protests by appearing as their own lawyers. They questioned witnesses—often each other—alongside licensed attorneys in a "hybrid defense." The courtroom thus witnessed multiple direct and cross examinations of the same person after a seemingly interminable presentation of opening statements. These hours on days on weeks of exposure to the defendants significantly familiarized the jury to the lives and personalities of the activists.

The tumultuous political landscape of the early 1970s further intensified the political stakes of the Camden 28 trial. By the time of opening arguments, the nation was already roiled by news about federal abuses of power and presidential cover-ups. The whistleblower Daniel Ellsberg was now a household name as a result of the Pentagon Papers scandal two years earlier. Americans remained polarized by the war, civil rights movement, and the sexual revolution, but increasingly united in a common mistrust of the federal government.

The cynicism escalated also as the Watergate scandal broke. The summer before the trial, five men were arrested for breaking into the Democratic National Headquarters at the Watergate building in Washington, D.C. Newspapers reported mounting evidence of White House involvement in the crime over the next several months. Toward the end of 1972, the *Washington Post* revealed that the Watergate burglary was part of a broader spying operation undertaken by President Nixon's reelection campaign. A trickle of government officials then resigned in the new year. Shortly before the jury handed down its decision on the Camden 28, the attorney general appointed special prosecutor Archibald Cox, a graduate of Harvard Law School, to lead an investigation of the Nixon campaign.[10]

As officials at the White House dealt unsuccessfully with this turmoil, the lawyers in Camden dove into a series of pretrial motions. Assistant U.S. attorney John Barry from the District of New Jersey sought to make a last-minute plea deal the evening before trial. The six-foot-tall, thirty-nine-year-old graduate of New York University law school, now at the U.S. Attorney's Office in Newark, led a team of government attorneys on the case.[11] Barry had already set the tone of events in ways he had not intended, however, when he met with some of the defendants to make a deal. He negotiated with five delegates from the Camden 28 to offer a settlement that would have ended the trial before adversaries picked the jury.

The delegation, which included Cookie Ridolfi, Terry Buckalew, Joan Reilly, Bob Williamson, and Ed McGowan, listened to Barry explain his offer of a misdemeanor plea with suspended sentences. The proposal was generous. Given the amount of evidence the FBI had collected against the twenty-eight activists, the raiders could not deny their guilt. Another federal prosecutor, David Hinden, confessed decades later that the defection of Robert Hardy from the prosecution had completely changed the dynamic of their case, however. Their star witness, the ex-Marine, was now a "big problem." The tides had turned in their favor, but with the defendants representing themselves, all faced a "long, tough, grind" in the months ahead.[12] Had the delegation accepted this offer, the entire group would have escaped all charges without felony convictions. The defense only had to agree to serve "unenforced" sentences for the crime, which amounted to time on paper but not in practice. They had to guarantee their good behavior and perform community service as well. For their complete freedom, the delegation needed only say "Yes." Before the terms of their "walk" could be worked out, however, the five representatives instead cut the meeting off with a curt "No."[13]

John Barry and his team of federal prosecutors continued with their efforts to undermine the defense into the next day with a pretrial motion. They moved to sever eight of the defendants from the larger group. Though apprehended for assisting with the raid preparations, Jayma Abdoo, Milo Billman, Gene Dixon, Keith Forsyth, Mel Madden, Lianne Moccia, Frank Pommersheim, and Sarah Tosi did not assist with the break-in to the same extent as the other defendants.[14] Prosecutors do not typically file motions to sever. Defense attorneys often use the pretrial stage to accommodate different goals or problematic relationships with this tool. They can sever defendants who might blame each other, feel mutual animosity, or lack a sufficient connection to maintain solidarity through a grueling trial. Here was an unconventional motion to sever by a prosecution team that, back in 1971, had chosen to join all the Camden 28 defendants together in one indictment. This motion revealed how far the entire context of the case had changed in favor of the defendants since that initial indictment. Now, the prosecution perceived a need to divide if it was to conquer.

Judge Fisher let the defense use the courtroom to deliberate this motion on February 5, 1973, and a contentious and emotional discussion ensued. Two points of view emerged during the morning's debate as the activists and their attorneys sat around five oblong tables. One side included Michael Doyle, who argued that the group should at least consider the prosecution's offer. He wanted to avoid conviction, especially since he was at risk for deportation back to Ireland. Ridolfi, Couming, Grady, and McGowan voiced the opposing perspective. Having immersed themselves in the draft board actions for many months, the four also wanted to avoid conviction, but only after taking advantage

A Prosecution Disarmed by Loving Kindness 149

of a full-blown trial to stage a public attack on the war. "The point was," reflected McGowan later, "to insist on having their day in court."[15] This trial had been a chance to bring "truth to power." By the end of the meeting, the defendants decided to go either way, announcing their acceptance of separate trials as well as their determination to endure the entirety of the trial together. They would continue to speak about themselves as one group, the Camden 28, though the court officially tried them as two distinct groups. In the meantime, the court granted the severance requested by the defense for William "Doc" Anderson and Martha Schemeley, who played minor roles in the action. Another of the original defendants, Anita Ricci, withdrew from the trial by taking a plea bargain on a lesser charge to remove herself from the proceedings. The larger group of seventeen, which faced harsher charges, came before their jury first.[16]

So much togetherness proved difficult in the months ahead, necessitating that the activists tolerate each other's habits and idiosyncrasies. They had bickered vigorously in the weeks before the trial but finally settled on a common strategy by the time of opening arguments. While deciding to not agree about every detail, they vowed to stay united, which carried them through the ordeal like a family. Just like in a family, the group was as dysfunctional as it was loving. The prosecutors had tried many times to divide the 28 against each other but found one plea deal refused after another. Yet the defendants could not prevent the government's motion to sever. Though it was rarely invoked, the prosecutors had the same right defendants had to seek severance. And it was the judge's decision to make. In the end he had granted the government's request, severing eight defendants for later trial.

But the defendants had a brilliant and unstoppable response. Courtrooms are open and trials are public in the United States. Nobody could keep the severed defendants out. So almost all of the 28 appeared together every day in court, even though the government was mounting its prosecution against only seventeen of them. Ed McGowan remembers the resolution to act together as a "euphoric" moment that transformed the meeting into a rally as the defendants walked out of the courtroom together chanting, "Let's go to trial."[17]

Jury selection occupied the next five days. The judge systematically questioned potential candidates from the pool of 130 men and women who appeared at the federal building to serve. Could they be "fair and objective?" he asked. "What is your opinion about the war?" "How do you feel about the involvement of clergy in civil disobedience? And how open are you to believing members of law enforcement who take the stand to testify?" After answering the judge's questions, the panel of prospective jurors then answered questions in turn from the prosecution and the defense.

The final group was an interesting mix of men and women, Black and white, Republican and Democrat. Though we can never know the full impact of the systematic jury research conducted by volunteers in the months leading up the trial, the Camden 28 mostly had the jury they sought. Filling the box were mostly working-class people whose life experience would suggest they could be persuaded by the activists' arguments against the war.

Ruth Blough of Vineland worked as a floor woman in a glassworks plant. She was Methodist, Republican, and white. Anna Marie Carmen was a German immigrant and mother of three children married to an RCA meter reader. A Catholic and a Democrat, she lived with her family in the working-class suburb of Lindenwold. Twenty-eight-year-old Daniel Bower worked as a machine operator at a linoleum and floor-covering plant. Fred Kaiser, a Catholic and a Democrat, was a computer operator with four children. The Republican and Protestant Bartlett Groveline was a Pine Hill housewife and mother of four grown children whose husband worked at RCA as a wireman. Eleanor Blaszczyk, also a housewife, lived in nearby Cinnaminson with her engineer husband and four children. The thirty-six-year-old Jane Butterbaugh was a Democrat and Lutheran who worked as a packer at Kerr Glass in rural Melville. Anna Bertino, a fifty-nine-year-old widow, owned a dress-making factory in New Jersey's blueberry capital, Hammonton. Sam Braithwaite, also fifty-nine, was a Black self-employed Methodist who worked as a cab driver in Atlantic City. He was a combat veteran of World War II and voted Democrat. Anna Mathis, a Republican and a Protestant, was a sewing machine operator at Nanette Manufacturing who lived in Gloucester City. Fifty-nine-year-old Ed Dobson lived in Camden. He was a Democrat and a Baptist. Fifty-one-year-old Jim Lomax of Penns Grove was a Black married man who worked at DuPont as a special operator and trouble-shooter. Lomax was politically active as president of the Penns Grove City Council and also of the Salem County Welfare Board. He was Methodist but had married into a Catholic family. There were also four alternate jurors, all white, Catholic, and Democrat. They never served.[18]

Opening statements finally started on the thirteenth day of the trial, Tuesday February 27, 1973. After the prosecution's turn, participants and observers immediately encountered the cacophony of defense voices that became a regular part of the trial. None denied responsibility; instead, they all sought to explain why they had committed the crime. At every opportunity over the ensuing weeks, the activists used their time on the stand to expose the government's crimes against its own citizens and the people of Vietnam. This unconventional approach also entailed a different means of addressing the judge, jury, and prosecutors—one that challenged the staid formality that typically governed courtroom behavior.

Father Ed McGowan put the reasons for the raid in terms of the larger principles of the Catholic Church: "We have an overwhelming respect for life." Peter Fordi declared, "I ripped up those files with my hands. . . . Standing here right before you, I'm not sorry I did it." Anne Dunham admitted that all the accusations made by prosecutor John Barry were true but insisted they did not amount to a crime. "The destruction of that paper was in no way an act of violence." Violence is perpetrated against people, she said, not paper. Dunham concluded her opening statement by reading verses from a poem by the Buddhist monk Thich Nhat Hanh, who ended with a dire warning: "Beware, turn around to face your real enemies, ambition, violence, hatred, greed."[19] Bob Good described his choice to drop out of school to join the movement. After his brother died in a rice paddy in the Mekong Delta and friends continued to be drafted, the lessons learned in a university classroom lost their meaning, said the Ohioan. "My dreams of helping people were being pondered away on textbooks," he continued, "while real people were dying."[20]

It was Cookie Ridolfi, though, who established the intimate and informal tone that would typify the defense's style with her opening words: "Hi, I'm Kathleen Ridolfi. Most people call me Cookie, I hope you get to know me that way." She noted that John Barry's job was to return a conviction in the trial but argued that the charges leveled by the prosecution were inappropriate for "the times in which we live." She said she wanted to introduce her defense team and acquaint the jury with them. "We are a group of brothers and sisters who have come out of a larger community of people opposing the war in this country for a long time." As she spoke their name, each defendant chimed in with "Good morning!" or "Hello!" Ridolfi then declared that, even though eleven of the group had been severed from the case by the prosecution, "they haven't been severed from us" and were still very much part of the case. She explained that even though only some of the defendants would appear in the trial, when each person spoke, they would "represent everyone." They had chosen the unorthodox pro se defense, even with lawyers, she said, because they believed they had to speak out the actions themselves, "from our hearts" (see figure 19).[21]

Ridolfi—who herself would one day finish college, attend law school,

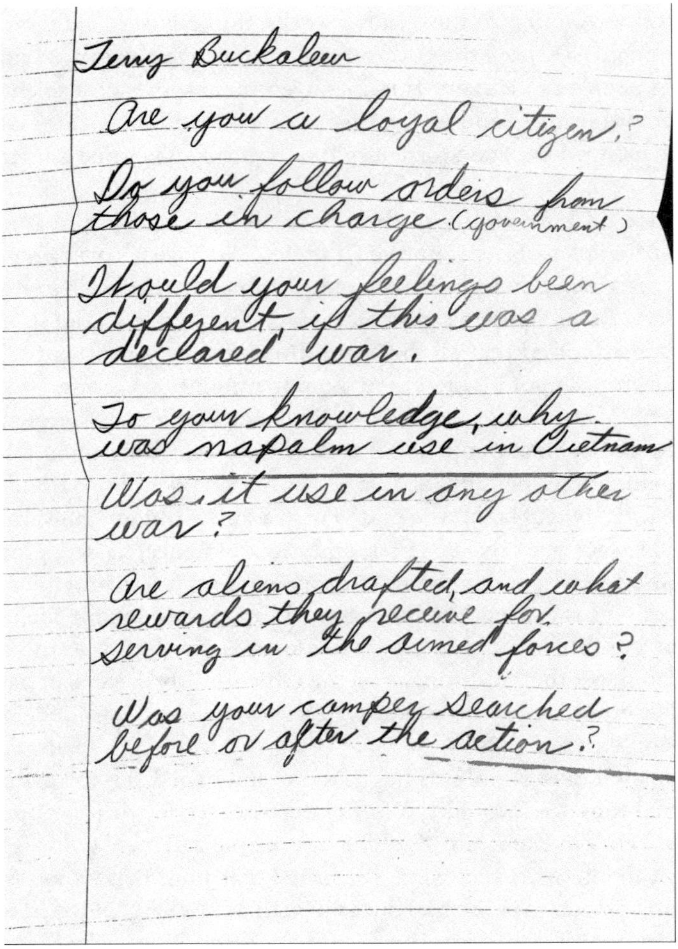

Terry Buckalew

Are you a loyal citizen?

Do you follow orders from those in charge (government)

Would your feelings been different if this was a declared war.

To your knowledge, why was napalm use in Vietnam

Was it use in any other war?

Are aliens drafted, and what rewards they receive for serving in the armed forces?

Was your camper searched before or after the action?

FIGURE 19. Handwritten Juror Note

Justice Clarkson Fisher shocked observers of the Camden 28 trial in 1973 with the tremendous latitude he gave the defense to make its case. Jurors took advantage of his allowances to submit handwritten notes with questions, which Fisher read out in the courtroom. Juror Sam Braithwaite, who submitted most of these notes, posed several queries to defendant Terry Buckalew. Image reproduced from Record Group 21: Records of District Courts of the United States U.S. District Court for the District of New Jersey, Camden, criminal case # 602-71, *United States of America v. William A. Anderson et al.*, https://catalog.archives.gov/id/71962676, courtesy of the National Archives and Records Administration, New York City.

A Prosecution Disarmed by Loving Kindness 153

and try cases as a professional lawyer—was nervous. After confiding her unease, she emphasized how vehemently she and her cohorts wanted to make a human connection with the jury. She would have preferred, she humbly explained, that these critical lines of communication could have opened "in our living room or yours, if you would have us; but since we have to do that through the confines of this courtroom, then I would ask that you bear with us and understand that we are trying very hard."[22] Ridolfi closed her remarks by inviting the jurors to pose questions throughout the trial as a means of demonstrating their right to a true understanding of the case. One juror, Sam Braithwaite, ultimately asked more than eighty questions.[23]

Father Doyle spoke the longest in an opening statement that would be celebrated for decades to come. He asked, with the permission of the judge, "to present a motion to a higher court than this one . . . and make a request that a blessing of truth and a spirit of truth would come upon the deliberations of this room in the months or the weeks ahead, with the hope that the judge and the jury, the prosecutors and the defendants, the counsel and the clerks might somehow be better because we met in this time and place." He begged everyone's patience and compassion, "without which I think that the pursuit of truth is not fruitful and could even be useless." He asked the jury to consider the question, "Who went too far?" Did the raiders push beyond the point of reason in breaking the law, or did the government do so by escalating and continuing the war for twelve years? Did the government go too far by assisting with the break-in?

Doyle declared that in order to explain the "present conscience" motivating him, he would trace the historical and Judeo-Christian ideas that formed the movement's "attitude towards life" and "non-violence." Doyle then referenced parts of the Bible, including stories about Jesus, who "pushed non-violence to its ultimate aim and ultimate end when he was killed to save those who killed him." In drawing jurors' attention to their own homes, as pieces of real estate they had labored to secure and protect, he said the defense aimed to help them understand "what bombs do to real estate and to flesh and to people." These activists would show that the United States had violated the law and brought the nation into a "war without honor."[24]

Doyle ended his statement by announcing that the defense would bring "Camden into this courtroom as the first piece of evidence" because there was a "connection between this city and the continuing war that has been waged. . . . Should a place as troubled as Camden," he continued, "exist in a nation as rich as the U.S.?" Rather than fight the war, Americans should be working on the conditions in "cities like this one, where their efforts could be made to rebuild it and save it." Moreover, understanding this relationship between Camden and the Vietnam War would help them understand "the complexity of this case and the conscience of the people involved."[25]

Defendant Michael Giocondo also spoke at length about Camden in his opening statements. Giocondo was one of the local residents who first planned the federal building raid. He was a close friend of Michael Doyle and, until the arrest, a friend of Bob Hardy as well. Born in Syracuse, New York, and trained as a journalist, Giocondo became fluent in Spanish after joining the Franciscan order as a brother and serving on a mission in Costa Rica. But Giocondo soon transferred to Camden as he was convinced there was meaningful work for him to do there, especially in the Latino and Black communities. By the time of the raid, he had dropped out of the Franciscan order but had continued his efforts in Camden by establishing the El Centro community center.[26]

Giocondo used his opening statement to discuss what he discovered from that project, including the problems of finding housing in a deteriorating city where "blocks had been destroyed for planned urban renewal or industrial development" that never came to fruition. He talked about his collaborations with Camden's BPUM, which in 1968 demonstrated against the lack of affordable housing by camping out at city hall, sleeping in chairs and on the floor of the lobby, and then moving outside to block the intersection of Broadway and Market Street. The riot of 1971 that coincided with the draft board raid resulted, he declared, from the same lack of organization and leadership. After demonstrating for a number of years by signing petitions, writing letters, and marching on Washington, Giocondo explained that his frustration with the neverending war had intensified. He came to believe that he and his fellow activists must assume "greater risks," and must do so in the spirit of "love and integrity."[27]

In these early days of the trial, no one knew how the judge would react to such arguments of conscience. The jury would decide the verdict, but Judge Clarkson Fisher ruled on what evidence could be advanced, who could appear, and what statements could stand.

Clarkson Fisher continued to astonish everyone by allowing the defendants almost everything. Fifty-two years old, the judge was a New Jersey native who had joined the federal judiciary in 1970. Since he lived near Trenton, where he typically presided, Fisher faced a long commute down Interstate 295 to the trial in Camden. He mostly stayed in a hotel, where he "lived on hotel food, drank hotel whiskey, and went home late Friday afternoons," according to one of his clerks.[28]

A devout Catholic, Fisher had attended parochial schools in the shore community of Long Branch and served in the Signal Corps during World War II before attending Notre Dame to earn BA and JD degrees.[29] The assignment of Fisher to the trial made the defense team nervous because he was a Republican and had been appointed by President Nixon. Though Fisher and the defendants had the church in common, he could have been among the legions of American Catholics who disapproved of the draft raids. He was also known to favor authority figures in his decisions, which resulted in mostly positive rulings for government and law enforcement officials.[30] At the same time, he had no tolerance for overzealous lawyers. Even assistant U.S. attorneys occasionally faced the mist of Fisher's "Bullshit Spray," an aerosol can labeled in bold print that sat on his desk. Fisher especially liked to keep it handy for settlement negotiations in chambers.[31]

As the trial proceeded, it became clear that the prosecution would execute an uncomplicated strategy that relied on the strength of its overwhelming evidence of the crime. The FBI had given the government's attorneys an open-and-shut case by extensively documenting the months-long investigation and early morning arrest. As defendant Joan Reilly recalled, they had "all the evidence they could possibly need." Their case was "complete."[32] With photographs of the break-in, reports from informant Bob Hardy, recorded conversations from wire taps, and tapes of the walkie-talkie communications during the crime, the charges simply could not be denied. The 28 had been caught red-handed—case closed.

Complicating this strategy, though, was the overreach of the FBI agents, who made sure to catch the raiders at the scene of the crime and accumulate a mountain of evidence to implicate anyone involved. Star witness Robert Hardy thus became the most problematic factor in the trial for prosecutors. He helped the defense demonstrate that the FBI contributed money, tools, and other resources to make the raid happen. The Camden 28 would never have gone through with the action on that morning in August, they argued, without the sustained assistance of the FBI through its informant, Hardy. The bureau, in other words, had financed and assisted in the crime itself.

The defense conceded early on that the case of the Camden 28 did not fit the case law definition of "entrapment," which could not apply if the defendants were "predisposed" to commit the crime. The 28 remained unapologetic about their predisposition throughout the trial—they meant to break the law and did so proudly.

Defense attorneys Stolar, Broege, and Kairys had to navigate the contorted history of prior cases to make this argument against the government. The young team of lawyers came to know each other through the

156 CHAPTER SEVEN

civil rights networks that had animated their legal work since law school. All were members of the National Lawyers Guild, an alternative bar association that was created in 1937 when the American Bar Association refused admission to Black lawyers. Subdued over the 1940s and 1950s by communist-baiting critics during the Red Scare, the organization surged back to life in the civil rights era. The three idealistic lawyers had been electrified by the movements for justice in the 1960s, and they gave enthusiastically of their time.[33]

Most of the government's witnesses were FBI agents, but first came Catherine Furlong, executive secretary of the local Selective Service Office. The fifty-six-year-old mother of three boys who supervised the draft boards for Camden County testified to the damage done in Room 508 of the federal building. The raiders destroyed safes, filing cabinets, binders, seven hundred draft files, and statistical reports amounting to a loss of $13,500 ($91,619 in 2023).[34] The raid delayed the operations of the draft board for about a year as the binders detailing the classifications had to be completely reconstructed. Furlong stated that the actual induction process had never stopped because the raiders destroyed the "wrong files," having shredded the lower-priority 1-As rather than the "acceptables" who were deemed ready to serve.[35]

The testimony of Catherine Furlong lasted the entire morning because, in addition to the attorneys, several of the defendants questioned her. This process of taking turns to cross-examine became the pattern for the next couple of weeks as a parade of FBI agents took the stand. John Barry was winding down the direct examination of Furlong when he asked about the pre-action reconnaissance visits by some of the defendants in preparation for the raid.

JOHN BARRY: Directing your attention to August 18th, 1971, did there come a time when three young girls [entered] into Room 508?

CATHERINE FURLONG: Yes.

ANNE DUNHAM: I object, your Honor. Three women, please. We are not girls.

Dunham's response launched a tense exchange among the women. Furlong responded that Cookie Ridolfi, Anne Dunham, and Rosemary Reilly had entered the draft board and misidentified themselves as representatives of the Friends Peace Center in Philadelphia who wanted to do research in the files on conscientious objectors (COs).[36]

In response, Dunham, Reilly, and Ridolfi then became the first defendants to cross-examine Furlong after the attorneys took their turn. Dunham prefaced her questions to Furlong by explaining that none of this interrogation was meant to "attack" her. She did not want the Furlong to think she meant anything personal by the questions that followed. "You said in your testimony," noted Dunham, "that the function of the draft board is to serve the public. Did you feel that sending young men to kill and be killed in Vietnam is also in a way a function of that Selective Service?" U.S. attorney Barry immediately barked an objection, which was sustained. Since the jury had just viewed several photographs of the mess and damage wrought by the action, Dunham also asked if Furlong knew the extent of property damage in Vietnam by men she drafted.[37] Furlong, of course, did not. When Cookie Ridolfi took over the cross-examination, she pushed this point further, quoting Furlong's earlier testimony about the "total wreck" that she found in the office after the raid.

COOKIE RIDOLFI: Do you think that the forty thousand Americans who returned home in caskets might be described as total wrecks?

CATHERINE FURLONG: Yes.

After some failed objections by John Barry, Ridolfi continued to push the matter, asking if Furlong knew what "carpet bombing does," and what "napalm bombing does to human flesh." Furlong actually conceded the point, responding that she was "alarmed" by the havoc wrought in her office by the defendants, but even "more alarmed" by the destruction in Vietnam.[38]

The next week featured hours of testimony from FBI agents who participated in the surveillance and arrest of the defendants. It was a systematic, if painstaking, process by which the prosecution guided agents through the voluminous evidence that they had gathered over the course of many weeks. Special agent Mason Smith of the Philadelphia field office, who led the investigation, had been in the bureau for twenty-one years. Smith appeared for three days on the witness stand. He described the process by which his team collected video footage of the defendants who were casing the federal building in the weeks leading up to the action. He explained how he hid in the federal building office during the months of July and August, using state-of-the-art video equipment to record the surveillance activity of the raiders.

Barry also questioned Smith about the hours of walkie-talkie communications between the defendants, which the FBI had recorded. The courtroom heard bits and pieces of these conversations, in which the raiders addressed each other in code names to report their whereabouts and observations.

Frank Pommersheim, going by the name "Filmore," was heard addressing Paul Couming, whom he called "Little Man." Couming updated

Pommersheim on the progress being made in the draft board raid, "My feeling is that, ah, game room number one should be secured before proceeding to game room number two. [pause] Over." In the minutes before the FBI descended on the draft board for the arrest, the defendants sounded upbeat about what they believed to be the conclusion of a successful raid. "Little Man to all units," said Couming as he watched his friends finish the work of shredding and bagging documents. "I want you all to know," he jokes, "that no matter what happens, my mother is still Irish." He instructs Joan Reilly, who identified herself as "Portico," to "give everybody around you a kiss for me" from her position across the street. After Couming reported that the raiding team would leave the scene within twenty minutes, he declared with alarm that he saw an FBI agent, whom he mistook for a guard, "There's a guard! There's a guard coming!"[39] When the tape ended, the judge called for a break and released the jury for the day.

The pro se defense proved particularly effective in the cross-examination of FBI agents because it afforded the advantage of repetition. Even though no agents ever admitted on the stand to drawing a weapon, several of the defendants raised questions about this disputed aspect of the arrests. The weapons had frightened and angered the nonviolent activists, who took turns recalling their distinct memories of looking down the barrel of a gun. Robert Williamson drilled special agent Robert Waller on this point.

WILLIAMSON: If I said there was a gun pointed at me, would I be mistaken?

(The prosecution objected, but Judge Fisher allowed the question.)

WALLER: There was no gun pointed at you, sir. There were no guns used in this whatsoever.

Williamson pressed for several minutes, however, asking Waller to clarify. Was he sure there were no guns, or that he did not *see* the guns, or that he did not remember? Neither Waller nor any of the other agents ever conceded, insisting that all side arms remained holstered the entire night, but Williamson and the other defendants sounded just as certain.

WILLIAMSON: Do you think that if someone ever pointed a gun at you that you would remember it pretty clearly?

WALLER: I am sure I would, sir.

Many Americans would have applauded agents for using weapons to stop a burglary and subdue criminals. The problem came down to the credibility of the federal officers as weighed against that of the defendants. Who was lying on the stand? The word of professional lawmen would typically have had more authority than that of criminal defendants, but trust in the government had reached an all-time low.[40]

Cookie Ridolfi asked the final questions for the defense in a long cross-examination on Friday March 30 that probed the role of the informant, Bob Hardy, in the crime. With the assistance of attorney Marty Stolar, she placed two stacks of paper before the jury, one representing the contributions to the crime by the defendants and the other, a higher stack, representing the contributions to the crime by the FBI. When she finished with her questions, she invited the jury to view the piles of evidence themselves and come to their own conclusion.[41] By the time court adjourned that day, the prosecution had rested its case.

CHAPTER EIGHT

No Guilt, No Apologies

Now it was the defendants' turn. The Camden 28 adopted a two-pronged strategy that made no attempt to demonstrate their innocence. While attacking the war, they also sought to show how the government had engineered their arrest on August 22, 1971. The activists on trial pushed for jury nullification to deliver a full acquittal. As John Grady told them in his opening, "you can actually take into account your own feelings, your own consciences . . . you have the power to ignore the law, to nullify it."[1] Aiming for nullification was bold and risky, but it was consistent with the strategy of recent movement trials. Only two states, Maryland and Indiana, granted jurors the right to know that power.[2] And federal law certainly did not.

In the 1960s, Leftists revived jury nullification as a popular defense strategy. This tool countered government escalation of its campaigns to arrest and jail demonstrators for acts of civil disobedience that, in many instances, involved intentional lawbreaking. The witness stand thus became a popular stage for broadcasting political messages—where defendants spoke directly to a captive audience of judge, jury, and courtroom staff as well as reporters and spectators. This "audience" was often quite large because the defendants in these trials, including Angela Davis, had achieved the status of political celebrities even before they had been charged.

The work of the Camden 28 Defense Committee became important, not only before the trial, but also during the proceedings. The CDC helped maintain larger numbers of Camden 28 supporters in the gallery, which contributed to the pressure for nullification. Daily attendance was one responsibility of a defense committee member.[3] The committee made a point of creating an affirming courtroom atmosphere for their "brothers" and "sisters" by filling the space with friendly faces that included family and fellow activists. Priests and nuns were strongly represented in the Camden courtroom, as well as parents with children. Restless kids took advantage of the breaks to play in the judge's chair or walk on the jury rail like a tightrope. Babies sucked on their bottles or crawled under the benches.[4]

A full schedule of evening and weekend events during the months of the trial also boosted the morale of the Camden 28 and their supporters. Comedian George Carlin came to raise money for the defendants in the midst of the trial, squeezing in an appearance for fellow war protesters into his busy touring schedule. Famous for social critiques as searing as they were hilarious, Carlin performed at Cherry Hill Auditorium on March 29, 1973, just as the prosecution was resting its case. The hurried planning and late notice gave the Camden 28 Defense Committee little time to broadcast the event. The CDC nevertheless sold the five-dollar tickets at area bookstores, including Nook of Knowledge in the Cherry Hill Mall.[5] Carlin stayed at the nearby home of activist Bill Stearn and, after a moving introduction by the folk-rock artist Kenny Rankin, gave a rousing two-hour concert to the Camden 28 supporters.[6]

The night after the Carlin performance, supporters could attend another fundraiser at Rutgers University, where the CDC hosted a benefit rock concert. A crowd of mostly twenty-somethings donated $1.75 at the door of the student center to hear local talent, including groups called We the People and High Treason. Defendant John Swinglish made an appearance to share reports of the trial and pass a hat around for extra funds.[7] Five nights later, Daniel Berrigan gave a talk at Glassboro State College, which drew five hundred people.[8]

The defense committee also collected food donations for the defendants, most of whom were staying at one of four houses in Camden during the trial. CDC volunteer Nora Sutherland collected nonperishable items at different drop-off locations, including the Baptist church she attended in nearby Moorestown, before delivering the goods to the defendant residences. Supporters could also share in meals with the defendants by joining them for dinner in Camden every Wednesday evening.[9]

A student at the University of Pennsylvania, John Khanlian, became interested enough in these activities that he wrote an ethnographic study of the trial for one of his classes. "Anthropology for Teachers" invited its budding secondary-school instructors to venture out into their region as cultural anthropologists. In addition to interviewing members of the defense committee, Khanlian attended many of their events during the trial. He observed that, in addition to their base of support in the youthful radical resistance community, the Camden 28 drew interest from wealthy liberals in the suburbs as well. Khanlian participated in a wine

162   CHAPTER EIGHT

and cheese party "sponsored by a divorcee [*sic*] in Cherry Hill," where
he recognized affluent Moorestown residents he knew from various political activities sponsored by the Quakers.[10]

Jury nullification, which was always part of the defense strategy, also
served a political purpose. It allowed the defendants to argue the moral
implications of their actions directly. Every witness represented an
opportunity to explain why the jury should not convict them for the
crimes they readily admitted to committing. Attorneys, who were more
invested in securing an acquittal, could use their time before the jury
to keep their clients out of prison. The Camden 28 defendants, on the
other hand, appealed directly to the jury's sense of right and wrong.
They asked to be judged and sentenced based, not on the laws they violated, but on the principles that had inspired them to commit crimes
they did not deny. Juries could thus use their power to "nullify" bad laws
and ruthless government institutions. In so doing, the defense reversed
the very dynamic of the prosecution by putting the government on trial.
As Bob Williamson noted in his own reflections, it was much easier to
mount this more offensive "defense" when you were fully prepared to
go to jail.[11]

The first of more than thirty defense witnesses appeared on Tuesday
April 3. Father Michael Doyle took the stand for a direct examination
by his friend, fellow priest Ned Murphy. Doyle spoke for four days. The
gifted storyteller related events of his rural childhood, growing up on a
small farm that taught him the value of life, its holiness, and its beauty.
Though his family was financially poor, he recalled an upbringing rich
with love and without hunger. His father was a hardworking farmer who
plowed his fields in a suit jacket, which Doyle described as a marker of
his dignity. As proud and reverential as he was about this youth close
to the earth, the parish priest spoke bluntly about the unjust history of
colonial oppression that disrupted economic relationships in Ireland.
From the early Viking and Norman invasions to the eighteenth- and
nineteenth-century penal laws, which suppressed Catholic Gaelic culture to the benefit of Protestantism, he gave a detailed history of Angli-
can overlords in Ireland. Doyle felt deeply connected to wars against
imperialism because of this history.[12]

After describing the early twentieth-century Easter Uprising, which
ultimately liberated Ireland from Great Britain, Doyle compared the
brutal execution of Irish leaders to the bloodbath in Vietnam. Doyle
also read a poem, "The Fool," by Pádraic Pearse, one of the dissident
Irish patriots he admired. In "The Fool," Pearse recognized that many
observers judged him and his activist cohorts as buffoons on a hare-

No Guilt, No Apologies 163

brained quest. Its irony invokes Don Quixote, the fictional Spanish hero who adopts the fantasy that he is a gallant knight on a chivalric mission. Unlike author Miguel Cervantes, who never revealed back in 1612 whether he meant to portray his protagonist as stupid or wise, Pearse was clear that his "fools" are recklessly brave souls, figures who are "pitied" by critics for clinging to their dreams. Doyle quoted Pearse's denouncement of haughty lawyers, who "have sat in council, the men with the keen, long faces." The so-called foolish were thus the wisest, giving their all "lest ye lose what is more than all."[13]

Doyle also gave some insight into why so many priests and sisters felt compelled to raid draft boards. He admitted that celibacy came with obligations as well as opportunities. He could live the risky life of a "fool" because he had no wife or children to support. As a pastor in Camden, he had witnessed a very different kind of poverty than the scarcity of his rural childhood. The struggling city felt to him raw, bereft, and hollowed out by racism. The Selective Service System exploited these problems through the processes of draft slavery.[14]

Doyle illustrated Camden's hard times with a graphic slide show. Prosecutor John Barry strongly objected to this presentation, but Fisher allowed it. With more than seventy slides, Doyle juxtaposed photographs of Camden and Vietnam, underscoring the profound ruin linking these two distant places. The screen flashed images of burned-out, boarded-up houses captured by Doyle's camera in his own community, and the smoky rubble of Vietnamese villages documented by war photographers. Camden was, in Doyle's words, "a casualty of the war."[15]

In its cross-examination of Doyle, the prosecution deployed the strategy it would use to attack all the defendants who took the stand in the remaining days—rebut, rebut, rebut. Barry and his team poked holes in defense statements about the what, the where, and the when of testimony to undermine credibility and cast doubt on the sincerity of good intentions. It was an uphill battle that grew steeper for the prosecution as the trial progressed and the defendants gradually humanized themselves to the jury. How does a lawyer dress down witnesses who are so invested in hiding nothing and revealing, in Doyle's words, the "truth" of themselves? At one point, the prosecutor asked Doyle if it was his prerogative to pick and choose which laws he would follow or disobey. The priest responded, "No." He said that laws should only be broken if they forced people to take lives, to "use the instruments of war."[16]

Robert Hardy, the most anticipated witness, took the stand on Tuesday, April 10. He faced questions for three days. None of his testimony surprised the court, since its most relevant parts had appeared in the affidavit and media reports weeks before the trial even started. What

164 CHAPTER EIGHT

mattered now was how Hardy's story could affect the jury. All the parties—the defense, the prosecution, and the judge—knew that his words could do the heavy lifting in proving that the government's intervention was instrumental in executing the crime. Attorney David Kairys conducted the direct examination, guiding the witness step-by-step through his involvement in the action. Hardy explained how he became aware of the raid preparations, how he approached the FBI, how the FBI established his role as informant, and how he ultimately fulfilled that role. This final aspect, how he carried out the duties of informant, stood out as the most damaging part of his testimony. Hardy parsed the multiple ways he had actually prompted and assisted with the raid at the FBI's behest.

Using money given to him by FBI agents, Bob Hardy bought the activists tools and groceries. He also trained them. As an ex-Marine and contractor, he knew how to eyeball room measurements and scale ladders quickly. Hardy stated repeatedly and in no uncertain terms that through him, the FBI became a critical participant in the crime itself. Technically, Hardy's testimony did not substantiate a bona fide "entrapment" defense as dictated by judicial precedent since it could not disprove the defendants' earlier intent to commit the crime. The witness did, however, help the defense by detailing the heavy-handed tactics of J. Edgar Hoover's FBI. Agents paid him "approximately twenty-five hundred dollars," according to Hardy ($16,966.10 in 2023).[17]

The Catholic convert said he had accepted the money and informed on his friends not only because he opposed the crime, but because he wanted it stopped before the activists perpetrated a felony. The FBI had promised him that the raiders would be apprehended before the break-in and "would be given. . . . suspended sentences . . . [and] that if they were in jail it would only be for a couple of hours." One agent, according to Hardy, said that the people "involved in this plan, to do something here at the draft board, were not really criminals . . . they were just misguided." Bob and his wife, Peg, were both "reassured that our friends would not receive any jail time for my involvement in this thing."[18]

John Barry sought to discredit Bob Hardy's testimony in the hours of cross-examination over April 11 and 12. Starting with questions about the affidavit, Barry tried to portray Hardy's narrative as confusing and error ridden. He asked about misstatements in the affidavit (which Hardy corrected in later months), calling attention to a date wrong here and a name wrong there. Barry then turned to the issue of how much the action preparations relied on assistance from the FBI.[19] The prosecutor walked Hardy through the various automobiles belonging to the defendants, not the FBI, as well as the living quarters, recording devices, binoculars,

No Guilt, No Apologies 165

and other equipment purchased with their own funds. He then asked about the expertise of different participants, the "old actors" who brought their collective experiences to the action in Camden. The prosecutor used his time with Hardy to undercut the argument for government entrapment. In his questioning he enumerated the different tasks that did not require the witness's instruction or help. "You didn't assist them up the ladder, did you? . . . Did you teach them to rip up files? . . . Did you teach them to wear gloves?" No FBI support needed, implied John Barry.[20]

On Thursday April 12, the court called Bob Hardy back to the stand, even though Barry had finished cross-examining the informant. Hardy answered questions that Sam Braithwaite, juror #10, had brought to the judge. "Were you ever threatened by the FBI in this case?" asked Fisher on behalf of Braithwaite. Hardy responded "no" at the time. Later, after the trial, he told other people that this was, in fact, a lie and that one agent had actually warned him he might get hit by a truck someday.[21]

On April 24, Joan Reilly took the stand and answered questions from her sister, Rosemary. The jury became acquainted with the sisters' different personalities. Ro Ro was a radical risk-taker who had fallen away from the church. She was one of the eight defendants who performed the break-in and theft of the federal building. Joan was devout and sensitive. She did much of the prep work for the movement, such as casing the building and preparing meals. Joan was also worried about her parents, who suffered as they watched their daughters drop out of school and go to jail. The FBI, in fact, had tried to separate Joan from the rest of the group by letting her leave jail shortly after the arrest so she could be with her parents on Long Island. Federal prosecutors had also offered a deal: Joan Reilly's testimony against the 28 in exchange for her freedom. Joan's concern for her parents compelled her to consider it, but after much prayer she decided to reject the offer and stand trial with everyone else.[22]

Joan used her time on the stand to explain this choice. As their parents watched from the gallery, Rosemary walked her sister through the life events that led to the Camden raid. Joan explained how she and her siblings had grown up "in a very Christian tradition" that involved numerous community projects in addition to parochial schools and weekly Mass. "I had a lot of opportunity to become familiar with the New Testament. . . . I saw in Christ a man whose very interest [was] in serving other people, who chose to give and work among the poor and the oppressed, whose message was one of love. . . . And he was also aware of the sacredness of human life."[23] She talked about hearing Daniel Berrigan give a sermon on peace that moved her deeply when she was at Marymount.[24]

Rosemary then invited Joan to read from that sermon. John Barry objected on the grounds of its inadmissible hearsay status, but Judge Fisher once again astonished observers by allowing the untraditional testimony. Fisher even acknowledged that he was out of bounds. "I am going to allow it," he declared, "even though technically I'm probably wrong, ladies and gentlemen, because it has something to do with this young lady's life during that period."[25] Berrigan's sermon addressed the severe costs of waging peace, noting how hard it had become for societies to disrupt the stability of their everyday lives for the purposes of stopping wars. "We want peace with half a heart and half a life and half a will," she read, though the making of war was "at least as disruptive, at least as liable to bring disgrace and prison and death in its wake."[26] After another fruitless objection from the prosecutor, Joan showed photographs of the My Lai massacre from *Life* magazine, recalling to the jury how they shook her—pictures of dead bodies in piles and in ditches, dead children, and thatched roofs on fire. [27]

The second phase of the defense introduced a series of character witnesses. These academics, poets, clinicians, clergy, representatives of the U.S. military, and family members testified to the "present conscience" that motivated the defendants to commit their crime. Parents of the defendants delivered some of the most moving testimony. Others spoke of the historical, psychological, and moral conditions behind the lawbreaking. At one point, Judge Fisher declared that he was tired of hearing about Watergate, that the presidential scandal had nothing to do with the trial.[28] But nonetheless, he let this defense strategy continue with almost no interference, even when the defendants and their counsel seemed to take advantage of the latitude. Fisher's clerk later recalled one moment when the defense "really frosted him." The judge "got up and stormed off the bench," he remembers, "without even excusing the jury." He "fumed" to the clerks in his chambers, promising that he was "going to give those bastards a fair trial whether they deserved it or not."[29]

That outburst stood out among other moments in chambers that helped law clerk Charles Clancy III understand why his boss gave the Camden 28 so much leeway. Fisher was concerned that any obstruction would jeopardize the ruling, since most of the high-profile movement trials of the 1960s were eventually overturned. Clancy remembers Fisher instructing him that "nobody ever got reversed for letting something in" and that "patience is the most important quality for a judge."[30]

Fisher knew well the cautionary experience of the Chicago Seven trial, in which a federal judge lost control of his courtroom by trying too hard to exercise rigid oversight. Activists who led demonstrations at the 1968 Democratic National Convention faced charges of conspiracy to incite a riot. Defendants Rennie Davis, David Dellinger, John Froines, Tom Hayden, Abbie Hoffman, Jerry Rubin and Lee Weiner were some of the most famous leaders of the New Left when they appeared in court that September 1968. Justice Julius Hoffman took the opposite approach of Clarkson Fisher by repeatedly silencing the radicals and cutting off their attorney. Prosecutors severed an eighth defendant, Bobby Seale, after the trial's most horrific moment—when Hoffman ordered the Black Panther gagged and bound to stop him from interrupting. Seale was chained to a chair and muzzled with a piece of cloth. Hoffman ultimately sentenced the activists, including Seale, to lengthy prison stays for contempt of court after the jury acquitted them all on conspiracy. However, an appeals court subsequently overruled Hoffman's sentences. Clarkson Fisher did not want a media circus and made it clear, according to lawyer David Kairys, that he did not want confrontations with defendants.[31] The Camden 28 judge "felt it wiser," according to Clancy, "to let it all in and be patient than to enforce traditional conventions" because "if there is anything a judge likes less than trying a tough case, it's trying it again."[32]

The Camden 28 trial was thus quite different from that of the Chicago Seven. Over the course of three months, the relationship between the judge and the defendants warmed. Bob Williamson remembers that he had little respect for the judge at first, but then saw that Fisher "got to where he liked us." To demonstrate his own good faith effort to keep the trial respectful in contrast to the media circus that devoured the Chicago Seven proceedings, Williamson quietly maintained a hunger strike throughout those many days. Bob lost twenty pounds, but no one called attention to his fast because no one knew about it. Wearing dashiki robes that hid his changing body, Williamson made a point to only tell the judge what he was up to. Clearly this was no publicity stunt; he simply wanted Fisher to witness his commitment. He lived on soup, juice, and water. "Whenever he [Fisher] would see me," remembers Williamson, "he would ask me how I was doing. And I could tell he was concerned for me."[33]

This new phase of the defense started with La Ann Tu, a representative from the American Friends Service Committee. Tu was working for the National Action/Research on the Military-Industrial Complex (NARMIC), a project studying the impact of war and militarism on the American people. Tu was a native of Thailand who lived in the United States as a permanent resident. She spoke about the "pacification" program, whereby the military sought to control people in Vietnam by moving them out of their villages into camps or cities. By 1973, ten thousand South Vietnamese, more than half the population, had been forced out of their homes and turned into refugees. This program aimed

168 CHAPTER EIGHT

to counter the influence of Ho's Viet Cong, which successfully converted and recruited adherents in mostly rural hamlets.[34] As political scientist Samuel P. Huntington wrote in a 1988 article about the problem in *Foreign Affairs*, "The most dramatic and far-reaching impact of the war in South Viet Nam has been the tremendous shift in population from the countryside to cities." He described the impact as "heart-rending," especially for the people trapped in "horrendous" conditions in the refugee camps.[35] The removals caused vast swaths of the countryside to become depopulated. Tu said that because the United States has failed at winning "hearts and minds," it had to "physically" control them in this manner.[36]

She also spoke at length about the Phoenix program, launched by the Central Intelligence Agency in 1967, which targeted suspected communist operatives in villages for assassination.[37] The prosecutor objected strenuously to Tu's appearance, arguing that her testimony was not "relevant." Its links to the defendants' motivations were "tenuous," he asserted. Rosemary Reilly, who was questioning Tu, objected to the objection. "I think that your definition of relevance has to do with your case solely, not ours." Fisher gently corrected Reilly, since it was Barry's right to object, but he ultimately ruled that the direct examination could move forward as evidence to the defendants' motivation.[38]

After lunch break one day, Terry Buckalew questioned a Vietnam veteran by the name of Robert Neil Steck who was pursuing his PhD in philosophy at Yale.[39] Steck had served with an aircraft unit that patrolled the Cambodian border. He described watching gunners spray rounds of fire on Vietnamese villages from a helicopter and seeing a fellow soldier shoot a man who appeared completely unarmed, probably a civilian. Steck described the "double standard" that governed combat in the Indochina war. This "gook rule" deemed the lives of Vietnamese people to be less valuable than the lives of Americans.[40]

The first of three priests to speak as expert witnesses was Father Joe Daoust. Daoust was the St. Joseph's University instructor who had served as the spokesperson for the defendants when they awaited arraignment after their arrest. As a Jesuit, Daoust also knew three of the other defendants—Edward McGowan, Ned Murphy, and Peter Fordi— all of whom had studied with him at the Woodstock Seminary. Bob Williamson, Daoust's former student, started the direct examination by asking the witness to explain the inner-city project he started in 1969. This educational endeavor had proved transformative for Williamson, ultimately leading him into the antiwar movement. Daoust described a social ethics class that offered summer credit to students who lived in a shared apartment and provided community services to people

No Guilt, No Apologies

in the neighborhood of North Philadelphia. He described Williamson's position at the Open House community center, where he became a rent escrow agent, which put him into acrimonious relationships between tenants and landlords. In this role, Williamson collected rents and held them until the building's owners performed required maintenance, such as fixing leaking pipes and replacing caving roofs.[41]

Daoust said that this experience shaped Williamson's motivations to join the Catholic Resistance because he learned what "the cities of America were up against" as well as "the frustrations of not being able to change them." The students in Bob's commune were forced to share the worries and fears of North Philadelphia residents. That summer they faced the same intense gang wars and drug trafficking in nearby abandoned buildings. Evenings brought the group together into conversations with Daoust about the unemployment, poverty, and inadequate housing, talks that took "deep philosophical turns."[42] The professor remembered that this experience seemed to move Williamson in particular. "He wasn't just talking about ideas"; he seemed to be feeling their impact at a deeper level. Since much of this discussion sprung from questions about how such struggles could happen in a nation with so much wealth, the class often turned its attention to the U.S. defense budget and the Vietnam War. "You can . . . have a society that defends Asia, that prepares for all possible wars and any possible future, and the result is going to be that resources are simply not available to handle problems like a roof over your head."[43] Williamson engaged in what Daoust described as "band-aid work," treating the impact of these problems on a case-by-case basis, while pondering the larger structural forces that caused them. Daoust remembered that the relationship between urban poverty and Vietnam had really "sunk in" for Bob after he joined fellow students at the massive "moratorium to end the war" demonstration that brought a half-million people to the capital in 1969.[44]

Daoust and the other priests who took the stand addressed the moral and spiritual underpinnings of the antiwar movement. True, the ex-Catholic Williamson was no longer a believer. He nevertheless urged Daoust to explain to the jury the soul-searching they had done together. Daoust obliged. He recalled their discussions about the traditions of nonconfrontation that had been popularized by Martin Luther King Jr. and Mahatma Gandhi. Like the nonviolent example of Christ, explained Daoust, one could actively deal with crisis not only by refusing to kill, but also by refraining from "psychological violence" meant to destroy opponents. The lessons of the Gospels urged Christians to stay "face to face" with their enemies rather than turning away.[45]

170   CHAPTER EIGHT

Ned Murphy continued with the examination after Williamson's questions, asking Daoust about their common values as Jesuits. Like other priestly orders, the Society of Jesus vowed to serve the people whom they encountered in need, "the people that God gave them to love," in Daoust's words. The society commanded that Jesuits do this by participating directly in these communities—by assuming their struggles. Though not politically aligned in any uniform way, remarked Daoust, priests in his order had a long history of going to jail to change society, a history of "four or five hundred years."[46] He elaborated on the biblical examples of prophets and of Christ's refusal to denounce sinners from mountaintops and assuming, instead, the dangers and burdens of their struggles. Such stories illustrate the Catholic Social Justice principle of accompaniment.

Cookie Ridolfi broke in to ask if this was a responsibility only for priests or for all Christians. Daoust replied, "all people." Paul Couming followed up on these questions by asking if the witness had ever spoken with Bob Williamson about breaking the law. They had spoken often, he replied, since the law is a serious matter in Catholic tradition. "You have to speak for the law. It's a creation of the people." At the same time, "the law is not supreme" because, as a human creation, it can also inflict harm. He paraphrased Thomas Aquinas, who said that the most serious form of violence is done through unjust laws.[47]

The defense treated the jury to further discussions of theology the following day when it called Daniel Berrigan to the stand as an expert witness. Ned Murphy asked the Jesuit to recall their discussions of the Catonsville draft board raid. Berrigan said that these talks centered on "how we could really live the Gospel in such a time and whether it was possible for us to wear the religious garb and to appear before the people in public or in the pulpits or in classrooms unless we were really standing somewhere, unless we were objecting to the murder of children." The raids represented their decision to break the law "non-violently in favor of human life."[48]

Daniel's brother Philip appeared on April 27. Defendant John Swinglish performed the direct examination of the younger Berrigan, guiding his witness through a philosophical and theological explication of Catholic Resistance that was framed around recollections of conversations. The two men had been active in the Catholic Peace Fellowship (CPF), which brought the Vietnam veteran Swinglish into the antiwar movement. Phil Berrigan talked about the numerous ways in which he sought to resist the war by legal means, from civil disobedience to personal discussions with government officials. Troubled by the daily slaughter

No Guilt, No Apologies 171

in Vietnam that was unfolding while they were arguing with legislators, he and three others had executed the first draft board raid in 1967.

Juror Sam Braithwaite asked three questions of Berrigan in a note passed to Judge Fisher. "What position do men of the cloth take on war?" "Why was Dr. Martin Luther King criticized for his stand on the war?" and "Who punishes the leaders when they in turn fail the people?" In answer to the first question, Berrigan noted that the majority of Christian denominations in the United States had condemned the war yet most Catholic clergy either supported it or "have been passive in the face of war." He responded to the second question by identifying the Nuremberg trials for Nazi war crimes as a good model for holding leaders accountable, but he acknowledged that it could not work in United States, where the perpetrators of the war remained in power. Americans had, therefore, to use the court of public opinion and nonviolent resistance to hold them accountable. As for Martin Luther King Jr.'s stance against the war, he explained that others in the civil rights movement had expressed concern that shifting attention to crimes in Vietnam would take the focus off the most important target, racism.[49]

Fisher addressed Berrigan, who still considered himself a priest, as "Father," even though the recent Harrisburg Seven trial had revealed his marriage to Elizabeth McAlister. Within weeks of the Camden verdict, the couple publicly announced their official nuptials, whereupon the church promptly excommunicated them.[50]

The final and most riveting expert to take the stand appeared directly after Philip Berrigan on April 27. Historian Howard Zinn revived the spirits of the defendants after a morning of disappointment. Judge Fisher had ruled in chambers that entrapment could not be used as a defense strategy. He declared that the recent (1962) *Russell v. United States* decision circumscribed the definition of entrapment to exclude cases where intent to commit the crime was established. The defense had already committed many hours of testimony to explain the reason underlying the intent to carry out the break-in. They had made their motivations part of the defense. Though the lawyers had anticipated the possibility of this ruling and had prepared the defendants for it, the ruling nevertheless came as a disappointment.[51]

Fortunately, the day ended with questions posed by Cookie Ridolfi to Zinn. The professor's comments about the war made the impact on the courtroom that the defense team had hoped they would. Zinn's untraditional path into academe worked in his favor with the jury. He only started college after working for several years in a shipyard and serving as a bombardier in World War II. After Zinn received a PhD at Columbia

University in Chinese and East Asian studies, his background as an industrial worker and city employee shaped his teaching style and career as a public intellectual. He took a position as chairman of the history department at Spelman College in Atlanta, Georgia, in 1956. He assumed that position in this historically Black women's college at the height of the civil rights movement where he became deeply involved with civil disobedience while lecturing and writing about the southern freedom struggle. This activism led Zinn into the peace movement. After he was fired from Spelman in 1963 by university officials who feared that he was radicalizing students, Zinn became a professor of political science at Boston University. Picking up his political activism in New England, Zinn came to know many of the defendants through his involvement in the resistance community there, including Paul Couming, Ned Murphy, Barry Musi, and Cookie Ridolfi.[52]

John Barry reiterated the objection he had raised for many defense witnesses, that Zinn could not speak for "what influenced any particular defendant in this case." Ridolfi replied that she was not asking the witness to talk about what influenced her or the other defendants, but to discuss the Pentagon Papers, which did affect their decision to raid. Judge Fisher denied the objection, and Zinn proceeded to talk about motivations, not of the defendants, but of the government's involvement in Indochina.[53]

In the next several minutes, Zinn gave testimony about the history of colonialism in Vietnam, ending with U.S. involvement. These words would be quoted for years to come. After describing the host of lies revealed about U.S. support for the dictator Ngo Dinh Diem, the Gulf of Tonkin incident, and Soviet influence on Ho Chi Minh, Zinn mentioned the earliest interest of the United States in the peninsula, dating back to 1941. The Pentagon Papers contained a memo by secretary of state Cordell Hull about Japanese occupation of Indochina, a possibility that concerned Hull because the region possessed raw materials that the United States needed. "Lots of tin," said Zinn, "lots of rubber, lots of oil."[54] Therefore, when "high officials" gathered in confidential meetings, they discussed the wealth to be harvested. The Pentagon Papers had been enormously influential, argued Zinn, because they revealed how imperial designs, far more than anticommunism or self-determination, shaped U.S. foreign policy in the region.[55]

The final character witnesses to appear were the mothers and fathers of defendants, who testified at the end of April. By calling parents to the stand, the defense further personalized the trial. They were parents, not only of activists, but of men in uniform as well. They all had struggled

No Guilt, No Apologies 173

with the loyalty and concern they felt for their children even as they disapproved of their decisions to break the law. Jurors heard their heartfelt opinions about how this criminal activity troubled them. While they all had expressed either anger or deep discomfort with their children's lawbreaking, they also described how they came to support and feel pride in these actions. These were stories of hard lessons learned from offspring who shocked and challenged their parents. Their testimony resonated with the jurors and courtroom observers, many of whom had found themselves in similar predicaments between loved ones for and against the war.

Tom and Rita Couming testified first. They had three older sons who served in the armed forces. Rita explained that one, Tom, had been stationed in Berlin for the air force but came home for a month's leave to talk Paul out of applying for conscientious objector status. "Instead," she recalled, "Paul reasoned with Tom. He changed his mind about a good many things even though he was serving in the armed forces." According to Rita, Paul had always been "a lovable and loving person." When she learned of his involvement in the draft board actions, she was afraid for him yet could not help "but feel proud."[56] Couming said she blamed her generation for the mess in Vietnam. Her contemporaries were "lax." "We didn't do our duty. We were so complacent and myself included, I am sure, that the war was something way over there. It wasn't affecting me to that degree. It wasn't affecting those around me." She watched Christmases come and go while men in uniform remained in Vietnam. "We were still living our lives pretty well here and we weren't concerned enough. We did nothing." Rita said that she admired the younger generation for acting more like Christians. "They are not concerned with the material things of life that we have fought so hard for and thought were so important. . . . They don't care about themselves." She knew no group of people more "Christ-like" than Paul and his fellow activists.[57] She believed they had to raid the draft boards in order to "wake the rest of us up."[58]

The testimony of Betty Good, mother of raider Bob Good, was wrenching. Her emotional comments moved the entire courtroom—judge included—to tears. In contrast to her son, Betty Good was a conservative Catholic and staunch supporter of the war. Her commitment to victory in Vietnam had been shaped by the participation and ultimate sacrifice of another son, GI Paul Good. The trial profoundly changed her attitude, however. Mrs. Good's transformation happened quickly and dramatically the day before while she listened from the gallery to the testimony of historian Howard Zinn. Zinn's description of U.S. interests in Indochina's "rubber, tin, and oil" shook her. In response, she fled

174   CHAPTER EIGHT

the courtroom sobbing and inconsolable. The reaction made her son nervous, but she asserted that she wanted to testify; and she did so with an unforgettable account of this metamorphosis. [59]

Good started by describing how she learned of her son's death, news that came to her first as a bad feeling. She experienced a deep sensation of sadness that forebode trouble. "I couldn't explain it. I just knew that all of a sudden something was wrong." She was eerily certain that a representative from the army would soon appear at her doorstep with the news. "We have a kind of long driveway. . . . I had a feeling I would see him walking." Her inkling was correct; when an officer came to her door, she said she had been expecting him. The officer responded that she should not get "excited," Paul Good was only missing in action at that point. She remembers replying, "No, he's gone."[60]

That same officer arrived later that week to confirm Paul's death. Good said that until she heard Zinn's testimony, she "tried to hang on to that theory that my boy died for his country." But now she was furious. "I really feel guilty—I feel guilty that we have sat aside and let them take our boys." She agreed with Zinn that those men who were serving in Vietnam had been "kidnapped." "I am ashamed of the day I took my son to that airplane and put him on it." She was still proud of him because it was not his job to know the reasons for the invasion; his job was to serve. "We should have known," and not Paul. It was a crime "to take that lovely boy and to tell him, 'You are fighting for your country.' . . . Can anybody," she asked the courtroom, "stand here and tell me how he was fighting for his country?"[61]

The defense continued to question its witnesses until the middle of May, when the prosecution and the defense gave their summations. Judge Fisher finally gave his instructions to the jury on May 17. Although he did not tell them that they could nullify the verdict, his instructions offered hope to the defendants, who nervously waited to hear about their fate. Fisher said the jurors could acquit if they determined that the government had overreached by using its informant to set up the raid. It had already been determined, weeks before, that the arrests could not be considered "entrapment" because the defendants had admitted that they were predisposed to commit the crime. In this instance, though, the judge told the jurors that they had to decide if the 1971 arrest "reached an intolerable degree of overreaching government participation."[62]

Both the prosecutors and defense lawyers told *New York Times* correspondent Donald Janson, who had been covering the trial, that they had never heard of a judge issuing such instructions. It was shocking. And indeed, to this day, this may be the only federal criminal trial in which a judge ever instructed the jury on a defense of outrageous governmental conduct. Fisher also said that since he had already ruled that the FBI's activities did not constitute entrapment, the predisposition of the defendants "[did] not matter." In other words, the jury only had to concern itself with how the arrests had been made. The actions of the government were all that mattered.[63]

This instruction, however, also meant that Fisher discounted the hours upon hours of testimony regarding the motivations of the draft board raiders as irrelevant. The moral, political, and spiritual elements presented in weeks of opening statements, cross-examination, direct examination, and closing arguments should not, he declared, shape the verdict. But how could they not have an influence? This question worked to the advantage of the defense because testimony presented so forcefully and sincerely could not be ignored.

Left now to confer with each other, the jurors deliberated for several hours before the court sequestered them for the night. This process continued for another three days and included some hiccups. An initial tentative vote among the jurors revealed some divisions. Half wanted to acquit while the other half included some who were undecided, some leaning to a not-guilty verdict, and some open to a not-guilty verdict. Those who favored acquittal argued to the others that the government had overreached. On the second day of deliberations, the jury came back to the courtroom and asked to once again hear the testimony of Robert Hardy as well as special agents Mason Smith and Robert Waller with respect to the night of the arrest. They also wanted further clarification from the judge about the count of conspiracy leveled by the prosecution and the "government activity" argument of the defense.

Before breaking at a 2 p.m. for lunch that second day of deliberations, Fisher read the requested testimony out loud to the jurors from the trial transcripts and then answered their questions to help them better understand the charges. The holdouts on the jury needed to hear this because even though they opposed the burglary, as one revealed later to the *Philadelphia Inquirer*, "The FBI participation changed their minds."[64] They did not approve of the trap set by the government to catch the defendants.

Saturday brought yet another delay when the jury declared that it needed to choose a new foreman. Bartlett Groveline confessed that she was feeling extreme stress from that burden as a member of her family had been pressuring her to decide against the defendants. Since she did not want to be in the position to deliver a verdict, Fisher invited the jury to choose another foreperson either by voting or drawing lots.

The defendants and lawyers felt the weight of the moment and did what they could to honor its importance. With the arguments now finished, it was time to manage the stress of uncertainty. Prosecutor John Barry headed to the closest bar at the Plaza Hotel, where he drank with some of the defendants and their friends. The judge eventually showed up, too. Saturday night brought parties, where defendants and their supporters found comfort in music, socializing, drinking, and recreational drugs. Some decamped for the Jersey shore, about an hour's drive from the courthouse, where they caught the sunrise. As light streamed through the cloudy morning, they erupted in cheers.

Deliberations ended Sunday at noon, followed by a two-hour flurry of communication and preparation to gather everyone into the courtroom. Some raced down the New Jersey Turnpike from New York.[65]

After everyone took their place in the courtroom, the new foreman, Jim Lomax, finally started to read the verdicts: "Not guilty on all counts for all defendants." The response was silence, and then someone gasped. Shortly thereafter, someone else started singing "Amazing Grace" and others joined in until the room filled with song. The joy was ecstatic; cheers, hugs, and tears ensued. Once the jury left the courtroom, John Barry made his way to the defense table for the customary shaking of hands with his adversaries but found himself embracing them instead as he moved from one defendant to the next. He eventually approached freelance journalist Betty Medsger and told her, "It ended the way it should have ended."[66]

Medsger was also one of the few to notice John and Bonnie Raines in the courtroom. These two raiders of the Media FBI office, whom the government never succeeded in identifying as perpetrators, shared in the exaltation. "They were radiant," remembers Medsger, "smiling widely, thrilled, amazed at the verdicts, and shedding a few tears of joy."[67] Juror Sam Braithwaite left a note for the defendants, delivered to them by the court clerk, congratulating them on a job well done.[68]

That Sunday night after the verdict, the defendants celebrated with a victory party at St. George's church in the Lithuanian section of Camden. All of the federal marshals showed up along with many of the jurors.[69]

CHAPTER NINE

Aftermath and Results

When the jury foreman announced the Camden 28 acquittals in 1973, he tipped the defendants over a turning point that would forever structure their lives, marking an axis dividing the "before" and "after" times. Bob Good described the experience as "singular," one that established a transformative "arc" in his life's history that makes it impossible to fathom how the subsequent years could have unfolded without that pivotal moment. He and the other defendants relished that day for decades to come, even as the future provided few opportunities for the Camden 28 to work together again. "I loved being on trial," remembered Father Michael Doyle in 2018. "To be able to cross-examine FBI agents — imagine that! I was a peasant from Ireland doing that, and I loved it."[1] Despite having been disciplined by superiors for his public protests against the Vietnam War, Doyle came out on the other side of the trial invigorated and ready to fight more battles for the disenfranchised people of Camden. He set a standard of pastoral care that earned him the honored title of "monsignor" and celebrity status in the region.

The victory of this verdict did not extend to every aspect of the Catholic Left agenda, though, especially when it came to reforming the church itself. While politicians seeking congressional seats or the White House can no longer seriously entertain military conscription as a policy proposal, the hoped-for reforms of Catholic radicals did not materialize. The nation and the church turned rightward in subsequent years while the military-industrial complex expanded. Hoped-for liberalizations, like opening the ranks of clergy to include women and married priests, never came close to fruition.

The social movements of the 1960s produced changes that church leaders remained ill-equipped to handle, from the proliferation of divorce and birth control to same-sex marriage and stem cell research. The scandal of child sexual abuse by the clergy stands as perhaps the most egregious instance of a church that was inclined to repress and cover up crimes rather than make thorough-going changes to address root causes. The problematic but consensual sexual liaisons of the Catholic Left, including the dalliances of John Peter Grady and Edward McGowan, never rose to the level of abuse, but still harmed people, and especially women, who grew up in a culture in which virginity, innocence, and reserve represented feminine virtues. Not unlike in the 2020s, the church could not reckon with sex outside the boundaries of heteronormative, cisgender marriage.

That same refusal to face the realities of sex and gender allowed abuse to quietly destroy lives within the walls of schools, seminaries, and rectories. The Vatican, in this respect, "danc[ed] on the edge of the volcano" at the second council, observes historian Stephen Schloesser. In its forceful reckoning with totalitarianism, the Holocaust, nuclear weapons, and other nightmares of the previous era, the church failed to recognize that transformations in gender and sexuality were already challenging ecclesiastical and doctrinal structures.[2] Catholic Social Teaching did not promote sexual abuse, but it failed to provide sufficient guidance for how to deal with these changes. As the church reacted by pushing back and attempting to protect its power, many of its Catholic critics disengaged from religious life or left the fold altogether.

The Camden 28 represented the latter category, though not all of them made a hard break from Catholicism. After the posttrial celebrations, they scattered in different directions and mostly lost touch with each other. Their life paths brought them to different places such as New Mexico, California, Minnesota, and South Dakota. With the central objectives of stopping the draft and U.S. hostilities in Vietnam having been achieved, activists had fewer reasons to maintain movement momentum. Most of the Camden 28 established full, rich lives on the right side of the law after the 1973 trial. They did not continue to work with organizations that put them at risk of serving jail time to realize goals.

Many of the defendants reenrolled in school, while others started careers and families. A few chose to continue living alternative lifestyles for a while, but most trod more conventional paths into jobs and parenting. With the exception of Bob Williamson, who went into the world of finance and real estate, and John Swinglish, who became a wedding photographer, the defendants pursued employment in education and service. They made peace with the liberal world order but avoided making a living from government or corporate jobs. They remained attuned to and engaged with the challenges facing American society but mostly worked through organizations that had no relationship to religious institutions. The path from Catholic to secular-oriented politics first embarked on by antiwar activists in the Vietnam era found its completion by the end of the century.

A handful of the Camden 28 stayed in the New York and Philadelphia metro areas, including the Reilly sisters. Joan Reilly married a community activist, and the couple raised four children in the Kensington neighborhood of Philadelphia. She remained a devout Catholic, even though she became frustrated over the years as the church took a harder line against abortion and gave cover to sexual predators in the clergy. Over the next few decades, she became active in the regional nonprofit world, eventually becoming president and chief operating officer of the Mural Arts Project, which earned Philadelphia the nickname, "Mural City." The organization engaged formerly incarcerated people, their families, and their neighborhoods in a project of creative self-expression that, over thirty-five years, has yielded award-winning works of art.[3]

Rosemary Reilly, who was already finished with the church when she became involved in Vietnam resistance, never regained an interest in Catholicism or any other religion in the years that followed. She married one of the Camden 28 lawyers, Carl Brogue, with whom she raised a daughter in New York City. The couple eventually divorced, and Reilly supported herself as a bookkeeper while staying active in political organizing projects.[4]

Most of the defendants from Boston relocated back to their hometown. Barry Musi and Sarah Tosi moved to Dorchester, Massachusetts, where they busied themselves with community activism. Paul Couming also returned to New England, where he worked as a nursing assistant and, after completing his RN degree, developed a career in health care. Lianne Moccia lived and worked in a restaurant collective called Common Stock with a former teacher, the Boston radical Anne Walsh. Moccia and her husband met while both were in the collective. After the restaurant closed, Moccia learned American Sign Language and became an interpreter for people with hearing loss.

Michael Doyle, Ned Murphy, and John Peter Grady stayed active in the world of Catholic activism. Grady moved to upstate New York where he took a job at Ithaca College and turned his attention to the injustices of mass incarceration. He quit drinking and spent his final years in the orbit of his five children, all of whom walked in the footsteps of John and Teresa Grady by devoting their lives to peace and economic justice.[5]

Father Michael Doyle became pastor at Sacred Heart Church in Camden, New Jersey. He traveled back to Ireland for several weeks every summer to visit his family but committed his life to the struggling city, his adopted home. Over the decades, Camden continued its steep decline. Doyle responded by doubling down on the efforts of his urban ministries, eventually starting a housing nonprofit in 1984 called "Heart of Camden" that rehabilitated more than 250 structures in the city to house local people.[6] Though the parish drew white, middle-class, and affluent parishioners from surrounding suburbs, Sacred Heart became an important community institution to city residents. Doyle's prolific writing also contributed to his local celebrity status, including his nickname, the "Poet Priest." For years he sent a mailing list of over five thousand people numerous handwritten letters, many of which were condensed into a documentary film narrated by the Catholic actor and activist Martin Sheen.[7]

Ned Murphy also continued with his life in the priesthood, serving with the Society of Jesus for his remaining days in New York City, where he was born, raised, and educated through his lengthy university and seminary years as a Jesuit. He was jailed another nine times before settling into a life of more lawful witness.[8] Murphy became a counselor to homeless youths in the Times Square area, eventually establishing a residence for this population in the North Bronx.[9] By 1982, that program grew into a Catholic Charities–funded agency providing food, services, and legal representation to struggling people.[10]

Keith Forsyth and Mike Giocondo turned their interest to the cause of labor. While working at an automotive stamping plant in Philadelphia at the time of the trial, Forsyth joined a reform caucus in the United Auto Workers. He then grew more deeply involved with the labor movement over the 1970s and 1980s. Forsyth eventually stopped organizing and enrolled in night school at Drexel University, where in 1989 he completed his degree as an electrical engineer.[11] Though happy to drop out of organizing for many years while raising his children, Forsyth always felt a political itch. "I could never get over what happened at the end of the '70s," he remembered years later. He eventually became interested in the problem of gerrymandering, which led him to a grassroots organization called Fair Districts PA, an offshoot of the League of Women Voters.[12] In his retirement, he became chairman of its state coordinating team. Forsyth and other redistricting reformers were effective in the late 2010s when the Pennsylvania Supreme Court struck down the new Republican map and ordered the legislature to start over and follow the guidelines in the state constitution.[13]

Michael Giocondo, who had already left the Franciscan order by the time of the Camden 28 trial, resumed his earlier career as a journalist but spent the rest of his years documenting the struggles of meatpackers, steelworkers, coal miners, and other working people for the communist

Daily World and *People's World* newspapers. He also covered the election of Chicago's first African American mayor, Harold Washington.[14]

Several defendants went into higher education in various fields. After working as a librarian and legal researcher and earning a BA and MA, Jayma Abdoo became an assistant dean at Columbia University's Barnard College, where she advised students. Anne Dunham also completed BA and MA degrees before working as a librarian in the different communities where she and Frank Pommersheim lived and raised their children. Ex-priest Ed McGowan taught sociology at community colleges and a small Catholic university in New York City before relocating to Ithaca, New York, where he taught and performed the Irish fiddle.[15]

Cookie Ridolfi and Frank Pommersheim built successful careers in law and academe where they helped to pioneer innovative forms of advocacy. Spending two years with the prospect of going to prison had motivated Ridolfi to get serious about her life and a career. "My ass was on the line," she remembers, "I had to face the fact that I was looking at prison. . . . It was just life changing. And then after it was all over, it was like . . . it was so boring to be back to ordinary life."[16] The twenty-four-year-old wrote a letter to Rutgers University explaining that in the past she had tried to change the world as an outlaw, and now she wanted to do it within the parameters of the legal system. Rutgers gave her a full scholarship.[17] After graduation, she became a consultant assisting in jury selection. She also worked at her own private investigative agency, Nancy Drew Associates.

Ridolfi earned her JD from Rutgers in 1982. This ambition caught her by surprise. "When I was growing up," she recalled later, "I didn't even think I would have graduated from high school. . . . Where I came from, people didn't even graduate from high school."[18] In her first job as an attorney, she represented Philadelphia's urban poor as a public defender. Then, in 1990, Ridolfi joined the law faculty at the City University of New York. She built on the jury research she did as a defendant in the Camden 28 trial in her professional work at the National Jury Project, where she led the development of expert testimony in cases of battered women charged with killing abusive partners. She eventually became a professor of law at Santa Clara University in California, where she founded the Northern California Innocence Project.[19] Her scholarly research focused on prosecutorial overreach, wrongful conviction, and clemency (see figure 20).[20]

Frank Pommersheim followed a similar path into law. At the time of the Camden 28 trial, Pommersheim wondered if he was about to lose his newly minted JD. The acquittal set him on a new and unanticipated path. He and wife, Anne Dunham, moved to the Rose Bud Sioux reservation

FIGURE 20. Kathleen Ridolfi Teaching Law at Santa Clara University
Kathleen "Cookie" Ridolfi was one of the eight burglars who broke into the Camden Federal Building to raid the draft board. Despite the lack of ambition that characterized her youth, she used her experience as a defendant to launch a long and successful career as an attorney and law professor. Photo by Jeff Chiu / *San Francisco Chronicle*.

in South Dakota, where Pommersheim took a job teaching at Sinte Gleska College and Dunham, who did not yet have her BA, worked at a mission school. When Pommersheim joined Sinte, it was a junior college with no campus. Instead of meeting in university buildings, the instructors went out to teach the students at community centers or churches. Sometimes classes met in Pommersheim's office, which was located in a condemned building owned by the Bureau of Indian Affairs.[21] This experience transformed Pommersheim, especially when the residents of Rose Bud welcomed this reserved and soft-spoken man and his wife into their community.[22]

Bob Good and Terry Buckalew also went to work at universities. Good completed his BS in civil engineering at the Rochester Institute of Technology. Starting with a student job he took with a professor who operated a biomechanics lab, Good spent the rest of his career there. Buckalew similarly earned his BA while earning his income at a university job. He started taking classes when he was working as a landscaper for the University of Pennsylvania and raised his family on a university property that he cared for as a facilities manager.[23]

Terry Buckalew thinks that the intense life of the movement ulti-

Aftermath and Results   183

mately broke down many of its participants, leading to the divorces, nervous breakdowns, lost jobs, and severed family ties that followed. They were a "cast of characters" who enjoyed themselves, he recalls, adding, "We did some good stuff, but really, it took a human toll."[24] He views the tragic suicide of Anita Ricci in 1986 as one such outcome.[25] Buckalew's suspicions regarding Ricci cannot be confirmed, however, since the details of her life after the trial have proven elusive.

Bob Williamson's feelings about his role in the draft board raids changed over the next several decades. He is proud of his involvement, but he also watched with sorrow as accomplishing his main objective—-U.S. withdrawal from Vietnam—failed to bring an immediate end to the violence in Southeast Asia. He regards the Camden 28 trial as "one of the greatest experiences of [his] life," and he takes pride in having played an active part. In witnessing the continued bloodshed in Vietnam, however, Williamson learned the "law of unintended consequences." He believes he shares responsibility for the negative impact of the sudden U.S. withdrawal, including the suffering of Vietnamese refugees and the murders of over a million Cambodians in state-sponsored genocide, even as he continues to be grateful for the outcome of his trial. Williamson, whose politics skew libertarian now, is the first to tell you that he has changed a lot since the 1960s. He nevertheless retains a "fondness" for Weed-Ex. One of the best memories of his younger self, reflects Williamson, was that he "managed, some of the time at least, not to take himself too seriously."[26]

Robert Hardy veered in a different direction away from the lay activists of the Camden 28. As most of them pursued their social reform objectives through secular institutions, he drew closer to the church. After the trial, he and his wife, Peggy, had more children—there were eight altogether. In March 1987, Peggy and their daughter Cathy survived a brutal car accident that left Peggy paralyzed. Bob cared for her at their farmhouse in Pedricktown, New Jersey, which he converted into a wheelchair-accessible home. She died of cancer eight years later.

Hardy's life grew richer after this tragedy, even as it continued to be difficult. Though four of the Hardy children were grown, Peggy's death left Hardy to be the single parent of three daughters. He married Florence Collins of Delaware and the two settled in Wilmington, Delaware, where they welcomed a growing family of grandchildren and great-grandchildren. They also became indispensable to their local parish. Hardy led men's groups, youth groups and retreats. He also became a prison chaplain. The church ordained him as a deacon, bestowing on him priestly duties like celebrating the sacrament of baptism. The Catholic convert who barely left Camden as a young man managed to visit

184   CHAPTER NINE

Ireland and Israel with his brother Patrick in his later years. He also experienced the sorrow of losing another child, as well as a grandchild.[27] In 2017, Hardy published a spiritual memoir recounting his experiences of grief and how God had led him through the accumulating losses.[28] He died in December 2022, less than forty days after the death of Monsignor Michael Doyle.[29]

The Catholic Left movement lived on after the Camden 28 trial through new efforts with updated goals. Campaigns to support refugees and stop nuclear armament directed spiritual fervor against the American national security state. Over the next fifty years, the word "progressive" came to describe Catholics who embraced the antipoverty, social justice, and peace agenda advanced by the Vietnam generation. The activists who keep their Catholic faith at the forefront of their work adapted the Vietnam-era church rituals and symbols to new targets of opposition.

In 1980, a group of priests, nuns, and Catholic laypeople unlawfully entered General Electric's Space Systems Division in King of Prussia, Pennsylvania, and revived a ritual of the Vietnam-era raids by pounding hammers and squirting blood (their own) on nose cones for nuclear missiles. The Plowshares Eight, as they became known, distributed materials explaining their moral rationale to the plant's security guards as they circulated pamphlets declaring that they chose "to obey God's law of life, rather than a corporate summons to death." They were, it continued, "beating swords into ploughshares to . . . enflesh this biblical call."[30] The statement invoked the Old Testament command to redirect the work of war-making to the task of peace-making issued by the prophet Isaiah: "They shall beat their swords into plowshares, and their spears into pruning hooks. Nation shall not take up sword against nation; neither shall they learn war anymore."[31]

The defilement of the weapons technology reinvigorated the radical witness of Christ's incarnation with corporal and symbolic acts. From the red blood drawn from their own veins to the bodily occupation of the plant, the peaceful face-to-face confrontation with the guards, and the physical hammering of weapon parts, the trespassers carried out spiritual gestures meant to invoke the carnality of Catholic liturgy. The Plowshares Eight aimed to, once again, draw attention to the global threat to human life posed by the U.S. military. In response, a jury sent them to prison. And as with the Catholic Left of the Vietnam era, the arrest, trials, and jail time begot more actions.[32]

Over the next four decades, Plowshares activists trespassed on government property and damaged weapons in more than eighty actions from coast to coast, as well as in Germany, Sweden, Australia, the Netherlands, Great Britain, and the Irish Republic.[33] Some, like the Prince of Peace Plowshares, invoked Christian messianic theology, while others, like Trident Plowshares and Griffiss Plowshares, chose names that referred to the weapon or location of the action.[34] Catholics have played a prominent role in the Plowshares movement, but it attracts Christians from other denominations as well. The octogenarian Sister Megan Rice of the Society of the Holy Child came to embody this persistence when she and fellow activists broke into the Oakridge, Tennessee, Y-12 National Security Complex in 2012. On release from jail, Rice declared that her only regret was not having started these demonstrations seventy years earlier.[35]

As a direct outgrowth of the Vietnam-era Catholic Left, Plowshares became the next logical step for the devout Catholic vanguard of the 1960s. Activists included not only the Berrigan brothers and Elizabeth McAlister, but also Phillip Berrigan and Elizabeth McAlister's children. The family of John Grady participated as well. Operating from the Jonah House community and sanctuary space in Baltimore, activists developed a way to launch actions and help raise each other's families while parents served their time behind bars. Martha Hennessy, the granddaughter of Dorothy Day, along with all five children of John Peter Grady, have carried on a family tradition of doing time for peace.[36]

Other movements brought Catholic theology into new areas of resistance. Many Catholics and fellow Christians joined secular volunteers in nonviolent campaigns against U.S.-supported dictatorships in Latin America. Many embraced the emerging social justice vision called "liberation theology," which ignited spiritual resistance to antidemocratic regimes that protected U.S. economic interests in the region. Strongly influenced by Marxist class critiques, liberation theologians focused on the concerns of oppressed people both by providing services and by creating an awareness of the sins perpetrated by government and socioeconomic elites. First articulated by Catholic scholars, most notably the Peruvian Dominican priest Gustavo Gutierrez, liberation theology ultimately galvanized many different strains of spiritually inspired activism in Latin America and beyond. The Salvadoran Archbishop Oscar Romero drew global attention to the movement by taking on its animating concerns. Until his assassination in 1980, he criticized the torture, economic injustice, and other political crimes of authoritarian regimes, including those supported by the United States. The elevation of Romero to sainthood illustrates a grudging acceptance of liberation theology by the church, though not a willingness to be transformed by it in the ways that activists had hoped.[37]

Organizations like the Quixote Center in Maryland have raised millions of dollars in the United States to develop aid projects in Latin America. Founded in 1976 to advance women's equality in the Catholic Church, the center launched a religious task force in El Salvador four years later. Its medical aid project grew into the Quest for Peace campaign, which raised $27 million for the poor citizens of Nicaragua to counter, dollar for dollar, the U.S. congressional aid package for the contra rebels. Another influential organization called Witness for Peace (WFP) sponsored volunteer trips that placed Americans in villages where they gathered information on community conditions to report on their return home.[38] Founded in 1983, WFP volunteers documented the murders of more than five hundred civilians by the U.S.-supported contras. Within ten years, it had sponsored 253 trips that brought forty-five hundred volunteers to Nicaragua.[39] In the early 1980s, the married Camden 28 defendants Anne Dunham and Frank Pommersheim joined one of these WFP missions, which brought them to the countryside of Nicaragua. While staying with families, they assisted villagers with house repairs and visited rural cooperatives. Afterward, they gave talks in the United States about their experiences and observations.[40]

While the Quixote Center, WFP, and other organizations focused their attention on circumstances on the ground in Central America, the Sanctuary movement emerged to help refugees within the borders of the United States. Modeled after the antebellum Underground Railroad, Sanctuary anointed churches, universities, and even entire states as spaces of protection for fugitives, called "sanctuary jurisdictions."[41] Drawing activists from across denominations, it updated a tradition of asylum dating back to Ancient Greece and early Christianity to protect people fleeing state violence. "The Church viewed itself," notes one scholar, "as having a God-given power to grant sanctuary that superseded state power."[42] When religious leaders in the United States declare "sanctuary," they signal that their holy spaces are performing the work of protection.

Presbyterian minister John Fife launched the Sanctuary movement in Tucson in 1980 when he welcomed a group of Salvadorans who had been abandoned by a smuggler in the desert. Tucson's Southside Presbyterian church held weekly prayer vigils and welcomed a community of refugees, immigrant lawyers, and other advocates to discuss the struggles of migrants and develop solutions. In 1981, Quaker rancher Jim Corbett started a similar project after his friend picked up a Salvadoran man who was then arrested for hitchhiking in their community of Nogales, Arizona. He and other Quakers started hosting refugees in their homes and introducing them at worship services. The church soon declared itself a sanctuary as members expanded efforts to bring undocumented migrants to safety and protect them from deportation by the Immigration and Naturalization Service.[43] Over the course of the next eight years, until a landmark trial severely punished Sanctuary activists, the movement grew into a national interfaith effort, which was particularly strong in Tucson, Los Angeles, and Chicago. By 1983, forty-five houses of worship offered sanctuary and six hundred activist groups supported these efforts.[44]

Sanctuary had the support of the U.S. Catholic Conference (now the United States Conference of Catholic Bishops [USCCB]). The USCCB sternly rebuked federal prosecutors for indicting activists, including one nun, who violated U.S. laws by providing refuge.[45] The conference, which had already urged the government to place a moratorium on deportations back to El Salvador in 1981, denounced the fact that U.S. foreign policy had "creat[ed] conditions which evoke humanitarian and religiously based responses, and entangle people of good faith in criminal prosecutions." Catholic churches, moreover, constituted 78 of the 484 houses of worship that offered sanctuary.[46] As one scholar noted, Sanctuary activists expanded the Catholic Left into a new area of political life by putting social justice principles before the law: "The defining mark of the Catholic Left was just this willingness to dissent or even to break the law in order to protest what they saw as unjustified US militarism, to prompt church and state to live up to their governing principles without feeling that through this dissent they had betrayed either institution."[47]

Another organization of self-consciously progressive Catholics called Call to Action (CTA) focuses mainly on reforming the church itself. Formed in 1976 and based in Chicago, CTA grew out of a bishops' meeting in Detroit where 1,340 delegates from 150 dioceses adopted several controversial resolutions, including support for the ordination of women. The papacy of John Paul II galvanized its members (which were estimated to number 250,000 by the end of the twentieth century), who saw the Pope and his supporters moving the church away from the Vatican II–inspired reforms.[48] CTA developed quickly, notes sociologist Anthony Pogorelc, in part because the early and mid-twentieth-century movement called Catholic Action bequeathed leaders, goals, and themes to the new movement. The cauldron of progressive Catholicism in Chicago proved critical to both.[49] Though CTA included many priests and sisters and established a cooperative relationship with some bishops, including Cardinal George Bernardin of Chicago in the 1980s, the organization often fueled the ire of conservatives in the church. In 2006, Bishop Fabien Bruskewitz excommunicated CTA members in his Omaha, Nebraska, archdiocese for affiliating themselves with an organization he said was "irreconcilable with a coherent living of the Catholic Faith."[50]

The Survivors Network of those Abused by Priests (SNAP) and Voices of the Faithful (VOTF) emerged out of the sex abuse crisis, meanwhile, to become two of the most dynamic and assertive forces of reform. Originating in the United States—SNAP in 1989 and VOTF in 2002—both organizations have since expanded into other nations. The nonprofits apply steady pressure on U.S. bishops and other church leaders to deal with the trauma caused by the abuse. VOTF represents Catholics and focuses its efforts within the church, whereas the scope of SNAP grew beyond Roman Catholicism to develop branches that serve survivors of other Christian denominations as well as organizations like the Boy Scouts. SNAP also addresses problems of abuse by spiritual elders, including nuns and teachers. Its thousands of members continue to meet at conferences, file lawsuits, and provide direct support to survivors.[51]

A vibrant landscape of Catholic print media documents progressive political activity and provides a critical examination of developments on the right. *Commonweal, America* magazine, and the *Catholic Worker* newspaper have, in fact, been on the scene since the early twentieth century. Jesuits in the United States established *America* magazine in 1909 as a journal of religion and culture. Though affiliated with the church through the Society of Jesus, *America* has sometimes run afoul of the Vatican for its liberalism. In 2005, Rev. Thomas Reese stepped down as editor under pressure from Cardinal Joseph Ratzinger, who censured many liberals in his roles as prefect of the Congregation for the Doctrine of the Faith before becoming Pope Benedict XVI.[52]

Commonweal joined *America* magazine in the world of Catholic thought and letters in 1924. Operating independently of the church hierarchy, it brought Catholic writers like Jacques Maritain, Dorothy Day, and C. K. Chesterton, and also non-Catholics like Hannah Arendt, to the small but highly educated readership of Catholic intellectuals interested in liberal perspectives.[53] Well into the twenty-first century, the magazine has served as an important platform for dissent and new controversial ideas regarding the church. When, in 1993, it printed "The Case for a God-She" by the feminist theologian Elizabeth Johnson, the magazine advanced discussions about the place of women in Christian texts and Catholic teachings.[54]

The *Catholic Worker* newspaper continues to stand out for its raw but purposeful lack of sophistication. Published with similar ideas about the mission of the church and its social teachings since it first appeared in 1933, the *Catholic Worker* has maintained its focus on the problems of economic injustice at the cost of one cent an issue. The mix of pieces by nonprofessional and famous writers maintains a steady diet of inspiration for a loyal readership among activist Catholics oriented toward peace and justice issues.

The 1960s spirit of reform inspired another new outlet, the *National Catholic Reporter* (*NCR*). *NCR*'s founders brought professional journalists to the task of publishing news independently of the church hierarchy. The unapologetic progressivism of the *NCR* has sometimes put it at odds with Catholic officials. In the late 1960s, the head of the Kansas City diocese condemned the newspaper for its criticism of Pope Paul VI's encyclical *Humanae Vitae* (Of Human Life), and specifically its prohibition against birth control. When Bishop Charles H. Helmsing ordered *NCR* to remove "Catholic" from the title, its editors refused and took the opportunity to underscore that their organization would continue to report on the world of Catholicism—but not under the direction of church officials.[55] It has built its readership with a steady focus on domestic and foreign news that touches on the themes of peace and justice.

A split between feminists and the Catholic vanguard over reproductive rights blunted the impact of the Catholic Left. The pro-life mantra against abortion had taken root in Catholic peace politics before it became an expression of conservative antifeminism. Antiwar activists represented some the earliest opponents of abortion. The "choose life" shorthand for "stop abortion" emerged as a universal humanitarian cry to respect all life in the 1960s. Religious and nonreligious activists alike chanted the slogan at demonstrations. The Vatican had also denounced abortion and birth control in demands for the "sanctity of life" since both became more available in the 1930s, but the Vietnam-era peace movement broadened the scope of activism on behalf of life. As one historian notes, "Many pro-lifers were genuinely disturbed by the American government's disregard for human life in warfare, and they wanted the movement to speak out against all attacks on human life, whether those attacks were directed against an unborn baby in the womb, a convicted criminal in an electric chair, or a civilian in a Vietnamese village."[56]

The National Right to Life Committee, which was formed by Catholics before the 1973 *Roe v. Wade* decision, focused its attention on abortion as a single issue around which some progressives and conservatives thought they could unite. Daniel Berrigan wrote a blistering attack on abortion in the Christian magazine *Sojourners*. "I think that women do a great disservice by isolating the fate of the unborn as their own problem," he wrote in 1980. "I come to the abortion question," he continued,

190   CHAPTER NINE

"by way of a long, long experience with the military and the mainline violence of the culture expressed in war."[57]

The antiabortion movement thus represented a fork in the road for Vietnam-era Catholic radicals. Though the issue did not destroy the friendships, which had generally been fading anyway, it did prevent former collaborators from working together in the future. New issues and challenges sent peace activists in a variety of directions. The histories of the Camden 28 defendants illustrate this divergence. Cookie Ridolfi remembers the moment she told Daniel Berrigan she had no interest in fighting abortion. "I remember [him] calling me to ask me my position on it. I think they were looking for strong women who supported their position, but I didn't." Ridolfi and Berrigan ended the call with the usual warmth and respect they shared even though they would not collaborate on this issue.[58]

Elizabeth McAlister, Daniel Berrigan's sister-in-law, also wrote about abortion in *Sojourners*. Her argument against the pro-life movement offers insight into why many people, Catholics included, opposed abortion but could not join the national campaigns against it. "I believe our culture is morally bankrupt," she explained in 1980; "And I don't think it right or just to put the burden of transforming our moral values as a people onto the shoulders of young women who are, in most respects, victims of those values—being women and thus objects; being poor and thus a burden; being members of a society where the military and leadership have gone mad, and being thus expendable."[59]

The radical McAlister also continually wrote in defense of sex, but only within marriage. In 1996, she described sex outside committed relationships as representing a form of violence. She asserted that sex could not be separated from the creation of life, so couples who were not prepared to assume the duties of parenthood and child-rearing should refrain from it.[60]

Like Cookie Ridolfi, some activists failed to continue in the same direction as the Berrigans in part because the prophetic witness maintained by the more religious lay and clergy did not speak to them. As the Berrigans and friends developed Jonah House into a hub of Christian anticapitalism (which was labeled by the state of Maryland as a "site of ongoing criminal activity"), other alumni of the draft board raids decided they wanted to move on. The reformist impulse of the Berrigans, according to scholar Jason Bivins, buckled by the end of the Vietnam War, giving way to a growing "pessimism" about the church and government institutions. The antagonism toward state power that developed in those years of the Catholic Left, notes Bivins, became "enshrined at Jonah House," where residents held property in common and centered the Scripture in their lives of activism.[61] Most radicals put lockups and run-down rowhouses behind them.

The legacy of the Vietnam-era Catholic Left also persists in the reforms it forced on the FBI. In addition to hindering the conscription process, the burglars interfered with the government's ability to spy on its own citizens. By successfully resisting the FBI's attempts to sow division among them after their arrest, and thereby preventing the bureau from collecting information about the burglary of the Media, Pennsylvania, FBI office, the Camden 28 maintained the outflow of information about the government's illegal activities. Over the next ten years, this information damaged the FBI's reputation and that of its defining and longest-serving director, J. Edgar Hoover. The FBI's own error of focusing obsessively on John Peter Grady, who had nothing to do with the Media raid, prevented agents from identifying Camden 28 defendants Keith Forsyth and Bob Williamson as two of the burglars. Given how important Forsyth's role was in the Media FBI office raid, his severance from the larger group of defendants by the prosecution illustrates the failure of the bureau's intelligence gathering on the case. The prosecution put Forsyth, who proved vital to the exposure of government secrets, in the category of defendants who would face lesser charges than the seventeen others who stood trial first in 1973. The bureau, in other words, correctly identified the Catholic Left as the movement behind this fiasco but struggled fruitlessly to arrest and charge the right perpetrators. The damaging secrets thus continued to trickle out.

It took years for journalists, government investigators, and scholars to assemble all the pieces, but we now know how the events in Media and Camden forced the government to reckon with this malfeasance. This research revealed that the FBI's COINTELPRO program sought to subvert the efforts of American political activists, including the Reverend Dr. Martin Luther King Jr. The nation started to learn the true extent of this illegal activity, first leaked by the burglars in 1971, only after journalist Carl Stern at NBC successfully sued the government under the 1966 Freedom of Information Act. On December 6, 1973, Stern reported on NBC's *Nightly News* that Hoover had ordered the FBI to "harass and destroy New Left organizations." His objective was not merely to collect intelligence, but to "expose," "disrupt," and "frustrate" these political organizations. The bureau must not just contain these organizations, Hoover determined; it must "neutralize" them.[62]

As the full nature of COINTELPRO and other illegal activities in the FBI came to light, top officials in Washington, D.C., started to demand investigations. Seymour Hersch at the *New York Times* forced the issue with his December 22, 1974, story, "Huge CIA Operation Reported in U.S. against Anti-War Forces." Hersch reported that the Central Intelligence Agency maintained thousands of files on antiwar activists in violation of its charter. In January 1975, the Senate established the Senate Select Committee to Study Governmental Operations with Respect to Intelligence Activities, better known as the Church Committee for its chair, Democrat Frank Church of Idaho. The committee in turn prompted the Church hearings of 1975 to probe the extent of unlawful activity by U.S. intelligence organizations.[63]

Unfortunately, the closed Church Committee hearings had little impact on the American public, but they did bring the government's attention to illegal operations, including Hoover's Security Index. Through this program, the director maintained files on people living in the United States whom the FBI recommended for detainment should the United States come under attack by a foreign power.[64] In response to the shocking revelations about this abusive surveillance, Congress passed reforms aiming to regulate spy activities by the government, which were still in effect almost fifty years later. The Senate Select Committee on Intelligence continues to provide oversight and study the intelligence work of the U.S. government.[65] The revelations also led to the passage of the Foreign Intelligence Surveillance Act of 1978 (FISA), which established the system by which government officials from the president on down must obtain a court-authorized warrant to conduct wiretaps and other surveillance for foreign intelligence information.[66]

These investigations also revealed that Hoover did not close the COINTELPRO program despite saying he had. The Church Committee determined in 1976 that the FBI had conducted at least three COINTELPRO-like operations after Hoover officially closed the program in 1971. Barbara Banoff, the committee's staff counsel, pointed out that congressional investigations could not possibly access all the five hundred thousand case files to accurately determine if the bureau actually ceased these operations.[67] In one instance, the FBI obtained information about the attorney of the Pentagon Papers whistleblower Daniel Ellsberg, which it leaked to a news organization to damage his reputation.[68] When Hoover was still alive and in charge, the FBI spied extensively on John Kerry of Massachusetts, the leader of Vietnam Veterans against the War, and shared reports with Richard Nixon, who regarded Kerry as a possible political opponent.[69] As late as 1988 the FBI released files revealing a COINTELPRO-like bureau operation that targeted the Committee in Solidarity with the People of El Salvador.[70] Illegal activity by the FBI thus persisted, but new institutions of oversight and whistleblowing activity mean that twenty-first-century Americans have more

Aftermath and Results

tools than Americans of the twentieth century to discover and act on this abuse of power.

Catholics on the Right, meanwhile succeeded in stealing the religious thunder of the left by infusing their political expression with spiritual fervor. After 1970, conservative Catholics also cultivated alliances with Christians in other denominations to curtail liberalism. The culture wars of the 1980s became a platform from which opponents of feminism, multiculturalism, and gender diversity could unite and attack the forces of modernization. As conservatives at the Vatican consolidated power in this period, conservative Catholics in the United States cultivated orthodox liturgy. Traditionalists revived Latin Masses, head coverings, and other practices that Vatican II had all but eliminated. The rise of the Catholic Right contributed to the rise of the American Right, and its striking impact conceals myriad ways that church progressives continue to shape politics under the radar.

Unlike the subjects of this investigation, who generally wanted Vatican II to go further with liberalization, other Catholics did not approve of the reforms it had introduced in the first place. A backlash against the council mirrored the political backlash against progressive change in the United States. A series of conservative encyclicals aimed at restricting sexual rights aligned with and fueled a "pro-family" movement that gained ground among American Catholics and Protestants in the Republican Party. Following the sweeping modernizations introduced under John XXIII, Pope Paul VI started shoring up rules on marriage and family life—a process that would continue with subsequent papacies stretching into the twenty-first century. Released in 1968, *Humanae Vitae* condemned birth control, prohibited abortion under any circumstances, and mandated that sex be tied to the holy duty to procreate.[71]

Paul's successor, John Paul II, further tightened the church's policies in *Evangelium Vitae* (Gospel of Human Life). This 1995 encyclical reaffirmed his predecessor's declarations on abortion and birth control and added that "such practices are rooted in a hedonistic mentality unwilling to accept responsibility in matters of sexuality, and they imply a self-centered concept of freedom, which regards procreation as an obstacle to personal fulfilment."[72] During the twenty-seven-year papacy of John Paul II, the church played a substantive role in the American antiabortion movement, a campaign that succeeded in galvanizing religious activists on the Right more than any other single issue.

Catholics on the Right aligned themselves with other Christians in claiming that their religious ideals made them more patriotic and authentically American than liberals. By grounding their interpretation of

194   CHAPTER NINE

capitalism in the church's social teachings, conservatives also succeeded in attracting rich donors into their orbit. The neoconservative scholar Michael Novak, for example, promoted capitalism from his office at the American Enterprise Institute by developing a theological basis for the free market. His 1990 book *Towards the Theology of the Corporation* argues that the organizational structures of corporations promote human dignity and that capitalism has fulfilled God's divine plan.[73]

The political strategist and lobbyist Paul Weyrich helped solidify the marriage of Christianity and capitalism by directing funds to the cultural battles of the religious Right. Vatican II prompted Weyrich to convert from Roman Catholicism to the more traditional Melkite Greek Catholic Church, in which he served as a deacon while juggling his many political projects.[74] Weyrich helped establish the conservative Heritage Foundation think tank in 1973 and, two years later, the American Legislative Exchange Council. Credited with coining the term "Moral Majority," he helped wed the economic and social platforms around which conservatism congealed in the 1980s.[75]

The rise of Weyrich coincided with that of the most influential Catholic woman on the American right, Phyllis Schlafly. Schlafly became a central figure in national politics when she led the successful Stop Taking Our Privileges (STOP-ERA) movement to block passage of the Equal Rights Amendment during the 1970s. In doing so, she developed an expansive grassroots network through her nonprofit Eagle Forum, which grew into a powerful lobbying organization for religious conservatives. By training her supporters to organize through their places of worship, Schlafly also made churches a critical base of activism for the emerging Right.[76] In 1980, she and Weyrich joined evangelical leaders Jerry Falwell and Timothy LaHaye on the stage of the National Affairs Briefing Conference in Dallas. In front of fifteen thousand conservative Christians, they endorsed Ronald Reagan, the Republican nominee for president. Though Reagan himself was not very religious, his warm relationship with the Christian Right underscored their influence in the halls of power.[77]

Conservatives gained yet more influence in the church with the elevation of Pope Benedict XVI, Joseph Ratzinger of Germany, to the papacy in 2005. His conservative influence at the Vatican had been developing for fifteen years. After a successful university career as a theologian, when he was quite liberal before Vatican II, the scholar prelate ascended through the College of Cardinals as the prefect for the Congregation for the Doctrine of the Faith in 1981. For decades, he was the premier enforcer of dogma. In 1981, Ignatius Press released an interview with the future Pope called the "Ratzinger Report," which resonated with conservatives inside and beyond the church for its reasoned condemnation of contraception, nonmarital sex, queer sexuality, and "radical feminism."[78] At the core of these problems, argued Ratzinger, was the decoupling of sexuality from biological reproduction, a process he describes as "biological manipulation."[79] Benedict continued to push the church in a more traditional direction by reviving Latin Tridentine Masses and inviting excommunicated members who opposed Vatican II back into the church. He then cut his papacy short by stepping down in 2013.[80]

The more progressive Jorge Mario Bergoglio of Argentina took over the Holy See as Pope Francis in 2013, but the enthusiasm for traditional liturgy and family values in the Catholic Church endured. Media executive Steve Bannon, who advised President Donald Trump after years as editor of the conservative Breitbart News site, played a significant role in this resurgence. He joined the Italy-based Dignitatis Humanae Institute, which ran political bootcamps at a thirteenth-century monastery to teach Catholics how to "defend the west" until the Italian Ministry of Culture shuttered the institution.[81]

"Defending the west" in the United States meant fighting immigration. Bannon and his supporters argued that the United States was fundamentally a "Christian" nation threatened by the rise of Islam and secularism.[82] A host of well-funded institutions lined up to promote this view. In 2011, the Jesuit priest Robert Spitzer and the Orange County, California, attorney, real estate mogul, and hotel-chain owner Timothy Busch established the Napa Institute to stimulate a conservative response to growing secularism.[83] Like many Catholic organizations across the spectrum, the Napa Institute aimed to confront the problems of clergy sexual abuse and declining faith, but it also promoted a stringent observance of sexual ethics and purification.[84] The institute celebrated the anniversary of the *Humanae Vitae* encyclical, claiming that "divorce, out-of-wedlock births and abortions are causally linked, and have wreaked havoc on the poor" while depriving "more than half of American children with the presence of their father."[85]

Spitzer and Busch also worked together in the Magis Center, an intellectual organization formed to bring science, reason, and faith together to revitalize Catholicism. Contrary to Pope Francis's work on environmental stewardship, however, conservatives in the Magis Center and other organizations downplayed or denied the impact of human-induced climate change.[86]

Conservative Catholics have succeeded in promoting these ideas by launching powerful media outlets. One of the largest religious broadcast networks in the world, the Eternal World Television Network (EWTN), was started in a converted garage in the early 1980s. Mother Angelica from the Order of Saint Clare founded the network not far from the cloistered Alabama monastery that she called home. EWTN became popular among viewers for its daily Mass and recitations of the rosary. It broadcast holiday ceremonies and installations of bishops and cardinals as well as nightly news "from a Catholic perspective." The successful television station grew over four decades, and by 2019 it had established a West Coast headquarters at a former evangelical megachurch in Orange County, California, known as the Crystal Cathedral. It launched free radio programming across five hundred U.S. and international affiliates, as well as SIRIUS/XM and IHeartRadio.[87]

With a budget in excess of $50 million, this outlet for devotion evolved into a conservative political organ where figures like the Catholic U.S. Speaker of the House of Representatives Paul Ryan and the nominal Christian Donald Trump promoted themselves through religious messaging. As early as 1993, Mother Angelica herself had become a political figure when she spoke at the annual World Youth Day conference to denounce church progressives. "I'm so tired of you, liberal church in America," she declared; "You do nothing but destroy." Much like the 1930s demagogue Father Charles Coughlin, the conservative nun invoked populist discontent among the faithful to bemoan how liberalism victimized ordinary Catholics.[88] As one journalist for the progressive *NCR* noted about EWTN's influence, the network has no counterpart in the world of Catholic progressives.[89]

The 2020 presidential election solidified the dominance of Republicanism among Catholics in the United States. Though the triumph of Joseph Biden brought the only member of the church to the White House since John F. Kennedy, exit polls indicate that roughly half of American Catholics voted for the incumbent, Donald Trump.[90] Reliably blue for almost a century, American Catholics had severed the historically solid connection between their church and the Democratic Party.

CONCLUSION

Is There Anything Left of the Catholic Left?

President Donald Trump gave American conservatives cause to celebrate in fall 2020 despite the continuing grip of the COVID-19 pandemic. Republicans across the country joyfully watched the White House Rose Garden ceremony televised on September 26, which marked the realization of a major conservative movement goal. Trump officially announced his appointment of Notre Dame law professor Amy Coney Barrett to the U.S. Supreme Court that sunny afternoon. A crowd of more than one hundred unmasked attendees sat shoulder to shoulder to hear these remarks, many of them infecting each other with coronavirus disease. The recent death of Justice Ruth Bader Ginsburg had provided the White House with an opportunity to fulfill one of the most popular campaign promises of the 2016 election—to seat conservatives in the judiciary who could be relied on to carry out the religious agenda of the Christian Right. Eliminating the legal protections of abortion rights represented a top priority.[1]

The role of Catholicism in this enormous victory for conservatism is hard to overlook. Indeed, the 2020 appointment of laywoman Barrett deepened the court's conservative majority by adding her to the bench alongside recent appointees Neil Gorsuch and Brett Kavanaugh. The seating of these conservatives also shifted the religious composition of the court. As of 2020, six of the court's nine members were Catholic.[2] This court delivered the most hoped-for outcome for the Republican base in the historic *Dobbs v. Jackson Women's Health Organization* decision of 2022, which overturned *Roe v. Wade* (1973) and *Planned Parenthood of Southeastern Pennsylvania v. Casey* (1992), two prior decisions that had asserted women's fundamental right to an abortion.[3]

By unifying around the goal of stopping abortion, religious conservatives succeeded not only in fulfilling their objective of overthrowing *Roe,* but also in claiming the victory for God. The religious Right has been a recognizable force since the 1980s, with the Catholic Church a major player in this coalition and no recognizable religious Left to challenge its power. Regardless of how often House Speaker Nancy Pelosi and President Biden announced their membership in the Catholic Church, their prominence did not evoke a significant discussion about an emerging progressive Christianity.[4] The recommendations by conservative bishops to deny these two communion drew as much or more press attention as stories about their religious backgrounds and beliefs. The subtext driving this public discussion, or lack thereof, is that Pelosi, Biden, and other Catholics on the Left represent the past—a time when the church represented a force in the Democratic Party.[5]

The attention paid to Catholics as conservatives, however, obscures the steady work of religious progressives whose faith shapes their effective political endeavors. Can we observe a "Catholic Left" or "Catholic Resistance" at work in the twenty-first century? We can, but not as a movement in the way movements operated fifty years ago. Though it generates less discussion than their Vietnam-era predecessors, the current generation continues to break laws, destroy government property, and spend significant time in jail, much as the draft board raiders once did. Some of these activists bridge both generations, though the elder radicals are fading from the scene. It might surprise people to learn that the Plowshares movement executed at least as many documented actions as the Vietnam-era Catholic Left. The media pays far less attention to it, however, probably because the campaigns against nuclear proliferation did not cause as much social upheaval as Vietnam resistance once did.[6]

While Plowshares and other movements have continued to hold up the cross and announce their work for God, most progressive Catholics work invisibly—or at least their Catholicism operates invisibly. Catholic progressives increasingly affiliate with nonreligious organizations as favored venues for political demonstration. While Catholic Social Justice principles like the preferential option for the poor, the common good, and personalism still ground their spiritual lives, these twenty-first-century Christians tend not to wear religion on their sleeves. Instead, they blend into secular and interfaith communities of activism.[7] Since they do not sign their emails with "God Bless" or talk about Jesus outside church settings, their religious identity falls under the radar. As one reporter noted in 2018, the "pink wave" of female candidates who ran for office in the wake of Donald Trump's election included progressive Catholic women who chose not to declare their religious affiliations even when spiritual ideals animated their ideology. These women are not, she observes, "overtly connecting themselves with the U.S. bishops and conservative elements in the church that identifies abortion, gay marriage and religious liberty as defining issues—issues that ultimately led about half of U.S. Catholic voters to choose Donald Trump in 2016."[8] "Catholic," in other words, has come to signal "conservative" in politics to the extent that Catholics on the Left risk a miscommunication of their positions if they foreground their religious affiliation.

The Catholic Left of the Vietnam War era is partly responsible for this lack of visibility even though, in contrast to their successors, members actually announced their faith without reserve. When priests, nuns, and laypeople started marching for civil rights and demonstrating for peace, they did not merely choose to represent their church in these movements like a sponsored float in a parade. The sixties generation of radicals opened their hearts to the truth claims and traditions of other faiths that were animating this activism. From Black and Latin American Christians, they learned the power of liberation theology. From Gandhi, they learned the peace philosophy of Satyagraha.[9] At the height of his influence as a writer, the Trappist monk Thomas Merton reportedly said that he wanted to "become the best Buddhist" he could.[10] He and Dorothy Day demonstrated how these traditions did not compete with Catholicism, but rather offered insight for how to be better Catholics.

Many progressive Catholics no longer belong to a parish yet still identify as Catholic. Some celebrate Mass in home-based gatherings because they find that the diocesan structure impedes, rather than animates, their spiritual life. To what extent can someone refer to their political activity as "Catholic" when they no longer belong to the church? Camden 28 defendant Paul Couming, for example, joined an evangelical congregation for several years but then again found himself worshipping in a Catholic parish.

In a church that defines membership tightly around the structures of the parish, it might seem logical to simply remove unaffiliated laypeople from the category of Catholicism. Church doctrine does not provide any clear basis for such a dismissal, however. Canon law, in fact, regards baptism as a seal that cannot be broken, affirming the old adage, "Once a Catholic, always a Catholic."[11] The life of draft board raider Anne Walsh provides a useful illustration of this ambiguity. A former nun, who married and raised her family with others in a religious collective outside Boston, she no longer attends Mass. She also chose not to hold a church funeral for her husband, the former priest Robert Cunnane. Though she is now active in a Unitarian congregation, Walsh says she would love to be a nun again in her old age. She left her order for a host of reasons but remained devoted of the Sisters of St. Joseph. "I love them," says Walsh; "I loved them all my life."[12]

Many Catholics today find themselves in a similar position, with one foot in the church and the other in the secular world. Frida Berrigan similarly lives a life inspired by her Catholic faith but outside any parish community. Though the daughter of Philip Berrigan and Elizabeth McAlister Berrigan describes herself as a practicing Catholic, she and her agnostic husband, Patrick Sheehan-Gaumer, belong to a Unitarian Universalist church. Her devout parents, who were excommunicated at one point, raised Berrigan and her siblings in a home where Catholic rituals and symbols infused their prayer life but actual church identification was less important. Berrigan and Sheehan-Gaumer have replicated many aspects of Jonah House in Baltimore, the Christian-based living community founded by Berrigan's parents. Their lifestyles also exhibit the values that both learned at the Catholic Worker House where the two met. Like Dorothy Day, Berrigan and Sheehan-Gaumer deliberately earned less than the level of taxable income in the United States so that none of their earnings went to fund the Pentagon.[13]

While considering the complex religious lives that make it difficult to identify the Catholic identity of many Catholic progressives, we should also take into account the overall retreat from Christian houses of worship in the United States. In contrast to Europe, religion remains a dominant social institution in the United States, but more Protestant churches are closing than opening while Catholics lead the pack in the rate of disaffiliation from Christian church membership.[14] Scholars digging into the secularization of America show us, however, that there is more to this story than a straightforward decline. Using valuable data, much of it from the Pew Center for Research, they break down the different directions taken by Christians who no longer affiliate as well as patterns in their explanations for these choices. Harder to assess would be the impact of the of the nonaffiliated but still spiritually animated Americans who apply the Gospels in other areas of life. Where—and through whom—might we see Catholic Social Justice at work in American politics if we looked beyond historical actors who proclaim their membership in the church?

Researchers have developed useful categories and concepts to make sense of this data. One group attracting significant attention since a Pew Center survey identified them are in the category labeled "None." When asked about their religion, this broad swath of the population identifies as either atheist, agnostic, or "nothing in particular." Gregory A. Smith at the Pew Center for Research reported in 2021 that 29 percent of Americans fit this classification. A 2020 guide for reevangelization published by the USCCB noted that for every American who converts to Catholicism, between six and seven have moved to the category of "former" Catholic and that 79 percent of Americans who disaffiliate from religious organizations do so before the age of twenty-four.[15]

Spiritual progressives do not fit this profile of the disengaged and uninterested. To evaluate their impact, we would need to look to a category of Americans more recently identified by scholars as "the dechurched," "church refugees," or "Dones." Having abandoned all denominations, this group seeks God privately and through relationships with people outside of institutionalized church settings. Church refugees include people who are open to finding a church community. According to sociologists Josh Packard and Ashleigh Hope, many dechurched people remain open to being rechurched though they struggle with the bureaucracy, hierarchy, dogma, or another aspect of organized religion. The secularization of American culture has made dechurching into an easy process even if it leaves many people longing for a spiritual home. One can withdraw from religious communities without suffering from the isolation that would have resulted from such a pivot in earlier times.[16]

The Packard and Hope study identifies another commonality among the Dones that suggests we might find a hidden political influence worth examining. This category of dechurched Americans rarely includes the free riders, who attend worship services and events but let others do the work. It tends to include the doers, the organizers and the leaders. "When the Dones walk out of the church," note Packard and Hope, "they take with them all of the institutional knowledge and training, all of their energy and talents, and all of their community and social connections that extend beyond the walls of the church." How might these spiritually driven people, with their talent and motivation, be expanding the influence of Christianity? "Their substantial energies and skills," suggest the authors, "are now poured daily into the activities and structures that happen completely outside the purview of organized religion."[17]

The growing collections of data on Dones interest leaders in American Christendom who are trying to develop new tools for attracting church refugees back into the fold. Some call attention to one area of American life that draws fervor that was once directed at religious worship—politics. In our polarized society, they note, people have made ideology into a replacement for theology as they sort themselves into opposing "Left" and "Right" camps. This trend demands our attention, as does the reality that in fact, religious belief drives much of this appetite for political engagement.[18] Just as we parse the evangelical and Catholic elements of the "Make America Great Again" movement that emerged in support of President Donald Trump, our understanding of religion's impact on American politics would benefit from studying the relatively invisible influence of religious progressives.

If we could identify and follow this group beyond the moment they stepped outside the walls of their former churches, we might very well find a world of people filled with faith. The inheritance of the Catholic Left would be found in this world. In battles to halt climate change, oil and gas pipeline construction, clergy sex abuse, capital punishment, mass incarceration, gun violence, and other injustices, we find the fruits of this legacy. The prophetic witness of Thomas Merton, Dorothy Day, and Camden 28 defendant Michael Doyle lives on in these campaigns. The War Resisters League and Witness Against Torture, where Frida Berrigan concentrates her efforts, represent two examples of this spiritual influence.[19] The Catholic Left persists through activists, affiliated and unaffiliated, who bend to the merciful work of serving marginalized communities, including people who are homeless, disabled, and displaced. They do not pour blood or say the rosary together, but they are prayerful. Although they do not call our attention to it, maybe it is time we took notice of their faith.

ACKNOWLEDGMENTS

I started research for this book to track down an incredible story that unfolded in my backyard. No one told me about the Camden 28 when I was growing up in South Jersey. I was born in Cooper Hospital five months before the Camden 28 raid, just blocks away from the draft boards. The project started after I watched a 2007 documentary by filmmaker Anthony Giacchino called *The Camden 28*. My father, who was raised in Camden, insisted that I watch the film. Though I was only two when the U.S. finally withdrew from Vietnam, the war hovered over our family life because my father's only brother died there in 1965. Ronald Nickerson enlisted in the U.S. Army before the 1964 escalation.

The defendants' story captured me for many reasons. I was shocked that no one had ever mentioned it to me given the geographic proximity of my home to all the events. I started my investigation with the documentary trail left by Giacchino at the Swarthmore College Peace Collection, outside Philadelphia. I was grateful for book research that brought me home to my family on my many research trips in New Jersey and Pennsylvania. It also brought me to California, South Dakota, New Mexico, and New York for individual interviews with the defendants and other participants. I benefited from generous fellowships and grants as well as support from a vast community of other scholars, as well as family and friends.

I am grateful for the support from many people and institutions that helped me track down the defendants and write this book. The College of Arts and Sciences (CAS) at Loyola University Chicago, my employer, helped me launch this work with a summer grant that funded the preliminary research. After that first trip into the archives, Loyola helped me time and again to follow up on those initial findings. CAS provided me with a research leave fellowship. The Gannon Center for Women and Leadership welcomed me into their offices with a generous semester of research leave as well. The Hank Center for Catholic Intellectual Heritage funded me generously, providing support for my research travel, recording equipment, and transcription fees. The University of Notre Dame became a second scholarly home in these years. Notre Dame's Cushwa Center for the Study of American Catholicism awarded me a grant to research the treasure trove of archival materials at the Hesburgh Library and bring me into contact with scholars in South Bend. The university's Center for Social Concerns funded my appearance at one of its Catholic Social Tradition conferences, boosting my education in this important history of the church. The final financial boost came from the Louisville Institute. Though the COVID-19 pandemic prevented my cohort of grantees from gathering in person, the institute's sabbatical research grant gave me leave to write many of the book's chapters.

Helping me take advantage of this financial support were the many people who hosted me on my research travels. Annie and Jon Coleman welcomed me in their home in South Bend on more than one occasion. My parents, Allen and Brenda Nickerson, and my sister and brother-in-law, Jennifer Rosenberg and Chad Rosenberg, provided my home base in greater Philadelphia. My friends Sudha Wadhwani and Cheryl Koos put me up for research trips in New York City and Los Angeles, respectively. I am grateful to Aaron Sachs and Christine Evans, who gave me a room in their house for multiple days of research at Cornell University, and to Father Michael Engh SJ, then president of Santa Clara University, who made a university residence available to me when I came to do an interview in Northern California. Camden 28 defendants Anne Dunham and Frank Pommersheim were kind enough to accommodate me when I interviewed them in Vermillion, South Dakota.

The analysis and the storytelling in this book benefited from the input of many scholars and writers who read manuscript drafts over the years. These readers include Kathleen Belew, Philip Byers, Peter Cajka, Melissa Coles, Vanessa Cook, Darren Dochuk, Anthony Giacchino, Raymond Haberski, Andrew Hartman, Liz Hauck, Dan Hummel, Tim Lacy, Colleen McDannell, John McGreevy, Jennifer Ratner-Rosenhagen, Andrew Sandoval-Strausz, Heidi Schlumpf, Kevin Schultz, and Alyssa Smith. I started this project as a new assistant professor at Loyola University Chicago, hoping that this book would introduce me to scholars of Catholicism on my campus who could help me, and to my great good fortune, this plan succeeded. Mike Murphy at the Hank Center repeatedly hosted events to bring this research to an audience of helpful listeners.

Theologian Susan Ross and sociologist Kathleen Maas Weigert gave valuable feedback on the chapters covering the history of the church. Matthew Dunch helped with an earlier chapter of that history. At Loyola Law School, Tom Donnelly, Dean Strang, Mary Bird, William Elward, Alan Raphael, and Barry Sullivan helped me sort out the many details of the Camden 28 trial. Dean Strang also read multiple chapters. I was fortunate that I could also lean on incredibly talented scholars in my own Department of History to give me critical feedback, including Timothy Gilfoyle, Elliott Gorn, Robert Bucholz, Benjamin Johnson, and Stephen Schloesser. Administrators David Hays and Tim Libaris as well as chair Brad Hunt gave valuable support for cutting all the red tape.

I have also benefited from numerous invitations for speaking engagements and workshops to present this work as it progressed. I am grateful for the opportunities extended by the Political History Colloquium at Purdue University; the Midwest Intellectual History Group; the U.S. History Workshop at the University of Chicago; the Religion and American Culture seminar at Chicago's Newberry Library; the Tamiment Library at New York University; the Colloquium on Religion in American History at Notre Dame; the Sorbonne Nouvelle in Paris, France; and the Heidelberg Center for American Studies in Heidelberg, Germany.

Many talented students have assisted me with project over the years. At Loyola, I received help with the research from Juan Basadre, Jenny Clay, Katie Dubielak, Sarah LaVanway, Michael Malucha, Mark Neuhengen, Pedro Regalado, Lizzy Schmidt, Mikey Spehn, Joanna Surma, and Anna Wilmhoff. At Rutgers, students in Jennifer Mittelstadt's undergraduate "Power and Politics in New Jersey" workshop and Anthony Giacchino's seminar on New Jersey public history did valuable work in their studies of the Camden 28. I was fortunate to be included in their activities. Special thanks go to Rutgers student Thomas Callahan for his bold forays into new archives. Several people at the University of Pennsylvania helped me access materials that I could not locate remotely. Thank-yous also go to Timothy Horning, Gabriel Raeburn, and Brian Rosenwald.

Luckily for me, the University of Chicago Press has provided the gold standard of editorial support for *Spiritual Criminals*. Susannah Engstrom, Olivia Aguilar, Elizabeth Ellingboe, and Andrea Blatz supported this work in different stages. I am especially grateful to my editor, Timothy Mennel, for showing enthusiasm for this manuscript, even before it was actually a manuscript. And thank you, Tim, for encouraging me to make some important revisions.

Historians know that we are nothing without the behind-the-scenes contributions of archivists, curators, and librarians. Those who supported me include Wendy Chmielewski at Swarthmore; Jane Currie at

Loyola University Chicago; Debra Dochuk and Jean McManus at Notre Dame; Bill Fliss at Marquette; Nancy Freeman and Emily Reiher at Loyola's Women and Leadership Archive; Mindy Johnson and Julie Tozer at the Camden, New Jersey, County Library; Chris Gushman at the National Archives at New York City; and Michael Koncewicz at the Tamiment Library at New York University.

I am also grateful to the legions of people who supported me in some other way as I made my way on this journey of research and writing. They include Manfred Berg, Jay Brandenberger, Kathleen Sprows Cummings, Harry Dammer, Howard Gillette, Tikia Hamilton, Andrew Johnson, Stephen Johnson, Isaac Johnston, Robert Johnston, Catherine Korda, Wilfried Mausbach, Gil Medina, Betty Medsger, Lisa Meyerowitz, Emily Moore, Greg Moore, Peter O'Connor, Natalia Mehlman Petrzela, Carl Poplar, Bernhard Prusak, Bill Purcell, Jennifer Reed-Bouley, Kyle Roberts, Anja Schüler, Jan Stievermann, Pamela Walker, Welf Werner, Nicole Yeftich, and Heather Smith Yutzy.

Last but not least are the two people who kept me going on this project. Ben and Aspen Johnson were with me through thick and thin, providing the constant love and encouragement I needed to bring this book to the finish line. I am able to do what I do because of the home and the adventures they make with me.

ABBREVIATIONS

ACLU	American Civil Liberties Union
BPUM	Black People's Unity Movement
CALCAV	Clergy and Laity Concerned about Vietnam
CCRM	Camden Civil Rights Ministerium
CDC	Camden 28 Defense Committee
CORE	Congress of Racial Equality
CO	Conscientious Objector
CPF	Catholic Peace Fellowship
CPS	Civilian Public Service
CST	Catholic Social Teaching, or Catholic Social Tradition
CW	Catholic Worker
FCDA	Federal Civil Defense Agency
FHA	Federal Housing Administration
FISUR	Physical Surveillance (FBI)
FOR	Fellowship of Reconciliation
GI	Government Issued (refers to people in the armed forces)
HOLC	Home Owners Loan Corporation
MEDBURG	Media Burglary
NAACP	National Association for the Advancement of Colored People
NARMIC	National Action Research into the Military-Industrial Complex
NCCB	National Council of Catholic Bishops (precursor to USCCB)
NECLC	National Emergency Civil Liberties Committee
NLF	National Liberation Front
OPEN	Organization of People Engaged in the Neighborhood

PATCO	Port Authority Transit Corporation
PRI	Institutional Revolutionary Party
RCA	Radio Corporation of America
RIT	Rochester Institute of Technology
RSHM	Religious of the Sacred Heart of Mary
SAC	Special Agent in Charge (FBI)
SDS	Students for a Democratic Society
SI	Security Index (FBI)
SJS	scientific jury selection
SNCC	Student Nonviolent Coordinating Committee
SNDN	Sisters of Notre Dame de Namur
SSJ	Sisters of St. Joseph
UFM	United Farm Workers
USCCB	United States Conference of Catholic Bishops
WFP	Witness for Peace

NOTES

INTRODUCTION

1. Ken Burns and Lynn Novick, *The Vietnam War* (San Francisco, CA: PBS, 2018), DVD.

2. Catonsville 9 Defense Committee, "The Catonsville 9: An Act of Conscience," pamphlet, 1968, Enoch Pratt Free Library, http://c9.digitalmaryland.org/artifact.php ?ID=DPCN003&PT=1.

3. The archivist Hillel Arnold developed a website to track the numerous draft board raids between 1967 and 1971, "Draft Board Raids," accessed May 18, 2023, http://hillelarnold.com/draft-board-raids/.

4. Ronald Reagan to Glenn Dumbe, August 15, 1997, in Gilder Lehrman Institute of American History, "History Resources: Ronald Reagan on the Unrest on College Campuses, 1967," accessed September 29, 2023, https://www.gilderlehrman.org/history -resources/spotlight-primary-source/ronald-reagan-unrest-college-campuses-1967.

5. L. M. Baskir and W. A. Strauss, *Chance and Circumstance: The Draft, the War, and the Vietnam Generation* (New York: Knopf, 1978), 25.

6. According to U.S. Veterans Affairs, about 2.7 million Americans served in the Vietnam War. U.S. Department of Veterans Affairs, accessed September 29, 2023, https:// www.research.va.gov/topics/vietnam.cfm.

7. Baskir and Strauss, *Chance and Circumstance*, 11–12.

8. VISTA is short for Volunteers In Service To America. For a history of VISTA, see AmeriCorps, "VISTA: How It works," accessed September 29, 2023, https:// americorps.gov/partner/how-it-works/americorps-vista.

9. For more on the demonstrations at the 1968 Democratic National Convention and the New Left, see David Farber, *Chicago '68* (Chicago: University of Chicago Press, 1988).

10. Laurie Lahey, "'The Grassy Battleground': Race, Religion, and Activism in Camden's 'Wide' Civil Rights Movement," *ProQuest Dissertations and Theses* (PhD diss., George Washington University, 2013).

210   NOTES TO PAGES 5–16

11. Colleen McDannell, *The Spirit of Vatican II: A History of Catholic Reform in America* (New York: Basic Books, 2011); *Gaudium et Spes* (Joy and Hope) (Vyšehrad, Prague, 1969), 56–57, 66, 75.

12. I use the word "radicals" to describe the subjects of this book as it has historically applied to political activists who seek to change society by reforming its basic institutions, including the family, the economy, the education system, and religious institutions. "Radical" does not appear here as a substitution for "extremist."

13. Andrew M. Greeley, *The Catholic Imagination* (Berkeley: University of California Press, 2000).

14. For a historical and ethnographic exploration of the Catholic Imagination, see Robert A. Orsi, *History and Presence* (Cambridge, MA: Harvard University Press, 2016). For an investigation of this concept in a larger Christian context, see David Tracy, *The Analogical Imagination: Christian Theology and the Culture of Pluralism* (New York: Crossroad, 1981).

15. David Horowitz, "No Ideologue Left Behind," *Weekly Standard*, November 12, 2007; David Horowitz, *Dark Agenda: The War to Destroy Christian America* (West Palm Beach, FL: Humanix Books, 2018); Ronald Reagan, "The Morality Gap at Berkeley," speech at Cow Palace, May 12, 1966, in *The Creative Society* (New York: Devin-Adair, 1968), 125–29.

16. "Abernathy, Ralph David," Martin Luther King, Jr. Research and Education Institution, Stanford University, accessed June 4, 2023, https://kinginstitute.stanford.edu/encyclopedia/abernathy-ralph-david.

17. Jason Bivins, *The Fracture of Good Order: Christian Antiliberalism and the Challenge to American Politics* (Chapel Hill: University of North Carolina Press, 2003), 9.

18. Betty Friedan, *The Feminine Mystique* (New York: W. W. Norton, 1963).

PART ONE

1. Lianne Moccia, interview by author, July 14, 2020, 12.

2. Moccia, interview, 5.

3. Moccia, interview, 13.

4. Moccia, interview, 13.

CHAPTER ONE

1. P. Murray Polner and Jim O'Grady, *Disarmed and Dangerous: The Radical Lives and Times of Daniel and Philip Berrigan* (New York: Basic Books, 1997), 174–75.

2. U.S. General Services Administration, "U.S. Custom House, Baltimore," accessed July 3, 2023, https://www.gsa.gov/historic-buildings/us-custom-house-baltimore-md.

3. Polner and O'Grady, *Disarmed and Dangerous*, 176.

4. Shawn Michael Peters, *The Catonsville Nine* (New York: Oxford University Press, 2012), 51; George Mische, "Oral History Interviews of the Vietnam Era Oral History Project," Minnesota Historical Society, St. Paul, 2019, 29.

5. Historical weather report found at https://www.wunderground.com/history/daily/KBWI/date/1967-10-27.

6. Polner and O'Grady, *Disarmed and Dangerous*, 173.

7. Polner and O'Grady, *Disarmed and Dangerous*, 174–77; Peters, *Catonsville Nine*, 35.

8. Polner and O'Grady, *Disarmed and Dangerous*, 177.

9. United States Conference of Catholic Bishops, "The Eucharist," 2023, https://www.usccb.org/eucharist; "What Do Catholics Mean When We Say the Eucharist Is 'the True Body and Blood' of Christ?," *America Magazine*, November 12, 2021, https://www.americamagazine.org/faith/2021/11/12/eucharist-real-presence-241625.

10. Andrew M. Greeley, *The Catholic Imagination* (Berkeley: University of California Press, 2000), 39–52.

11. For more on sacramentality, see Richard P. McBrien, *Catholicism*, rev. ed. (San Francisco, CA: Harper San Francisco, 1994).

12. For more on sacramentalism and the Catholic Imagination, see Robert A. Orsi, "'The Infant of Prague's Nightie': The Devotional Origins of Contemporary Catholic Memory," *U.S. Catholic Historian* 21, no. 2 (2003): 1–18; Stephen Schloesser, "The Unbearable Lightness of Being: Re-Sourcing Catholic Intellectual Traditions," *Cross Currents* 58, no. 1 (2008): 65–94.

13. Andrew Greeley, "Why They Stay," in *The Catholic Revolution: New Wine, Old Wineskins, and the Second Vatican Council* (Berkeley: University of California Press, 2004), 108.

14. James M. O'Toole, *The Faithful: A History of Catholics in America* (Cambridge, MA: Harvard University Press, 2009), 147–48.

15. Karen J. Johnson, *One in Christ: Chicago Catholics and the Quest for Interracial Justice* (New York: Oxford University Press, 2018), 54.

16. Johnson, *One in Christ*.

17. Peters, *Catonsville Nine*, 39–40.

18. Michael S. Foley, *Confronting the War Machine: Draft Resistance during the Vietnam War* (Chapel Hill: University of North Carolina Press, 2003), 35.

19. Foley, *Confronting the War Machine*, 39.

20. L. M. Baskir and W. A. Strauss, *Chance and Circumstance: The Draft, the War, and the Vietnam Generation* (New York: Knopf, 1978), 30–31. See also "U.S. Military Service and LGBT Policy," *The Oxford Encyclopedia of LGBT Politics and Policy* (New York: Oxford University Press, 2021).

21. Foley, *Confronting the War Machine*, 36.

22. Foley, *Confronting the War Machine*, 50–54.

23. Foley, *Confronting the War Machine*, 21–22.

24. Foley, *Confronting the War Machine*, 43.

25. Foley, *Confronting the War Machine*, 41.

26. Foley, *Confronting the War Machine*, 349.

27. Baskir and Strauss, *Chance and Circumstance*, 9.

28. Baskir and Strauss, *Chance and Circumstance*, 10.

29. Foley, *Confronting the War Machine*, 38.

30. Baskir and Strauss, *Chance and Circumstance*, 14–15.

31. Baskir and Strauss, *Chance and Circumstance*, 27.

32. Baskir and Strauss, *Chance and Circumstance*, 14–15, 27; Peter Shapiro, "Freshman Deferments End as Nixon Signs New Draft Legislation," *Harvard Crimson*, September 29, 1971.

33. Baskir and Strauss, *Chance and Circumstance*, 67–69.

34. Baskir and Strauss, *Chance and Circumstance*, 78.

35. Foley, *Confronting the War Machine*, 364.

36. Peters, *Catonsville Nine*, 108–10.

37. Peters, *Catonsville Nine*, 116.

38. Peters, *Catonsville Nine*, 116.

39. "Musings from Baltimore City Jail," *Commonweal*, November 17, 1967, https://www.commonwealmagazine.org/musings-baltimore-city-jail.

40. Peters, *Catonsville Nine*, 121.

41. Peters, *Catonsville Nine*, 121.

42. John Deedy, "News and Views," *Commonweal*, June 1, 1968.

43. "Vietnam War" (Letter to the Editor), *Criterion*, November 3, 1967, 3, quoted in Penelope Moon, "Loyal Sons and Daughters of God," *Peace & Change* 33, no. 1 (January 2008): 10.

44. Moon, "Loyal Sons and Daughters of God," 8.

45. "Walker Percy," *Commonweal*, September 4, 1971, 431, quoted in Peters, *Catonsville Nine*, 124.

46. Augustine, *City of God*, 19.13.1.

47. Augustine's political *Contra Faustum Manichaeum*, penned around 400 CE, stands as the main text from which theologians have developed his theories of just warfare into doctrine. He continued to develop these theories in *City of God*. For more on Augustine's theories regarding just war, see John Langan, "The Elements of St. Augustine's Just War Theory," *Journal of Religious Ethics* 12, no. 1 (1984): 19–38.

48. See Thomas Aquinas, *Summa Theologica*, II of II, q. 40, a. 1. American bishops updated the criteria for just warfare in a 1983 pastoral letter. See National Conference of Catholic Bishops, *The Challenge of Peace: God's Promise and Our Response: A Pastoral Letter on War and Peace: Summary*, May 3, 1983, https://www.usccb.org/upload/challenge-peace-gods-promise-our-response-1983.pdf. For a recent theological justification of war, see Nigel Biggar, *In Defence of War* (Oxford: Oxford University Press, 2013).

49. See Andrew Preston, *Sword of the Spirit, Shield of Faith: Religion in American War and Diplomacy* (New York: Knopf Doubleday Publishing Group, 2012).

50. Preston, *Sword of the Spirit*.

NOTES TO PAGES 25–28

51. John J Burke, "Special Catholic Activities in War Service," *Annals of the American Academy of Political and Social Science* 79, no. 1 (1918): 213.

52. "Background: On American Catholics and World War One," American Catholic History Classroom, American Catholic History Research Center and University Archives, Catholic University of America, accessed May 13, 2022, http://cuomeka.wrlc.org/exhibits/show/american-catholic-participatio/catholics-wwi.

53. Patricia McNeal, "Catholic Conscientious Objection during World War II," *Catholic Historical Review* 61, no. 2 (1975):\, 226.

54. McNeal, "Catholic Conscientious Objection," 226.

55. Isaiah 2:4 (New International Version [NIV]); Matthew 5:9 (NIV).

56. For more on peace churches, see Albert N. Keim and Grant M. Stoltzfus, *The Politics of Conscience: The Historic Peace Churches and America at War, 1917–1955* (Eugene, OR: Wipf and Stock, 2000); and Lisa Sowle Cahill, *Blessed Are the Peacemakers: Pacifism, Just War, and Peacebuilding* (Minneapolis, MN: Fortress Press, 2019), chap. 8, "A Witness for the Kingdom: Humanist, Anabaptist, and Quaker Pacifists," 247–82.

57. Joseph Kip Kosek, *Acts of Conscience: Christian Nonviolence and Modern American Democracy*, Columbia Studies in Contemporary American History (New York: Columbia University Press, 2009), 2.

58. Polner and O'Grady, *Disarmed and Dangerous*, 119.

59. Paul VI, *Address of the Holy Father Paul VI to the United Nations* (October 4, 1965), Vatican Website https://www.vatican.va/content/paul-vi/en/speeches/1965/documents/hf_p-vi_spe_19651004_united-nations.html.

60. Paul VI, *Christi Matri*, papal encyclical, September 15, 1966, Vatican Website, https://www.vatican.va/content/paul-vi/en/encyclicals/documents/hf_p-vi_enc_15091966_christi-matri.html.

61. "Roman Catholics: The Pastor Executive," *Time*, May 15, 1964, https://content.time.com/time/subscriber/article/0,33009,871039,00.html.

62. For more on American pluralism in this period see Richard Steele, "The War on Intolerance: The Reformulation of American Nationalism, 1939–1941," *Journal of American Ethnic History* 9, no. 1 (October 1989): 9–35.

63. Colleen McDannell, *The Spirit of Vatican II: A History of Catholic Reform in America* (New York: Basic Books, 2011), 35.

64. James H. Cone, *A Black Theology of Liberation*, 20th anniversary ed., Twentieth Century Religious Thought (Maryknoll, NY: Orbis Books, 1990); James H. Cone, *Risks of Faith: The Emergence of a Black Theology of Liberation, 1968–1998* (Boston, MA: Beacon Press, 1999).

65. McDannell, *Spirit of Vatican II*, 36.

66. Will Herberg, *Protestant, Catholic, Jew: An Essay in American Religious Sociology* (Garden City, NY: Doubleday, 1955); Kevin Michael Schultz, *Tri-Faith America How*

Catholics and Jews Held Postwar America to Its Protestant Promise (Oxford: Oxford University Press, 2011).

67. James Carroll, *An American Requiem: God, My Father, and the War That Came between Us* (New York: Houghton Mifflin Harcourt, 1997); "Roman Catholics: The Pastor Executive," *Time*, May 15, 1964; Thomas J. Shelley, "Slouching toward the Center: Cardinal Francis Spellman, Archbishop Paul J. Hallinan and American Catholicism in the 1960s," *U.S. Catholic Historian* 17, no. 4 (1999): 28, 32, 34; "Vatican II Re-educates the American Bishops," *New York Times*, November 22, 1964; "Francis Joseph Cardinal Spellman (1889–1967)," Eleanor Roosevelt Papers Project, accessed May 14, 2022, https://erpapers.columbian.gwu.edu/francis-joseph-cardinal-spellman-1889-1967.

68. Ross Labrie, "Contemplation and Action in Thomas Merton," *Christianity & Literature* 55, no. 4 (2006): 475; Paul Elie, *The Life You Save May Be Your Own* (New York: Farrar, Strauss and Giroux, 2003), 405–10.

69. Labrie, "Contemplation and Action," 475.

70. "Work Hard and Pray Hard: On Dorothy Day and Thomas Merton," *U.S. Catholic* 76, no. 11 (November 2011): 18–21.

71. Patrick F. O'Connell, "Peace," in *Merton Encyclopedia*, ed. William H. Shannon, Christine M. Bochen, and Patrick F. O'Connell (Maryknoll, NY: Orbis Books), 354–55.

72. Thomas Merton, *Thomas Merton on Peace* (New York: McCall Publishing, 1971), 13.

73. Thomas Merton, *Raids on the Unspeakable* (New York: New Directions, 1966), 45–47.

74. Elie, *The Life You Save*, 405.

75. Gordon Oyer, *Pursuing the Spiritual Roots of Protest: Merton, Berrigan, Yoder, and Muste at the Gethsemani Abbey Peacemakers Retreat* (Eugene, OR: Cascade Books, 2014), 27.

76. Oyer, *Pursuing the Spiritual Roots of Protest*, 28–40.

77. Oyer, *Pursuing the Spiritual Roots of Protest*, 35–36, 43.

78. Polner and O'Grady, *Disarmed and Dangerous*, 21–66.

79. Polner and O'Grady, *Disarmed and Dangerous*, 21–66.

80. Oyer, *Pursuing the Spiritual Roots of Protest*, 27.

81. Oyer, *Pursuing the Spiritual Roots of Protest*, 135.

82. Daniel Berrigan, *The Bow in the Clouds: Man's Covenant with God* (New York: Coward-McCann, 1961), 102.

83. The USCCB lists the church's social justice principles on its website, United States Conference of Catholic Bishops, "Seven Themes of Catholic Social Teaching," 2023, https://www.usccb.org/beliefs-and-teachings/what-we-believe/catholic-social-teaching/seven-themes-of-catholic-social-teaching.

84. Pope Leo XIII, "*Rerum novarum*," Vatican Website (Vatican, May 15, 1891), accessed May 13, 2022, http://www.vatican.va/holy_father/leo_xiii/encyclicals/documents/hf_l-xiii_enc_15051891_rerum-novarum_en.html.

85. See Thomas Massaro SJ, *Living Justice: Catholic Social Teaching in Action* (New York: Rowman and Littlefield, 2008).

86. James J. Farrell, "Dorothy Day and the Sixties," *Records of the American Catholic Historical Society of Philadelphia* 108, nos. 1–2 (1997): 30.

87. For more on the Catholic church and progressive politics in the United States, see Robert D. Cross, *The Emergence of Liberal Catholicism in America* (Cambridge, MA: Harvard University Press, 1958). For more on the history of liberal Christianity after World War II, see Leilah Danielson, *American Gandhi: A. J. Muste and the History of Radicalism in the Twentieth Century* (Philadelphia: University of Pennsylvania Press, 2014); Leilah Danielson, Marian Mollin, and Doug Rossinow, eds., *The Religious Left in Modern America: Doorkeepers of a Radical Faith* (London: Springer International Publishing, 2018); Sean T. Dempsey, *City of Dignity: Christianity, Liberalism, and the Making of Global Los Angeles* (Chicago: University of Chicago Press, 2023); Mark Wild, *Renewal: Liberal Protestants and the American City after World War II* (Chicago: University of Chicago Press, 2019); and Douglas Charles Rossinow, *Visions of Progress: The Left-Liberal Tradition in America* (Philadelphia: University of Pennsylvania Press, 2008).

88. Walter Rauschenbusch, *A Theology for the Social Gospel*, Apex Books, E7 (New York: Abingdon Press, 1917), 4–5.

89. E. L. Fortin, "'Sacred and Inviolable': *Rerum Novarum* and Natural Rights," *Theological Studies* (Baltimore) 53, no. 2 (1992): 223.

90. Mark Edward Ruff, *The Battle for the Catholic Past in Germany, 1945–1980* (Cambridge: Cambridge University Press, 2017).

91. James Chappel, *Catholic Modern: The Challenge of Totalitarianism and the Remaking of the Church* (Cambridge, MA: Harvard University Press, 2018), 100–102.

92. The Editors, "In the Face of the World's Crisis," *Commonweal*, August 21, 1942, https://www.commonwealmagazine.org/face-worlds-crisis; John T McGreevy, *Catholicism and American Freedom: A History* (New York: W. W. Norton, 2003), 201–2.

93. John T McGreevy, *Parish Boundaries: The Catholic Encounter with Race in the Twentieth-Century Urban North* (Chicago: University of Chicago Press, 1996), 204–6.

CHAPTER TWO

1. Dorothy Day, "On Pilgrimage," *Catholic Worker*, April 1, 1968, 1, 6, https://catholicworker.org/252-html/; 1 Corinthians 15:31 (NIV).

2. John Loughery and Blythe Randolph, *Dorothy Day: Dissenting Voice of the American Century* (New York: Simon & Schuster, 2020), 36–72.

3. For more on Dorothy Day and the Catholic Worker movement, see Patrick G. Coy, *A Revolution of the Heart: Essays on the Catholic Worker* (Philadelphia: Temple University Press, 1988); Dorothy Day, *The Duty of Delight: The Diaries of Dorothy Day* (Milwaukee, WI: Marquette University Press, 2008); Paul Elie, *The Life You Save May Be Your Own: An American Pilgrimage* (New York: Farrar, Straus and Giroux, 2004); Jim Forest, *All Is*

216   NOTES TO PAGES 39–42

Grace: A Biography of Dorothy Day (Maryknoll, NY: Orbis Books, 2011); Kate Hennessy, *Dorothy Day: The World Will Be Saved by Beauty: An Intimate Portrait of My Grandmother* (Simon & Schuster, 2017); Anne Klejment; *American Catholic Pacifism: The Influence of Dorothy Day and the Catholic Worker Movement* (Westport, CT: Praeger, 1996); Anne Klejment and Nancy Roberts, "The Catholic Worker and the Vietnam War," in *American Catholic Pacifism: The Influence of Dorothy Day and the Catholic Worker Movement*, ed. Anne Klejment and Nancy Roberts (London: Praeger, 1996), 153–70; Anne Klejment, "Dorothy Day and César Chávez: American Catholic Lives in Nonviolence," *U.S. Catholic Historian* 29, no. 3 (2011): 67–90; Anne Klejment, "The Spirituality of Dorothy Day's Pacifism," *U.S. Catholic Historian* 27, no. 2 (2009): 1–24; Mel Piehl, *Breaking Bread: The Catholic Worker and the Origin of Catholic Radicalism in America* (Philadelphia: Temple University Press, 1982); John Loughery and Blythe Randolph, *Dorothy Day: Dissenting Voice of the American Century* (New York: Simon & Schuster, 2020); Nancy Roberts, *Dorothy Day and the Catholic Worker* (Albany, NY: SUNY Press, 1985).

4. Loughery and Randolph, *Dorothy Day*, 149–67.

5. Dorothy Day, "We Go On Record: CW Refuses Tax Exemption," *Catholic Worker*, May 1972, https://www.catholicworker.org/dorothyday/articles/191.html.

6. Loughery and Randolph, *Dorothy Day*, 192–95.

7. Loughery and Randolph, *Dorothy Day*, 160.

8. The *Catholic Worker* first started articulating its radical pacifism through articles about the civil war in Spain. Most Catholics in the United States and Europe supported the fascist president Francisco Franco and viewed the conflict as a battle between the Christian world and communism. The *Catholic Worker* remained neutral and pacifist on the issue. Then Dorothy Day directly criticized the U.S. entry into World War II, arguing that the church's teaching demanded peace in all circumstances.

9. Loughery and Randolph, *Dorothy Day*, 213–26; Sandra Yocum Mize, "'We Are Still Pacifists': Dorothy Day's Pacifism during World War II," *Records of the American Catholic Historical Society of Philadelphia* 108, nos. 1–2 (1997): 7.

10. Dee Garrison, *Bracing for Armageddon: Why Civil Defense Never Worked* (Oxford: Oxford University Press, 2006). See also Laura McEnaney, *Civil Defense Begins at Home* (Princeton, NJ: Princeton University Press, 2000).

11. Mel Piehl, *Breaking Bread: The Catholic Worker and the Origin of Catholic Radicalism in America* (Philadelphia: Temple University Press, 1982), 85.

12. Loughery and Randolph, *Dorothy Day*, 263–67.

13. Dorothy Day, "Theophane Venard and Ho Chi Minh," *Catholic Worker*, May 1954, 1, 6.

14. Day, "Theophane Venard," 2.

15. Paul Harvey, "Civil Rights Movements and Religion in America," *Oxford Research Encyclopedia: Religion*, 2018, https://oxfordre.com/religion/view/10.1093/acrefore/9780199340378.001.0001/acrefore-9780199340378-e-492. For a history of Black nuns in

the civil rights movement, see Shannen Dee Williams, *Subversive Habits: Black Catholic Nuns in the Long African American Freedom Struggle* (Durham, NC: Duke University Press, 2022).

16. Raj Dhananjay and Rityusha Mani Tiwary, "Gandhi and Satyagraha—A Quest for Global Transformation: A Review Essay on the International Seminar," *Social Change* 51, no. 1 (2021): 121–33.

17. Stanley Rowland Jr., "2,500 Here Hail Boycott Leader; Head of Montgomery Negro Bus Protest Gets Hero's Welcome in Brooklyn," *New York Times*, March 26, 1956.

18. Dorothy Day, *Catholic Worker*, June 1967, https://www.catholicworker.org/dorothyday/articles/853.pdf.

19. Bill Wylie-Kellermann, "'An Act of Prayer': Dorothy Day's Influence on Daniel Berrigan (and Even Vice Versa)," *Radical Discipleship* (blog), November 29, 2021, https://radicaldiscipleship.net/2021/11/29/an-act-of-prayer-dorothy-days-influence -on-daniel-berrigan-and-even-vice-versa/#_edn20; Daniel Berrigan, *To Dwell in Peace* (San Francisco: Harper & Row, 1986), 71.

20. Wylie-Kellermann, "An Act of Prayer"; Jim Forest, *At Play in the Lion's Den* (Maryknoll, NY: Orbis Books, 2017), 40.

21. Wylie-Kellermann, "An Act of Prayer"; Forest, *At Play in the Lion's Den*, 121.

22. Wylie-Kellermann, "An Act of Prayer"; Anne Klejment, "War Resistance and Property Destruction," in *A Revolution of the Heart*, ed. Patrick Coy (Philadelphia: Temple University Press, 1988), 285.

23. See Bryan Burrough, *Days of Rage: America's Radical Underground, the FBI, and the Forgotten Age of Revolutionary Violence* (New York: Penguin Press, 2015).

24. P. Murray Polner and Jim O'Grady, *Disarmed and Dangerous: The Radical Lives and Times of Daniel and Philip Berrigan* (New York: Basic Books, 1997), 171.

25. Christine Emba, "This Is What White Privilege Is," *Washington Post*, January 22, 2023, https://www.washingtonpost.com/opinions/this-is-what-white-privilege-is/2016/01/22/57166c72-c093-11e5-83d4-42e3bceea902_story.html.

26. Ann Walsh, interview by author, February 14, 2022, 7.

27. For a history of the Josephites, see Diane Batts Morrow, "'Undoubtedly a Bad State of Affairs': The Oblate Sisters of Providence and the Josephite Fathers, 1877–1903," *Journal of African American History* 101, no. 3 (2016): 266–68.

28. Martin Luther King Jr., *Letter from Birmingham Jail* (London: Penguin Books, 2018).

29. Paul Murray, "54 Miles to Freedom: Catholics Were Prominent in 1965 Selma March," *National Catholic Reporter*, March 7, 2015, https://www.ncronline.org/news/justice/54-miles-freedom-catholics-were-prominent-1965-selma-march.

30. Shawn Michael Peters, *The Catonsville Nine* (Oxford University Press, 2012), 227.

31. Bob Good, interview by author, December 6, 2017, 8.

32. Peters, *Catonsville Nine*, 168.

33. Peters, *Catonsville Nine*, chaps. 14–17.

34. Peters, *Catonsville Nine*, 264–66.

35. Charles A. Meconis, *With Clumsy Grace: The American Catholic Left, 1961–1975* (New York: Seabury Press, 1979); Hillel Arnold, "Draft Board Raids," accessed May 18, 2023, http://hillelarnold.com/draft-board-raids/.

36. Jim Boyle, "Nearly Fifty Years Later Draft Protestor Has No Regrets," *Elk River* (Minnesota) *Star News*, March 7, 2014, https://www.hometownsource.com/elk_river _star_news/news/local/nearly-years-later-draft-protestor-has-no-regrets/article _a55ee516-e0fa-507a-98ae-bf3b6f4e1587.html.

37. Meconis, *With Clumsy Grace*, 54–55.

38. Meconis, *With Clumsy Grace*, 54–55.

39. R. G. Riegle, *Crossing the Line: Nonviolent Resisters Speak Out for Peace* (Eugene, OR: Wipf & Stock Publishers, 2013), 100.

40. Sara Evans, *Personal Politics: The Roots of Women's Liberation in the Civil Rights Movement and the New Left*, 2nd ed. (New York: Vintage, 1980), 105–25.

41. Marian Mollin, *Radical Pacificism in Modern America: Egalitarianism and Protest* (Philadelphia: University of Pennsylvania Press, 2006), 173.

42. Robert Orsi, "U.S. Catholics Between Memory and Modernity," in *Catholics in the American Century: Recasting Narratives of U.S. History*, ed. R. Scott Appleby and Kathleen Sprows Cummings (Ithaca, NY: Cornell University Press, 2012), 37.

43. Polner and O'Grady, *Disarmed and Dangerous*, 246.

44. Mollin, *Radical Pacifism*, 172–73.

45. Mollin, *Radical Pacifism*, 176–77.

46. Marian Mollin, "Women's Struggles with the American Radical Pacifist Movement," *History Compass* 7, no. 3 (2009): 1079.

47. Polner and O'Grady, *Disarmed and Dangerous*, 246.

48. Polner and O'Grady, *Disarmed and Dangerous*, 170.

49. Daniel Berrigan, *The Berrigan Letters: Personal Correspondence between Daniel and Philip Berrigan*, ed. Daniel Cossachi and Eric J. Martin (Maryknoll: Orbis Books, 2016), 143–44.

50. Peters, *Catonsville Nine*, 57–68.

51. Peters, *Catonsville Nine*, 57–68.

52. Peters, *Catonsville Nine*, 72–73.

53. Peters, *Catonsville Nine*, 73–74.

54. For more on *aggiornamento* and the impact of Vatican II, see John W. O'Malley, "Vatican II: Did Anything Happen?," *Theological Studies* 67 (2006), 13–14.

55. Amy L. Koehlinger, *The New Nuns: Racial Justice and Religious Reform in the 1960s* (Cambridge, MA: Harvard University Press, 2007), 9.

56. Angelyn Dries, "Living in Ambiguity: A Paradigm Shift Experienced by the Sister Formation Movement," *Catholic Historical Review* 79, no. 3 (July 1993): 478–79.

NOTES TO PAGES 53–57

57. Eileen Egan, "The Struggle of Pax," in *American Catholic Pacifism: The Influence of Dorothy Day and the Catholic Worker Movement,* ed. Anne Klejment and Dorothy L. Roberts (Westport, CT: Praeger, 1996), 129.

58. Susan Fitzpatrick-Behrens, *The Maryknoll Catholic Mission in Peru, 1943–1989: Transnational Faith and Transformation* (South Bend, IN: University of Notre Dame Press, 2012); Colleen Doody, *Detroit's Cold War: The Origins of Postwar Conservatism* (Urbana-Champagne: University of Illinois Press, 2013); Michelle Nickerson, *Mothers of Conservatism: Women and the Postwar Right* (Princeton, NJ: Princeton University Press, 2012).

59. Richard McBrien, "Women Religious' Embrace of Vatican II Change Commendable," *National Catholic Reporter* 21 (November 2011), https://www.ncronline.org/blogs/essays-theology/women-religious-embrace-vatican-ii-change-commendable; Sara Ludewig, "In the Habit of Resistance," *American Catholic Studies* 133, no. 1 (Spring 2022): 1–26.

60. John XXIII, *Perfectae Caritatis,* Encyclical Letter, Vatican Website, October 28, 1965, https://www.vatican.va/archive/hist_councils/ii_vatican_council/documents/vat-ii_decree_19651028_perfectae-caritatis_en.html. See points 2a, 2b, 2c, and 3.

61. Ludewig, "Habit of Resistance," 5.

62. Letter from Mary Cain to the Maryland Province of Sisters of Notre Dame de Namur, October 24, 1969, Sister Mary Hayes Papers, Trinity Washington University Archives, as cited in Ludewig, "Habit of Resistance," 11.

CHAPTER THREE

1. Robert Orsi, *The Madonna of 115th Street: Faith and Community in Italian Harlem, 1880–1959* (New Haven, CT: Yale University Press, 1985).

2. Orsi, *Madonna of 115th Street,* 75–106.

3. Leslie Woodcock Tentler, *American Catholics: A History* (New Haven, CT: Yale University Press, 2020), 230–35.

4. John T. McGreevy, *Parish Boundaries: The Catholic Encounter with Race in the Twentieth-Century Urban North* (Chicago: University of Chicago Press, 1996), 19.

5. Michael Joseph Schuck, *That They Be One: The Social Teaching of the Papal Encyclicals, 1740–1989* (Washington, DC: Georgetown University Press, 1991), 181–83.

6. Orsi, *Madonna of 115th Street,* 83.

7. Franz Jägerstätter, Erna Putz, and Robert Anthony Krieg, *Letters and Writings from Prison* (Maryknoll, NY: Orbis Books, 2009).

8. Gordon C. Zahn, *In Solitary Witness: The Life and Death of Franz Jägerstätter* (New York: Holt, Rinehart and Winston, 1965).

9. Benjamin T. Peters, "A Completely Fresh Reappraisal of War: Americanism, Radicalism, and the Catholic Pacifism of Gordon Zahn," *American Catholic Studies* 128, no. 4 (2017): 1–27.

10. Francine du Plessix Gray, "The Ultra-Resistance," *New York Review of Books,*

September 25, 1969, reprinted in Jim and Nancy Forest, "The Ultra-Resistance: On the Trial of the Milwaukee 14," November 18, 2006, https://jimandnancyforest.com/2006/11/m14trial/.

11. Joan Cook, "The Troubled, Uneasy World of the Women in the Berrigan Case," *New York Times*, May 26, 1971, https://www.nytimes.com/1971/05/26/archives/the-troubled-uneasy-world-of-the-women-in-the-berrigan-case.html.

12. Joan Reilly, interview by author, July 22, 2014, 6.

13. Joan Reilly, interview, 5–6.

14. Marian Mollin, "Communities of Resistance: Women and the Catholic Left of the Late 1960s," *Oral History Review* 31, no. 2 (Summer–Autumn 2004): 39.

15. Mollin, "Communities of Resistance," 40.

16. Eleanor Blau, "Woodstock Jesuit College Here, Experimental Seminary, to Shut," *New York Times*, January 9, 1973; Peter McDonough, *Men Astutely Trained: A History of the Jesuits in the American Century* (New York: Free Press, 1992), 153–56; Jerry Filteau, "Woodstock Theological Center to Close in June," *National Catholic Reporter*, February 15, 2003, https://www.ncronline.org/news/theology/woodstock-theological-center-close-june; "The Jesuits' Search for a New Identity," *Time*, January 10, 2008. https://content.time.com/time/subscriber/article/0,33009,945242,00.html.

17. Blau, "Woodstock Jesuit College." See also Peter McDonough, "Metamorphoses of the Jesuits: Sexual Identity, Gender Roles, and Hierarchy in Catholicism," *Comparative Studies in Society and History* 32, no. 2 (1990): 325–56.

18. George Mische, "Oral History Interviews of the Vietnam Era Oral History Project," Minnesota Historical Society, 2019, St. Paul, Minnesota, 15; Shawn Michael Peters, *The Catonsville Nine* (Oxford University Press, 2012), 57–58.

19. John Swinglish, interview by Anthony Giacchino, March 8, 1998, 10, Anthony Giacchino Camden 28 [Motion Picture] Collection, Swarthmore College Peace Collection, Swarthmore, PA.

20. Swinglish, interview.

21. Bob Begin, interview by Naomi Randt, Protest Voices Oral History Project, July 21, 2016, https://engagedscholarship.csuohio.edu/crohc000/769/; Michael O'Malley, "The Rev. Bob Begin, Known as the Rebel Priest, Wins His Latest Battle to Keep St. Colman Church Open," *Plain Dealer*, June 16, 2009, https://www.cleveland.com/metro/2009/06/the_rev_bob_begin_know_as_the.html.

22. Bob Good, interview by author, December 6, 2017, 10.

23. Robert Williamson, "Janitor's Closet," unpublished memoir, n.d.; italics in the original.

24. Robert Williamson, interview by author, December 6, 2015, 8.

25. Kathy C, *My Life as the Spouse of a Member of the Philadelphia Resistance, WITF Stories*, May 5, 2017, https://vietnam.witf.org/my-life-as-the-spouse-of-a-member-of-the-philadelphia-resistance/.

26. Terry Buckalew, interview by author, July 3, 2020, p. 22.

27. Keith Forsyth, interview by author, August 14, 2017, 4, 7.

28. Forsyth, interview, 9–10.

29. Forsyth, interview, 10.

30. Paul Couming, interview by author, January 26, 2022.

31. Beth Healy, "Those Nuns Left the Convent But Never Each Other," *Boston Globe Magazine*, October 16, 2016, https://www3.bostonglobe.com/magazine/2016/10/16/?arc404=true.

32. Couming, interview, 1.

33. Couming, interview, 1–2; "The Jesuits Search for a New Identity," *Time*, April 23, 2003, accessed via Internet Archive, https://web.archive.org/web/20080111214616/http://www.time.com/time/magazine/article/0,9171,945242-1,00.html.

34. Bill Ayers, *Fugitive Days: Memoirs of an Antiwar Activist* (Boston: Beacon Press, 2009), 111.

35. Ayers, *Fugitive Days*, 110.

36. Anne Dunham and Frank Pommersheim, interview by author, March 3, 2020, 47.

37. Dunham and Pommersheim, interview, 46–47.

38. For a discussion of priest-nun marriages, see Peter Manseau, "When 'Priest Weds Nun,'" *New York Times*, August 31, 2019.

39. Mike Newall, "After Nearly a Half Century of Service, an Activist Turned City Honcho Walks Away, Hopeful," *Philadelphia Inquirer*, January 9, 2019, https://www.inquirer.com/news/columnists/mike-diberardinis-rebuild-soda-tax-ed-rendell-jim-kenney-parks-and-rec-philadelphia-20190109.html; Joan Reilly, interview by author, 7.

40. Ann Walsh, interview by author, February 14, 2022, 4.

41. Sara Ludewig, "In the Habit of Resistance," *American Catholic Studies* 133, no. 1 (Spring 2022): 12.

42. Ludewig, "Habit of Resistance," 15.

43. See also William O'Rourke, *The Harrisburg 7 and the New Catholic Left*, 40th anniversary ed. (Notre Dame, IN: University of Notre Dame Press, 2012).

44. O'Rourke, *Harrisburg 7*, 186–98.

45. P. Murray Polner and Jim O'Grady, *Disarmed and Dangerous: The Radical Lives and Times of Daniel and Philip Berrigan* (New York: Basic Books, 1997), 158–59, 253–54, 281–83.

46. "Marriage of Philip Berrigan to Sister Elizabeth Reported," *New York Times*, May 29, 1973, https://www.nytimes.com/1973/05/29/archives/marriage-of-philip-berrigan-to-sister-elizabeth-reported.html.

47. Sharon Erickson Nepstad, *Religion and War Resistance in the Plowshares Movement* (New York: Cambridge University Press, 2008), 52.

48. Daniel Berrigan, *Widen the Prison Gates: Writing from Jails* (New York: Simon and Shuster, 1973), 124.

49. Harry Cargas, "An Interview with Elizabeth McAlister," *Commonweal*, October 15, 1972, https://www.commonwealmagazine.org/interview-elizabeth-mcalister-1971.

50. Cargas, "Interview with Elizabeth McAlister."

51. Peter Cajka, *Follow Your Conscience: The Catholic Church and the Spirit of the Sixties* (Chicago: University of Chicago Press, 2021), 5.

52. Paul Vitello, "Paul Mayer, 82, Ex-Priest and Peace Activist, Dies," *New York Times*, November 29, 2013, https://www.nytimes.com/2013/11/30/nyregion/paul-mayer-82-ex-priest-and-peace-activist-dies.html.

53. Vitello, "Paul Mayer."

54. Lianne Moccia, interview by author, July 14, 2020, 19.

55. Polner and O'Grady, *Disarmed and Dangerous*, 240.

56. Gordon Oyer, *Pursuing the Spiritual Roots of Protest: Merton, Berrigan, Yoder, and Muste at the Gethsemani Abbey Peacemakers Retreat* (Eugene, OR: Cascade Books, 2014), 14–15.

57. Polner and O'Grady, *Disarmed and Dangerous*, 240–41.

58. Oyer, *Spiritual Roots of Protest*, 47.

59. Walsh, interview, 10.

60. Walsh, interview, 11.

PART TWO

1. Eugene Dixon, interview by author, January 25, 2018, 19.

2. Dixon, interview, 19.

3. "New Jersey Turnpike History," New Jersey Turnpike Authority, accessed June 4, 2023, http://www.njturnpikewidening.com/history.php; New Jersey Department of Transportation, "*Official Map of New Jersey* (H. M. Gousha Company, ca. 1960).

CHAPTER FOUR

1. Cookie Ridolfi, interview by author, December 3, 2020, 6–7.

2. "Jersey Raids: Draft Action 'Confessed,'" *Catholic Advocate*, February 25, 1971, Catholic Research Resources Alliance, https://thecatholicnewsarchive.org/?a=d&d=ca19710225-01.1.1&; Edward McGowan, *Peace Warriors: The Story of the Camden 28* (Nyack, NY: Circumstantial Productions Publishing, 2001), 22.

3. McGowan, *Peace Warriors*, 22. Eugene Dixon, interview with Anthony Giacchino, n.d., 9–10, Anthony Giacchino Camden 28 [Motion Picture] Collection, Swarthmore College Peace Collection, Swarthmore, PA (hereafter Giacchino Collection), 9–10.

4. Dixon, interview by author, 7.

5. Mark Oppenheimer, *Knocking on Heaven's Door: American Religion in the Age of Counterculture* (New Haven, CT: Yale University Press, 2003), 62, 80–81.

6. Dixon, interview by Giacchino, 19.

NOTES TO PAGES 76–79   223

7. Dixon, interview by author, 5.

8. Dixon, interview by Giacchino, 5–6.

9. Dixon, interview by Giacchino, 5.

10. Jeffry Dorwart, *Camden County, New Jersey: The Making of a Metropolitan Community, 1626–2000* (New Brunswick, NJ: Rutgers University Press, 2001), 97.

11. Jefferson Cowie, *Capital Moves: RCA's Seventy-Year Quest for Cheap Labor* (Ithaca, NY: Cornell University Press, 2019), 17–18.

12. Howard Gillette, *Camden after the Fall: Decline and Renewal in a Post-Industrial City* (Philadelphia: University of Pennsylvania Press, 2005), 24.

13. Dorwart, *Camden County*, 140; New York Shipbuilding Corporation, "List of Contracts," accessed July 3, 2023, https://newyorkship.org/ships/#more-9.

14. New York Shipbuilding Corporation, "A Shipbuilding Legacy: List of Contracts," accessed September 29, 2023, https://newyorkship.org/ships/#more-9.

15. Gillette, *Camden after the Fall*, 11; Camden County Road Map, 1965, Rutgers University Special Collections and Archives, accessed May 22, 2022, https://mapmaker.rutgers.edu/CAMDEN_COUNTY/CamdenHighway1965_3.gif.

16. U.S. Census Bureau, "1950 Census of Population, Detailed Characteristics, New Jersey," Table 87, 30.263, accessed July 3, 2023, https://www2.census.gov/library/publications/decennial/1950/population-volume-2/23024255v2p30ch2.pdf.

17. Laurie Lahey, "'The Grassy Battleground': Race, Religion, and Activism in Camden's 'Wide' Civil Rights Movement," *ProQuest Dissertations and Theses* (PhD diss., George Washington University, 2013), 12, 41.

18. U.S. Census Bureau, "1970 Census—Subject Reports: Puerto Ricans in the United States (June 1973)," Report PC(2)-1E, June 1973, 103, https://www.census.gov/library/publications/1973/dec/pc-2-1e.html.

19. Gillette, *Camden after the Fall*, 42.

20. Cowie, *Capital Moves*, 33.

21. For the redlining maps of Camden, NJ, from the 1930s, see "Mapping Inequality: Redlining in New Deal America," 2023, https://dsl.richmond.edu/panorama/redlining/#loc=12/39.924/-75.072&city=camden-nj; see also "Why Minorities in N.J. Are More Likely to Be Denied Mortgages, Explained," NJ.com, February 2018, https://www.nj.com/data/2018/02/modern-day_redlining_how_some_nj_residents_are_bei.html. For more on the history of housing discrimination and its relationship to racial discrimination in the United States, see David Freund, *Colored Property: State Policy and White Racial Politics in Suburban America* (Chicago: University of Chicago Press, 2007).

22. Edward C. Burks, "Camden: An Exodus of Whites," *New York Times*, June 25, 1972; U.S. Census Bureau, "1970 Census—Subject Reports: Puerto Ricans in the United States."

23. Burks, "Camden"; Gillette, *Camden after the Fall*, 48.

224   NOTES TO PAGES 79–85

24. Gillette, *Camden after the Fall*, 177–82.

25. Lahey, "Grassy Battleground," 7.

26. Lahey, "Grassy Battleground," 7.

27. Lahey, "Grassy Battleground," 178, 205.

28. Lahey, "Grassy Battleground," 177.

29. Gualberto Medina, interview by author, July 7, 2015, 18.

30. Lahey, "'Grassy Battleground"; Gillette, *Camden after the Fall*, 86–87.

31. Medina, interview, 18.

32. Gillette, *Camden after the Fall*, 85–86; Patrolman Gary Miller was indicted again in 1974 for excessive force. "Five Camden Police Indicted for Two Assaults on Black," *New York Times*, June 4, 1974. https://www.nytimes.com/1974/06/04/archives/5-camden -police-indicted-for-2-assaults-on-blacks-none-hurt.html. For more on the death of Raphael Gonzales, see Pedro A. Regalado, "Previous Grievances," *Camden Riots Research Project* (blog), July 24, 2013, http://camdenriots.blogspot.com/2013/07/the-chaos-that -puerto-rican-riots-story.html.

33. "Two Police Offers Who Killed Puerto Rican Declared Not Guilty," *Palante*, March 28, 1973.

34. For more on the history of St. Maria Goretti School, see Gloria Cipollini Endres, "The Golden Girls of Saint Maria Goretti," *Philadelphia Inquirer*, October 6, 2008, https://www.inquirer.com/philly/opinion/20081006_The_Golden_Girls_of_Saint _Maria_Goretti.html.

35. "Dearly Departed," *South Philly Review* (blog), October 13, 2005, https:// southphillyreview.com/2005/10/13/dearly-departed/.

36. Cookie Ridolfi, interview by author, February 25, 2014, 3.

37. Ridolfi, interview, 2014, 3–7.

38. Kathleen Z. Young, "The Imperishable Virginity of Saint Maria Goretti," *Gender and Society* 3, no. 4 (1989): 474–82.

39. Young, "Imperishable Virginity."

40. Ridolfi, interview, 2014.

41. Ridolfi, interview, 2014, 9.

42. Ridolfi, interview, 2014, 14.

43. Ridolfi, interview, 2014, 14.

44. Ridolfi, interview, 2020, 9.

45. McGowan, *Peace Warriors*, 22–23.

46. Dixon, interview, 9.

47. McGowan, *Peace Warriors*, 23.

48. *Poet of Poverty: Based on the Letters of Father Michael Doyle*, dir. Sean Dougherty, Tanna Ross, and Freke Vuijst (Huntley, IL: Green Room Productions, 2010), DVD.

49. *Poet of Poverty.*

NOTES TO PAGES 87–96

50. Michael Doyle, interview by Anthony Giacchino and Dave Dougherty, April 20, 1996, Giacchino Collection, 4.

51. McGowan, Peace Warriors, 266.

52. Doyle, interview by Giacchino and Dougherty, 12.

53. Doyle, interview by Giacchino and Dougherty, 5; McGowan, *Peace Warriors*, 23.

54. Medina, interview, 13.

55. McGowan, *Peace Warriors*, 23–24; Doyle, interview by Giacchino and Dougherty, 9–10.

56. McGowan, *Peace Warriors* 30.

57. McGowan, *Peace Warriors*, 30–31.

58. McGowan, *Peace Warriors*, 30.

59. "Camden Man Named Infiltrator in Draft Board Office Raid, Plot," *Courier-Post*, August 25, 1971.

60. McGowan, *Peace Warriors*, 30–31.

61. McGowan, *Peace Warriors*, 30–31.

62. David Kairys, *Philadelphia Freedom: Memoir of a Civil Rights Lawyer* (Ann Arbor: University of Michigan Press, 2009), 210.

63. Betty Medsger, *Burglary* (New York: Oxford University Press, 2014), 290; Kairys, *Philadelphia Freedom*, 210.

64. McGowan, *Peace Warriors*, 32–33.

65. Jeff Gammage, Joseph N. DiStefano, and Dwight Ott, "A Riot That Redefined a City 20 Years Ago: Camden Erupted," *Philadelphia Inquirer*, August 18, 1991.

66. Carmen Luz Morales De Martinez, Latino Life Stories Project, interview by Yamil Avivi, November 18, 2007, 23, https://www.npl.org/Pages/Collections/njhric/Martinez.pdf; Joseph A. Rodriguez, Latino Life Stories Project, interview by Yamil Avivi, December 17, 2007, 14–15, https://www.npl.org/Pages/Collections/njhric/Rodriguez.html.

67. Terry Buckalew, interview by author, July 3, 2020, 2–3.

68. Buckalew, interview, 2–3.

69. Buckalew, interview, 3–4.

70. Bob Good, interview by author, December 6, 2017, 19; McGowan, *Peace Warriors*, 36–38.

71. Good, interview, 19.

72. Good, interview, 19..

73. Ridolfi, interview, 2014, 6.

74. Ridolfi, interview, 2014, 7.

75. John Swinglish, interview by Anthony Giacchino, March 8, 1998, 10, Anthony Giacchino Camden 28 [Motion Picture] Collection, Swarthmore College Peace Collection, Swarthmore, PA, 11–12.

76. Anne Dunham and Frank Pommersheim, interview by author, March 3, 2020, 21–22.

CHAPTER FIVE

1. Edward McGowan, *Peace Warriors: The Story of the Camden 28* (Nyack, NY: Circumstantial Productions Publishing, 2001), 42.

2. Billboard Hot 100, February and March 1971, accessed July 3, 2023, https://www.billboard.com/charts/hot-100/1971-02-12/; "How Led Zeppelin's Classic Song Bombed on Its Belfast Premiere," *Belfast Telegraph*, February 27, 2016, https://www.belfasttelegraph.co.uk/life/features/how-led-zeppelins-classic-song-bombed-on-its-belfast-premiere/34490005.html; John Kendall, "Addict Can Be Programmed to Kill, Witness Tells Manson Jury: Manson Trial," *Los Angeles Times* (1923–1995), March 5, 1971.

3. Betty Medsger, *Burglary* (New York: Oxford University Press, 2014), 50–52.

4. Leilah Danielson, *American Gandhi: A. J. Muste and the History of Radicalism in the Twentieth Century* (Philadelphia: University of Pennsylvania Press, 2014).

5. Gordon Oyer, *Pursuing the Spiritual Roots of Protest: Merton, Berrigan, Yoder, and Muste at the Gethsemani Abbey Peacemakers Retreat* (Eugene, OR: Cascade Books, 2014).

6. "Fugitive Priest Speaks in Philadelphia," *New York Times*, August 8, 1970.

7. Patrick Catt, Interview with William Davidon at Haverford College, July 11, 1997, 2–3, https://www.aip.org/history-programs/niels-bohr-library/oral-histories/32356.

8. Medsger, *Burglary*.

9. Kenny Cooper, "How to Break into the FBI: 50 Years Later, Media Burglars Get Local Honors," WHYY, https://whyy.org/articles/how-to-break-into-the-fbi-50-years-later-media-burglars-get-local-honors/.

10. Medsger, *Burglary*, 52.

11. Medsger, *Burglary*, 433.

12. Medsger, *Burglary*, 61.

13. Medsger, *Burglary*, 100.

14. Medsger, *Burglary*, 101.

15. Beverly Gage, *G-Man: J. Edgar Hoover and the Making of the American Century* (New York: Viking, 2022), 701.

16. Gage, *G-Man*, 354–56.

17. Gage, *G-Man*, 702.

18. Medsger, *Burglary*, 252–58.

19. Michael E. Ruane, "'You Are Done': A Secret Letter to Martin Luther King Jr. Sheds Light on FBI's Malice," *Washington Post*, December 13, 2017, https://www.washingtonpost.com/news/retropolis/wp/2017/12/13/an-old-letter-sheds-light-on-fbis-malice-toward-martin-luther-king-jr/; D. J. Garrow, *The FBI and Martin Luther King, Jr.: From "Solo" to Memphis* (New York: Open Road Media, 2015).

NOTES TO PAGES 104–106

20. "Federal Bureau of Investigation (FBI)," Martin Luther King, Jr. Research and Education Institution, Stanford University, March 16, 1909 [*sic*; 1989?], https://kinginstitute.stanford.edu/encyclopedia/federal-bureau-investigation-fbi.

21. Medsger, *Burglary*, 342.

22. Ward Churchill and Jim Vander Wall, *The Cointelpro Papers: Documents from the FBI's Secret Wars against Domestic Dissent* (Boston: South End Press, 1990); John Drabble, "To Ensure Domestic Tranquility: The FBI, COINTELPRO, White Hate, and Political Discourse, 1964–1971," *Journal of American Studies* 38, no. 2 (2004): 297–328; Bryan Burrough, *Days of Rage: America's Radical Underground, the FBI, and the Forgotten Age of Revolutionary Violence* (New York: Penguin Press, 2015).

23. Medsger, *Burglary*, 346–47, 356.

24. Medsger, Burglary, 350.

25. For more information on the conspiracy theories driving the post–World War II anticommunist movement, see Michelle Nickerson, *Mothers of Conservatism: Women and the Postwar Right* (Princeton, NJ: Princeton University Press, 2012).

26. "The File on J. Edgar Hoover," *Time*, October 25, 1971, https://content.time.com/time/subscriber/article/0,33009,877302,00.html. See also "The 47-Year Reign of J. Edgar Hoover: Emperor of the FBI," *Life*, April 9, 1971; and Sally Quinn, "The Night the Director Stole," *Washington Post*, May 25, 1971, B1.

27. Tom Wicker, "The Heat on the FBI," *New York Times*, April 15, 1971. The bureau kept close tabs on Wicker as it did with all critical journalists. A source at Random House informed the bureau on possible plans for a critical Hoover biography by Wicker. John R. Bohrer, Capital New York, "What J. Edgar Hoover Did to a New York Times Critic of the FBI," *Atlantic*, April 11, 2012, https://www.theatlantic.com/national/archive/2012/04/what-j-edgar-hoover-did-new-york-time-critic-fbi/329439/.

28. Medsger, *Burglary*, 281.

29. Gage, *G-Man*, 701.

30. Medsger, *Burglary*, 273.

31. Medsger, Burglary, 273.

32. J. Edgar Hoover to SAC Albany, Counterintelligence Programs (COINTEL-PRO) Internal Security-Racial Matters, 4.28.71, accessed via Internet Archive, May 26, 2023, https://archive.org/stream/COINTELPROIndianapolis/157-IP-761-v-1-ARC-ID-5243502_djvu.txt; Frank Church (chair), *Hearings before the Senate Select Committee to Study Governmental Operations with Respect to Intelligence Activities: Federal Bureau of Investigation, November 18, 19, December 2, 3, 9, 10 and 11, 1975*, 94th Congress, 1st sess. (Washington, DC: U.S. Government Printing Office, 1976); https://www.intelligence.senate.gov/sites/default/files/94intelligence_activities_VI.pdf.

33. Medsger, *Burglary*, 288.

34. Joseph Crespino, *In Search of Another Country: Mississippi and the Conservative Counterrevolution* (Princeton, NJ: Princeton University Press, 2007), 116.

228 NOTES TO PAGES 106–111

35. Federal Bureau of Investigation (FBI) file 52-HQ-94527 re: March 1971 break-in at the FBI Media, Pennsylvania Resident Office, 1971–1972, November 21, 2011, 511, https://www.governmentattic.org/5docs/FBI-FileMEDBURG_1971-1972.pdf; Frederick Zollo et al., *Mississippi Burning* (Santa Monica, CA: MGM Home Entertainment, 2001) (DVD).

36. FBI Memo to Director from Philadelphia Division, August 23, 1971, personnel recommendations for Incentive Awards and Commendations, Giacchino Collection.

37. Federal Bureau of Investigation (FBI) file 52-HQ-94527, 209.

38. Robert Hardy, interview by Anthony Giacchino, ca. 2004, 1–2.

39. Anthony Giacchino, *The Camden 28*, documentary (First Run Features, 2007), http://www.camden28.org/; McGowan, *Peace Warriors*.

40. Medsger, *Burglary*, 288–89.

41. Philadelphia SAC to Director, FBI Memo Re: "MEDBURG," June 30, 1971, Giacchino Collection.

42. Giacchino, *Camden 28*; Ridolfi, interview, 2020, 3; FBI Memo to Director, August 3, 1971, Giacchino Collection.

43. FBI. Memo to Director, July 2, 1971, Giacchino Collection.

44. FBI, Surveillance Report, August 8, 1971, Giacchino Collection.

45. *United States of America v. William Anderson et al.*, 356 F. Supp. 1311 (D.N.J. 1973), Justia Law, https://law.justia.com/cases/federal/district-courts/FSupp/356/1311/1892560; transcripts, 16 (March 5, 1972): 2066–67, 2071, 2113–14; 18 (March 7, 1971), 2406–20.

46. FBI, Surveillance Report, August 27, 1971, Giacchino Collection.

47. A. Rosen to William Sullivan, FBI Memorandum, Re: MEDGBURG, July 7, 1971, 1–2, The Black Vault Intelligence Archives, accessed September 29, 2023, https://documents.theblackvault.com/documents/fbifiles/fbicia/0368692---62-HQ-80750---Section080(770838).pdf.

48. Louisa Guidaa, "Powelton Village," *American Preservation*, December 1978–January 1979, 44–52.

49. Donald M. Janson, "Philadelphia Fair 'Exposes' F. B. L.[*sic*]," *New York Times*, June 6, 1971, https://www.nytimes.com/1971/06/06/archives/philadelphia-fair-exposes-f-b-i-angry-powelton-residents-satirize.html.

50. Medsger, *Burglary*, 188–89; Janson, "Philadelphia Fair."

51. SAC Philadelphia to Director J. Edgar Hoover, Memorandum re. MEDBURG, 15–16.

52. SAC Philadelphia to Director J. Edgar Hoover, Memorandum re. MEDBURG, 15–16.

53. SAC Philadelphia to Director J. Edgar Hoover, Memorandum re. MEDBURG, 15–16.

54. SAC New York to SAC Philadelphia, Memorandum Re: John Peter Grady Misc. Info Concerning (MEDBURG SUBJECT) (OO:NY), May 27, 1971, https://www.governmentattic.org/5docs/FBI-FileMEDBURG_1971-1972.pdfl.

NOTES TO PAGES 111–115

55. One name was redacted from this list of people that Rosen hoped would participate in the raid. I suspect it was that of Joseph O'Rourke, a Jesuit priest who was active in the Catholic Left and whose name appears alongside Peter Fordi and Edward McGowan in other memos concerning principal subjects. Alex Rosen to William Sullivan, Memorandum re: Burglary of FBI Resident Agency, Media, PA., 3-8-71, July 19, 1971, https://www.governmentattic.org/5docs/FBI-FileMEDBURG_1971-1972.pdf.

56. Joan Reilly, interview by Giacchino, p. 10; Rosemary Reilly, interview by author, February 21, 2020, 14; Giacchino, *Camden 28*.

57. *U.S. v. Anderson et al.* (transcripts), 30 (March 28, 1971), 4157; 23 (March 15, 1971), 3120.

58. Dunham and Pommersheim, interview, 24.

59. FBI Memo to Director from Philadelphia Division, personnel recommendations for Incentive Awards and Commendations, Giacchino Collection.

60. Giacchino, *Camden 28*.

61. Burrough, *Days of Rage*.

62. Donald Janson, "Friend of Antiwar Activists Says He Still Prefers Jail to Testifying," *New York Times*, March 5, 1973.

63. Donald Janson, "Witnesses Freed after 14 Months: U.S. Appeals Court Acts on the Couple Who Would Not Testify on 'Camden 28' Immunity Granted New Subpoenas Planned More Subpoenaed," *New York Times*, March 2, 1973.

64. In the Matter of Patricia Grumbles and Donald Bruce Grumbles, Appellants, 453 F.2d 119 (3rd Cir. 1971), U.S. Court of Appeals for the Third Circuit, December 20, 1971, https://law.justia.com/cases/federal/appellate-courts/F2/453/119/385940/; Janson, "Witnesses Freed after 14 Months."

65. Tim Findley, "Farewell to the Fifth Amendment," *Rolling Stone*, December 7, 1972, https://www.rollingstone.com/politics/politics-news/farewell-to-the-fifth-amendment-115813/.

66. Findley, "Farewell to the Fifth Amendment."

67. *Beverly v. United States*, 468 F.2d 732, 747–49 (5th Cir. 1972). For the appeal of that decision, see *Briggs v. Goodwin*, 69 F.2d 486 (United States Court of Appeals, 1983).

68. Burrough, *Days of Rage*, 153–54, 233.

69. Cookie Ridolfi, interview by author, February 25, 2014, 12; The Grand Jury Reform Act of 1978, Appendix to Hearings before the Senate Subcommittee on Administrative Practice and Procedure, 95th Congress, 2nd sess. on S3405, Part 2 (Washington, DC: U.S. Government Printing Office, 1979), 608–16.

70. Ridolfi, interview.

71. "The Man Robert W. Hardy: Good Friend, or a Fink?," *Courier-Post* (Cherry Hill, NJ), August 26, 1971.

72. Joseph Daoust, interview by author, November 11, 2021.

73. "Jury Calls Draft Raid 'Tipster,'" *Courier-Post*, August 26, 1971.

230   NOTES TO PAGES 115–124

74. "Camden Man Named Infiltrator in Draft Board Office Raid, Plot," *Courier-Post*, August 25, 1971.

75. "Draft Suspects Blast Government—Not the Informer," *Vineland* (NJ) *Times Journal*, September 1, 1971.

76. Sandy Grady, "Hardy: 'Disagree with Method," *Courier-News* (Bridgewater, NJ), September 13, 1971.

77. Giacchino, *Camden 28*.

78. Bob Good, interview by author, December 6, 2017, 21.

79. Keith Forsyth, interview by author, August 14, 2017, 11.

80. Michael Doyle, interview by Giacchino and Dougherty, 49.

81. Sandy Grady, "A Boy Dies, Intrigue Is Forgotten," *Philadelphia Bulletin*, ca. October 8, 1971.

82. Giacchino, *Camden 28*; Robert W. Hardy, *Fallen Leaves* (Wilmington, DE: Cedar Tree Books, 2017), 5.

83. Giacchino, *Camden 28*.

84. Michael Doyle, interview by Giacchino and Dougherty, 49.

85. "Service Set for Son of Key '28 Witness," *Philadelphia Inquirer*, October 5, 1971.

86. Giacchino, *Camden 28*.

87. Giacchino, *Camden 28*.

PART THREE

1. Richard Chused, "Dream Vignettes," *New York Law School Law Review* 59, no. 1 (2014): 128.

CHAPTER SIX

1. Linda Charlton, "A Camden Suspect Linked to 2d Raid," *New York Times*, August 31, 1971; "Jury Indicts 28 in Camden Draft Raid," *Philadelphia Daily News*, August 28, 1971; Mitchell H. Cohen, Judge, U.S. District Court, "Statement of Reason," August 31, 1971, Jayma Abdoo Collected Papers, Swarthmore College Peace Collection, Swarthmore, PA; U.S. Bureau of Labor Statistics, CPI Inflation Calculator, accessed July 4, 2023, https://data.bls.gov/cgi-bin/cpicalc.pl?cost1=25%2C000.00&year1=197101&year2=202204.

2. Steven E. Barkan, "Political Trials and the 'Pro Se' Defendant in the Adversary System," *Social Problems* 24, no. 3 (1977): 1–5.

3. Joan Reilly, interview by Anthony Giacchino, ca. 2004, Anthony Giacchino Camden 28 [Motion Picture] Collection, Swarthmore College Peace Collection, Swarthmore, PA.

4. "Draft Raid is Balked," *Philadelphia Inquirer*, August 23, 1971; Cohen, "Statement of Reason"; Edward McGowan, *Peace Warriors: The Story of the Camden 28* (Nyack, NY: Circumstantial Productions Publishing, 2001), 48.

NOTES TO PAGES 124–130

5. "Arraignment of 27 in Draft Raid Case Delayed in Camden," *New York Times*, September 18, 1971.

6. Robert Williamson, interview by author, December 6, 2015, 15.

7. David Kairys, *Philadelphia Freedom: Memoir of a Civil Rights Lawyer* (Ann Arbor: University of Michigan Press, 2009), 192.

8. Edward McGowan, *Peace Warriors: The Story of the Camden 28* (Nyack, NY: Circumstantial Productions Publishing, 2001), 54.

9. McGowan, *Peace Warriors*, 54.

10. Martin Stolar had a busy year. Earlier in 1971, the U.S. Supreme Court had ruled in his favor when he challenged, on First Amendment grounds, the Ohio bar's demand that as a condition of membership, he disclose the names of all organizations to which he had belonged since law school. *In re Stolar*, 401 U.S. 23 (1971).

11. Williamson, interview, 16.

12. Mark Atwood Lawrence, *The Vietnam War: A Concise International History* (Oxford: Oxford University Press, 2008), 122.

13. Neil Sheehan, *The Pentagon Papers as Published by the New York Times* (New York: Quadrangle Books, 1971).

14. Sheehan, *Pentagon Papers*, x.

15. Sheehan, *Pentagon Papers*, 1.

16. *Sorrells v. United States*, 287 U.S. 435, 53 S. Ct. 210, 77 L. Ed. 413, 1932; *Sherman v. United States*, 356 U.S. 369, 78 S. Ct. 819, 2 L. Ed. 2d 848, 1958.

17. *United States v. Russell*, 411 U.S. 423, 93 S. Ct. 1637, 36 L. Ed. 2d 366, 1973.

18. Eileen Egan, "The Struggle of Pax," in *American Catholic Pacifism: The Influence of Dorothy Day and the Catholic Worker Movement*, ed. Anne Klejment and Dorothy L. Roberts (Westport, CT: Praeger, 1996), 141.

19. Egan, "Struggle of Pax," 142–43; National Council of Catholic Bishops, "Pastoral Letter on Human Life in Our Day," November 15, 1968.

20. *In the Name of Peace: Collective Statements of the United States Catholic Bishops on War and Peace, 1919–1980* (Washington, DC: National Conference of Catholic Bishops, 1983), 59.

21. David Kairys, Paul G. Chevigny, and Melvin L. Wulf, Amicus Brief, *United States v. Russell*, for the American Civil Liberties Union and the National Emergency Civil Liberties Committee, decided 1973; https://aclu.procon.org/view.background -resource.php?resourceID=003505&print=true.

22. For more on race and jury selection in the United States see Paul D. Butler, "Race-Based Jury Nullification: Case-in-Chief," *John Marshall Law Review* 30, no. 4 (1997): 911; Thomas Ward Frampton, "The Jim Crow Jury," *Vanderbilt Law Review* 71, no. 5 (2018): 1593–1654; and Tania Tetlow, "Discriminatory Acquittal," *William and Mary Bill of Rights Journal* 18, no. 1 (2009): 75.

23. The 1895 case of *Sparf and Hansen v. United States* was the first Supreme Court de-

cision regarding the right to keep juries ignorant of the power to ignore the instructions of judges and nullify the law. *Sparf and Hansen v. United States*, 156 U.S. 51 (1895). *Moylan* relied on that ruling in 1969. *United States v. Moylan*, 417 F.2d 1002 (4th Cir. 1969).

24. Williamson, interview, 17.

25. Anne Dunham and Frank Pommersheim, interview by author, March 3, 2020, 64–66; Cookie Ridolfi, interview by author, February 25, 2014, 14.

26. Camden 28 Defense Committee (CDC), solicitation, ca. 1971–1972, Jayma Abdoo Collected Papers, Swarthmore College Peace Collection, Swarthmore, PA.

27. CDC, "Some Background on the Camden Defense Committee," ca. 1971–1972, Anthony Giacchino Camden 28 [Motion Picture] Collection, Swarthmore College Peace Collection, Swarthmore, PA (hereafter Giacchino Collection).

28. Jayma Abdoo, "Jury Nullification," ca. 1972–73, Abdoo Collected Papers.

29. Jayma Abdoo, "Movement Affirms Spirit," *Trinity Times*, Trinity University, October 1971, Abdoo Collected Papers.

30. John Standring, "Bomb Scare Interrupts Peace Play," *Courier-Post* (Cherry Hill, NJ), January 17, 1972.

31. Kate Shellnutt, "Death Not Welcome Here," *Christianity Today* (Washington, DC) 66, no. 2 (2022): 25.

32. For more on the tradition of burning palm fronds, which dates back at least to the seventeenth century, see Jędrzej Kitowicz, "Ash Wednesday: Dark Matins," in *Customs and Culture in Poland under the Last Saxon King: The Major Texts of Opis Obyczajów Za Panowania Augusta III (Description of Customs during the Reign of August III) by Jędrzej Kitowicz 1728–1804*, trans. Oscar E. Swan (Budapest: Central European University Press, 2019), 73–77.

33. Craig Waters, "Grief, Home for Ash Wednesday," *Courier-Post*, ca. February 15, 1972.

34. Ash Wednesday Service at Johnson Cemetery, February 15, 1973, transcript of audio recording, courtesy of Sacred Heart Parish, Camden, New Jersey, Anthony Giacchino Personal Collection.

35. Ash Wednesday Service at Johnson Cemetery.

36. Carol Comegno, "Historic Camden Cemetery Resurrected," *Courier-Post*, May 25, 2015, https://www.courierpostonline.com/story/news/local/south-jersey/2015/05/25/historic-camden-cemetery-resurrected/27810481.

37. Ash Wednesday Service at Johnson Cemetery.

38. Dorothy Day, *The Duty of Delight: The Diaries of Dorothy Day* (Milwaukee, WI: Marquette University Press, 2008), 533–34.

39. "War Protesting Priest Loses Post in Camden," *New York Times*, February 19, 1972; "Father Doyle Is Relieved of Parish Duty," *Courier-Post*, ca. February 14, 1972.

40. Edward McGowan, *Peace Warriors: The Story of the Camden 28* (Nyack, NY: Circumstantial Productions Publishing, 2001), 59; "Jane Fonda to Visit South Jersey," *Courier-Post*, September 21, 1972, https://www.newspapers.com/image/181355402/.

NOTES TO PAGES 137–144   233

41. Herald P. Fahringer, "In the Valley of the Blind: A Primer on Jury Selection in a Criminal Case," *Law and Contemporary Problems* 43, no. 4 (1980): 116–36.

42. National Jury Project, *Jurywork, Systematic Techniques: A Manual for Lawyers, Legal Workers and Social Scientists*, ed. Beth Bonora et al. (Berkeley, CA: The Project, 1979).

43. McGowan, *Peace Warriors*, 62–63; Edward Tivnan, "Jury by Trial," *New York Times*, November 16, 1975, https://www.nytimes.com/1975/11/16/archives/jury-by-trial-there-are-now-computers-pollsters-media-analysts-and.html; Morton Hunt, "Putting Juries on the Couch," *New York Times*, November 28, 1982, https://www.nytimes.com/1982/11/28/magazine/putting-juries-on-the-couch.html.

44. Caroline B. Crocker and Margaret Bull Koverna, "Systematic Jury Selection," chap. 2 in *Handbook of Trial Consulting*, ed. R. L. Wiener and B. H. Bornstein (New York: Springer, 2011).

45. David Kairys, "Juror Selection: The Law, A Mathematical Method of Analysis and a Case Study," *American Criminal Law Review*, no. 3 (1972): 771.

46. Kairys, "Juror Selection," 800.

47. David Kairys, *Philadelphia Freedom: Memoir of a Civil Rights Lawyer* (Ann Arbor: University of Michigan Press, 2009), 139–46.

48. Mary Schmelzer, interview by author, July 10, 2014, 1, 6–8.

49. Schmelzer, interview, 13.

50. Schmelzer, interview, 15–16.

51. Schmelzer, interview, 22–24.

52. Schmelzer, interview, 21–22.

53. Jayma Abdoo, Notes, ca. 1972–73, Jayma Abdoo Collected Papers, Swarthmore College Peace Collection, Swarthmore, PA.

54. Abdoo, Notes.

55. Schmelzer, interview, 24.

56. Kairys, *Philadelphia Freedom*, 199–202.

57. Kairys, *Philadelphia Freedom*, 199–202.

58. Kairys, *Philadelphia Freedom*, 199–202.

59. Catholic Canon Law 983 § 1–2.

60. Robert Hardy, interview by Anthony Giacchino, ca, 2004, 105–7.

61. Hardy, interview, 105–7.

62. Hardy, interview, 109; McGowan, *Peace Warriors*, 226.

63. Anthony Giacchino, *The Camden 28*, documentary (First Run Features, 2007), http://www.camden28.org/.

64. Donald Jansen, "F.B.I. is Accused of Aiding a Crime," *New York Times*, March 28, 1972.

65. Robert Hardy, Affidavit filed in the Commonwealth of Pennsylvania, February 28, 1972, David Kairys Papers, University of Pennsylvania.

66. David Kairys and Carl Broege to the "Camden 28," letter, December 22, 1972, An-

234 NOTES TO PAGES 145–153

thony Giacchino Camden 28 [Motion Picture] Collection, Swarthmore College Peace
Collection, Swarthmore, PA.

CHAPTER SEVEN

1. Donald Janson, "Leader of Camden Draft Raid Asks Jurors to 'Ignore the Law':
Washington Is Cited," *New York Times*, February 28, 1973.

2. *United States v. Anderson*, 481 F.2d 685 (4th Cir. 1973) 59:8502.

3. Anne Dunham and Frank Pommersheim, interview by author, March 3, 2020, 37.

4. Cookie Ridolfi, interview by author, February 25, 2014, 15.

5. Rosemary Reilly, interview by author, February 20, 2020, 54.

6. Rosemary Reilly, interview by author, February 20, 2020, 41.

7. Joan Reilly, interview by Anthony Giacchino, ca. 2004, Anthony Giacchino Camden 28 [Motion Picture] Collection, Swarthmore College Peace Collection, Swarthmore, PA, 8.

8. Ridolfi, interview, 15.

9. Rosemary Reilly, interview, 54.

10. Betty Medsger, *Burglary* (New York: Oxford University Press, 2014), 331.

11. "John Barry, 60, Trial and Appellate Lawyer," *New York Times*, April 18, 2000;
"Maryanne Desmond Weds John Barry," *New York Times*, December 27, 1982.

12. Anthony Giacchino, *The Camden 28*, documentary (First Run Features, 2007),
http://www.camden28.org/.

13. Edward McGowan, *Peace Warriors: The Story of the Camden 28* (Nyack, NY: Circumstantial Productions Publishing, 2001), 63.

14. McGowan, *Peace Warriors*, 65; Donald Janson, "8 of the Camden 28 Face Separate Draft-File Trial," *New York Times*, February 6, 1973, https://www.nytimes.com/1973/02/06/archives/8-of-the-camden-28-face-separate-draftfile-trial-severance-move-in.html; "Acquittal Seen Vote on the War," *Courier-Post* (Cherry Hill, NJ), May 21, 1973, https://courierpostonline.newspapers.com/image/181337631/.

15. McGowan, *Peace Warriors*, 67.

16. *United States of America v. William Anderson et al.*, 356 F. Supp. 1311 (D.N.J. 1973), Justia Law, accessed May 31, 2023, https://law.justia.com/cases/federal/district -courts/FSupp/356/1311/1892560/.

17. McGowan, *Peace Warriors*, 67.

18. McGowan, *Peace Warriors*, 98–104.

19. *U.S. v. Anderson et al.* (transcripts), 13:1765–66.

20. *U.S. v. Anderson et al.*, 1818–19.

21. *U.S. v. Anderson et al.*, 1745–49.

22. *U.S. v. Anderson et al.*, 1745–49.

23. Betty Medsger, "Justice in a Camden Court," *Progressive*, October 1973, 5.

NOTES TO PAGES 153–161

24. *U.S. v. Anderson et al.*, 1743–56.

25. *U.S. v. Anderson et al.*, 1743–56.

26. "Mike Giocondo 85: Fighter for Justice at Home and Abroad," *People's World* (blog), April 23, 2014, https://www.peoplesworld.org/article/mike-giocondo-85 -fighter-for-justice-at-home-and-abroad/.

27. *U.S. v. Anderson et al.*, 13:1809–13.

28. Charles Clancy III, "Recollection on Judge Clarkson S. Fisher and the Camden 28 Trial," unpublished reflections shared with participants at a Camden 28 reunion, ca. 2002, 3.

29. David M. Herszenhorn, "Clarkson S. Fisher, 76, Is Dead; Was Federal Judge in New Jersey," *New York Times*, July 30, 1997, https://www.nytimes.com/1997/07/30/ nyregion/clarkson-s-fisher-76-is-dead-was-federal-judge-in-new-jersey.html.

30. Herszenhorn, "Clarkson S. Fisher."

31. Clancy, "Recollection on Judge Clarkson S. Fisher," 2.

32. Giacchino, *Camden 28*.

33. David Kairys, *Philadelphia Freedom: Memoir of a Civil Rights Lawyer* (Ann Arbor: University of Michigan Press, 2009), 194–95.

34. Bureau of Labor Statistics, CPI Inflation Calculator, accessed May 28, 2022, https://www.bls.gov/data/inflation_calculator.htm.

35. McGowan, *Peace Warriors*, 125–26.

36. *U.S. v. Anderson et al.*, 15:960.

37. *U.S. v. Anderson et al.*, 15:1985–86.

38. *U.S. v. Anderson et al.*, 15:1985–86.

39. *U.S. v. Anderson et al.*, 17:2314–22.

40. *U.S. v. Anderson et al.*, 26:3558–59.

41. McGowan, *Peace Warriors*, 372–73.

CHAPTER EIGHT

1. *United States of America v. William Anderson et al.* 356 F. Supp. 1311 (D.N.J. 1973), Justia Law, https://law.justia.com/cases/federal/district-courts/FSupp/356/1311/ 1892560; (transcripts), 13:1777.

2. Barkan, "Jury Nullification," *Social Problems*, 31 (1983): 30.

3. Bob Good, interview by author, December 6, 2017, 11.

4. Betty Medsger, "Justice in a Camden Court," *Progressive*, October 1973, 5.

5. Camden 28 Defense Committee, *Camden 28 Newsletter*, 4 (March 29, 1973), Anthony Giacchino Camden 28 [Motion Picture] Collection, Swarthmore College Peace Collection, Swarthmore, PA (hereafter Anthony Giacchino Collection); John F. Khanlian, "The Trial of the Camden 28: An Ethnography," University of Pennsylvania, 1973, 9, Anthony Giacchino Collection.

6. Edward McGowan, *Peace Warriors: The Story of the Camden 28* (Nyack, NY: Circumstantial Productions Publishing, 2001), 59.

7. Khanlian, "Trial of the Camden 28," 10.

8. Khanlian, "Trial of the Camden 28," 10.

9. Khanlian, "Trial of the Camden 28," 10.

10. Khanlian, "Trial of the Camden 28," 10.

11. Robert Williamson, interview by author, December 6, 2015, 19.

12. *U.S. v. Anderson et al.*, 34:4729–64.

13. Khanlian, "Trial of the Camden 28," 10.

14. *U.S. v. Anderson et al.* 34:4780.

15. *U.S. v. Anderson et al.*, 34:4799–4807.

16. *U.S. v. Anderson et al.*, 34:4835.

17. United States Bureau of Labor Statistics, CPI Inflation Calculator, accessed May 28, 2022, https://www.bls.gov/data/inflation_calculator.htm.

18. McGowan, *Peace Warriors*, 196–210.

19. *U.S. v. Anderson et al.*, 38:5313–97; McGowan, *Peace Warriors*, 196–205.

20. *U.S. v. Anderson et al.*, 39:5448–65.

21. McGowan, *Peace Warriors*, 225–26.

22. Joan Reilly, interview by Anthony Giacchino, ca. 2004, Anthony Giacchino Camden 28 [Motion Picture] Collection, Swarthmore College Peace Collection, Swarthmore, PA, 15.

23. *U.S. v. Anderson et al.*, 46:6480–81.

24. *U.S. v. Anderson et al.*, 34:4729–64.

25. *U.S. v. Anderson et al.*, 46:6490.

26. *U.S. v. Anderson et al.*, 6492.

27. *U.S. v. Anderson et al.*, 6494–95.

28. *U.S. v. Anderson et al.*, 29:4016–17.

29. Charles Clancy III, "Recollection on Judge Clarkson S. Fisher and the Camden 28 Trial," unpublished reflections shared with participants at a Camden 28 reunion, ca. 2002, 3.

30. Clancy, "Clarkson Fisher," 3.

31. Kairys, David Kairys, *Philadelphia Freedom: Memoir of a Civil Rights Lawyer* (Ann Arbor: University of Michigan Press, 2009), 218.

32. Clancy, "Clarkson Fisher," 3.

33. Williamson, interview, 18.

34. Mai Elliott, "The Terrible Violence of 'Pacification,'" *New York Times*, January 18, 2018, https://www.nytimes.com/2018/01/18/opinion/violence-pacification-vietnam-war.html.

35. Samuel P. Huntington, "The Bases of Accommodation," *Foreign Affairs*, July 1,

NOTES TO PAGES 168–176

1968, 648–49, https://www.foreignaffairs.com/articles/vietnam/1968-07-01/bases
-accommodation.

36. *U.S. v. Anderson et al.*, 42:5865–5932.

37. Edward Miller, "Behind the Phoenix Program," *New York Times*, December 29, 2017,
https://www.nytimes.com/2017/12/29/opinion/behind-the-phoenix-program.html.

38. *U.S. v. Anderson et al.*, 42:5884.

39. "Obituary for Robert N. Steck," O'Keefe Funeral Homes, March 9, 2015, https://
www.keefefuneralhome.com/memorials/Steck-RobertN/2080575/obituary.php.

40. *U.S. v. Anderson et al.*, 42:5958.

41. *U.S. v. Anderson et al.*, 6190–93.

42. *U.S. v. Anderson et al.*, 6190.

43. *U.S. v. Anderson et al.*, 6193.

44. *U.S. v. Anderson et al.*, 6210.

45. *U.S. v. Anderson et al.*, 6217.

46. *U.S. v. Anderson et al.*, 6217.

47. *U.S. v. Anderson et al.*, 6227.

48. *U.S. v. Anderson et al.*, 47:6694.

49. *U.S. v. Anderson et al.*, 49:7034–38.

50. *U.S. v. Anderson et al.*, 7034–38; "Marriage of Philip Berrigan to Sister Elizabeth
Reported," *New York Times*, May 29, 1973.

51. *U.S. v. Anderson et al.*, 48:6841–42.

52. *U.S. v. Anderson et al.*, 49:6978–7039.

53. *U.S. v. Anderson et al.*, 7081, 7982.

54. *U.S. v. Anderson et al.*, 7081, 7982.

55. *U.S. v. Anderson et al.*, 7081, 7982.

56. *U.S. v. Anderson et al.*, 47:6646–47.

57. *U.S. v. Anderson et al.*, 6648–49.

58. *U.S. v. Anderson et al.*, 6652.

59. *U.S. v. Anderson et al.*, 50:7127–38.

60. *U.S. v. Anderson et al.*, 7127–38.

61. *U.S. v. Anderson et al.*, 7127–38.

62. Donald Janson, "Judge Instructs 'Camden 28' Jury: Calls U.S. Role a Possible
Ground for Acquittal, Entrapment Not Issue, Role Described," *New York Times*, May 18,
1973.

63. Janson, "Judge Instructs 'Camden 28' Jury."

64. David Kairys, *Philadelphia Freedom: Memoir of a Civil Rights Lawyer* (Ann Arbor:
University of Michigan Press, 2009), 224.

65. Edward McGowan, *Peace Warriors: The Story of the Camden 28* (Nyack, NY: Circumstantial Productions Publishing, 2001), 372–73.

238 NOTES TO PAGES 176–181

66. Medsger, "Justice in a Camden Court," 25.

67. Betty Medsger, *Burglary* (New York: Oxford University Press, 2014), 327.

68. "Juror Lauds Camden 28 for a Job 'Well Done,'" *New York Times*, May 21, 1973.

69. Medsger, "Justice in a Camden Court," 25.

CHAPTER NINE

1. Kyrie Greenberg, "Camden 28 Revisit Court Where They Were Tried for '71 Break-In to Protest Vietnam War," WHYY, Dec. 6, 2018, https://whyy.org/articles/camden-28-revisit-court-where-they-were-tried-for-71-break-in-to-protest-vietnam-war/.

2. Stephen Schloesser SJ, "'Dancing on the Edge of the Volcano': Biopolitics and What Happened after Vatican II," in *From Vatican II to Pope Francis: Charting a Catholic Future*, ed. Paul G. Crowley and Stephen Schloesser (Maryknoll, NY: Orbis Books, 2014), 3–26.

3. Mural Arts Philadelphia, https://www.muralarts.org/programs/.

4. Rosemary Reilly, interview by author, February 20, 2020, 29.

5. "The Camden 28: Film Update," accessed June 4, 2023, http://archive.pov.org/camden28/film-update/2/; Patrick O'Neill, "Teresa Grady, Matriarch of Catholic Peace Activist Family, Dies," *National Catholic Reporter*, April 11, 2016, https://www.ncronline.org/eresa-grady-matriarch-catholic-peace-activist-family-dies. For a record of all the plowshares actions, see Plowshares Disarmament Chronology, 1988-2018, accessed September 29, 2023, https://ickevald.net/plowshares/plowshares-chronology-1980-2018.

6. Heart of Camden, accessed July 3, 2023, https://www.heartofcamden.org/.

7. Nick DiUlio, "Camden's Poet Priest," *NJ Monthly*, June 11, 2012, https://njmonthly.com/articles/jersey-living/camdens-poet-priest/.

8. George M. Anderson, *With Christ in Prison: Jesuits in Jail from St. Ignatius to the Present* (New York: Fordham University Press, 2000), 2, 13.

9. "Father Edward 'Ned' Murphy, S.J.," *Catholic New York*, May 17, 2012, https://www.cny.org/stories/father-edward-ned-murphy-sj,7522?.

10. "POTS Bronx," accessed May 22, 2020, https://potsbronx.org/; "Part of the Solution (POTS)," Catholic Charities of New York, July 1, 2015, https://catholiccharitiesny.org/our-agencies/part-solution-pots.

11. Keith Forsyth, interview by author, August 14, 2018, 15–18.

12. Fair Districts PA, "Fair Districts PA," January 1, 2020, https://www.fairdistrictspa.com/updates/p2.

13. Adam Liptak, "Justices Won't Block Pennsylvania Gerrymandering Decision," *New York Times*, February 5, 2018.

14. "Mike Giocondo, 85: Fighter for Justice at Home and Abroad," *People's World* (blog), April 23, 2014, http://www.peoplesworld.org/article/mike-giocondo-85-fighter-for-justice-at-home-and-abroad/.

NOTES TO PAGES 181–185

15. Edward John McGowan, obituary, accessed September 29, 2023, https://www
.lansingfuneralhome.com/obituaries/edward-mcgowan.

16. Cookie Ridolfi, interview by author, February 25, 2014, 18.

17. Ridolfi, interview, 19.

18. Ridolfi, interview, 19.

19. "Mission, Vision, and History," Northern California Innocence Project, accessed
July 3, 2023, http://ncip.org/about/.

20. "Kathleen M. Ridolfi, Professor Emerita," Santa Clara University School of Law,
2023, https://law.scu.edu/faculty/profile/ridolfi-kathleen/.

21. Anne Dunham and Frank Pommersheim, interview by author, March 3, 2020, 83.

22. Dunham and Pommersheim, interview, 8.

23. Terry Buckalew, interview by author, July 3, 2020, 30.

24. Buckalew, interview, 20.

25. Buckalew, interview; "Interview with Poet Maria Fama on SDS, the Catholic
Left, and the Camden 29," July 6, 2004, http://phillysound.blogspot.com/2004/07/
interview-with-poet-maria-fama-on-sds.html.

26. Robert Williamson, "The Janitor's Closet," unpublished reflections, 2023, 6.

27. "Robert W. Hardy," accessed July 3, 2023, http://www.lifecelebrationstudio.com/
robert-w-hardy/.

28. Robert W. Hardy, *Fallen Leaves* (Wilmington, DE: Cedar Tree Books, 2017); The-
resa Hardy to Anthony Giacchino, May 13, 2002, Anthony Giacchino Private Collection.

29. Kevin Riordan, "Services for Camden's Msgr. Michael Doyle Are Set for Friday
and Saturday," November 9, 2022, https://www.inquirer.com/obituaries/father
-michael-doyle-funeral-masses-viewing-interment-20221109.html.

30. K. Tobey, *Plowshares: Protest, Performance, and Religious Identity in the Nuclear Age*
(Philadelphia: Pennsylvania State University Press, 2016), 1–2.

31. Michael David Coogan, *The New Oxford Annotated Bible: New Revised Standard Version: With the Apocrypha: An Ecumenical Study Bible* (Oxford: Oxford University Press,
2010), 971.

32. "Plowshares Disarmament Chronology," accessed May 31, 2023, https://ickevald
.net/plowshares/plowshares-chronology-1980-2018.

33. S. E. Nepstad, "Appendix C: Chronological List of Plowshares Actions by
Region," *Religion and War Resistance in the Plowshares Movement*, Cambridge Studies in
Contentio (Cambridge University Press, 2008), 233–38.

34. Nepstad, "Appendix C," 233–34.

35. Clay Risen, "Sister Megan Rice, Fierce Critic of U.S. Nuclear Arsenal, Dies at 91,"
New York Times, October 17, 2021, https://www.nytimes.com/2021/10/17/obituaries/
megan-rice-dead.html.

36. "Anna Grady Flores," in *Doing Time for Peace: Resistance, Family, and Community*,
ed. Rosalie Riegle (Nashville, TN: Vanderbilt University Press, 2012), 310–13.

37. Mee-Ae Kim, "Liberation and Theology: A Pedagogical Challenge," *History Teacher* 46, no. 4 (2013): 601–12.

38. Barb Prosser, "Witness for Peace in Nicaragua" (Fall 1985), https://karen housecw.org/WitnessforPeaceinNicaragua.htm.

39. Edward T. Brett, "The Attempts of Grassroots Religious Groups to Change U.S. Policy towards Central America: Their Methods, Successes, and Failures," *Journal of Church and State* 36, no. 4 (1994): 778.

40. Dunham and Pommersheim, interview, 93.

41. Brett, "Attempts of Grassroots Religious Groups," 784.

42. Valerie J. Munson, "On Holy Ground: Church Sanctuary in the Trump Era," *Southwestern Law Review* 47, no. 1 (2017): 50.

43. Robin Lorentzen, "Women in the Sanctuary Movement: A Case Study in Chicago" (PhD diss., Loyola University of Chicago, 1989), 30–32.

44. Norma Stoltz Chinchilla, Nora Hamilton, and James Loucky, "The Sanctuary Movement and Central American Activism in Los Angeles," *Latin American Perspectives* 36, no. 6 (2009): 107.

45. Msgr. Daniel Hoye, USCCB, "Statement on the Sanctuary Movement," January 14, 1985, http://www.usccb.org/issues-and-action/human-life-and-dignity/global -issues/latin-america-caribbean/el-salvador/statement-on-sanctuary-movement-1985 -01-14.cfm.

46. Aaron Bekemeyer, "The Acme of the Catholic Left: Catholic Activists in the US Sanctuary Movement, 1982–1992" (PhD diss., University of Michigan, 2012), 8.

47. Bekemeyer, "The Acme of the Catholic Left," 6–7.

48. Anthony J. Pogorelc, "Movement to Movement Transmission and the Role of Place: The Relationship between Catholic Action and Call to Action," *Sociology of Religion* 72, no. 4 (2011): 426.

49. Pogorelc, "Movement to Movement Transmission," 426.

50. "Vatican Supports Excommunication of Call to Action Group," *Catholic News Agency*, December 7, 2006, https://www.catholicnewsagency.com/news/vatican _supports_excommunication_of_call_to_action_group.

51. Voices of the Faithful, accessed May 28, 2023, https://www.votf.org/; Survivors Network of those Abused by Priests, accessed May 28, 2023. See Tricia Colleen Bruce, *Faithful Revolution: How Voice of the Faithful Is Changing the Church* (New York: Oxford University Press, 2011); William V. D'Antonio and Anthony J. Pogorelc, *Voices of the Faithful: Loyal Catholics Striving for Change* (New York: Crossroad, 2007).

52. Laurie Goodstein, "Vatican Is Said to Force Jesuit off Magazine," *New York Times*, May 7, 2005.

53. "A Brief History of Commonweal," accessed May 12, 2020, https://www .commonwealmagazine.org/history.

NOTES TO PAGES 188–192 241

54. Elizabeth A. Johnson, "A Theological Case for God-She," *Commonweal* 120, no. 2 (January 29, 1993): 9.

55. A. Jones, *National Catholic Reporter at Fifty: The Story of the Pioneering Paper and Its Editors* (Washington, DC: Rowman & Littlefield, 2014).

56. Daniel K. Williams, *Defenders of the Unborn: The Pro-Life Movement before Roe V. Wade* (New York: Oxford University Press, 2016), 163.

57. Daniel Berrigan, "An Inkling of a Life Being Snuffed Out," *Sojourners*, November 1, 1980.

58. Cookie Ridolfi, interview by author, February 25, 2014, 19.

59. Elizabeth McAlister, "The Concern Is For Human Life," *Sojourners*, November 1980.

60. Elizabeth McAlister, "Is Marriage Obsolete?," *Sojourners*, March–April 1996, as quoted in B. Steensland and P. Goff, *The New Evangelical Social Engagement* (New York: Oxford University Press, 2013), 202.

61. Jason Bivins, *The Fracture of Good Order: Christian Antiliberalism and the Challenge to American Politics* (Chapel Hill: University of North Carolina Press, 2003), 126.

62. "NBC's Carl Stern Reveals COINTELPRO Spy Program," NBC News, January 7, 2014, https://www.nbcnews.com/video/nbcs-carl-stern-reveals-cointelpro-spy-program-109192259961; Betty Medsger, *Burglary* (New York: Oxford, 2014), 333; Athan G. Theoharis, *Spying on Americans: Political Surveillance from Hoover to the Huston Plan* (Philadelphia: Temple University Press, 1978), 151–52.

63. Senate Select Committee to Study Governmental Operations with Respect to Intelligence Activities, U.S. Senate, accessed July 3, 2023, https://www.senate.gov/about/powers-procedures/investigations/church-committee.htm; Medsger, *Burglary*, 340.

64. Medsger, *Burglary*, 340.

65. U.S. Senate Select Committee on Intelligence, accessed May 18, 2023, https://www.intelligence.senate.gov/about.

66. Bureau of Justice Assistance, U.S. Department of Justice, "The Foreign Intelligence Surveillance Act of 1978 (FISA)," accessed July 3, 2023, https://bja.ojp.gov/program/it/privacy-civil-liberties/authorities/statutes/1286.

67. Theoharis, *Spying on Americans*; "Final Report of the Select Committee to Study Governmental Operations with Respect to Intelligence Activities, United States Senate: Together with Additional, Supplemental, and Separate Views," accessed May 26, 2023, https://archive.org/stream/finalreportofselo3unit/finalreportofselo3unit_djvu.txt.

68. Theoharis, *Spying on Americans*, 151.

69. Reports on the White House from the Nixon years reveal conversations between the president and his staff regarding the problem of John Kerry and how to neutralize his political power. "FBI Shadowed Kerry during Activist Era," *Los Angeles Times*, March 22, 2004, https://www.latimes.com/archives/la-xpm-2004-mar-22-na

242 NOTES TO PAGES 192–195

-kerryfbi22-story.html; "Nixon Targeted Kerry for Anti-War Views," NBC News, March 15, 2004, https://www.nbcnews.com/id/wbna4534274.

70. "FBI: Close, But—," *Los Angeles Times*, February 6, 1988, https://www.latimes .com/archives/la-xpm-1988-02-06-me-10258-story.html; "General Accounting Office, International Terrorism: FBI Investigates Domestic Activities to Identify Terrorists, September 1990. Unclassified | National Security Archive," accessed May 23, 2023, https://nsarchive.gwu.edu/document/23870-general-accounting-office-international -terrorism-fbi-investigates-domestic; Wayne King, "An F.B.I. Inquiry Fed by Informer Emerges in Analysis of Documents," *New York Times*, February 13, 1988, https://www .nytimes.com/1988/02/13/us/an-fbi-inquiry-fed-by-informer-emerges-in-analysis-of -documents.html.

71. Paul VI, *Humanae Vitae*, encyclical letter, Vatican website, July 25, 1968, http:// www.vatican.va/content/paul-vi/en/encyclicals/documents/hf_p-vi_enc_25071968 _humanae-vitae.html.

72. John Paul II, *Evangelium Vitae*, encyclical letter, March 25, 1995, http://www .vatican.va/content/john-paul-ii/en/encyclicals/documents/hf_jp-ii_enc_25031995 _evangelium-vitae.html.

73. M. Novak, *Toward a Theology of the Corporation*, American Enterprise Institute Studies in Religion, Philosophy, and Public Policy (Washington, DC: AEI Press, 1990).

74. Bruce Weber, "Paul Weyrich, 66, a Conservative Strategist, Dies," *New York Times*, December 18, 2008.

75. Joseph A. D'Agostino, "Conservative Spotlight: Paul Weyrich," *Human Events* 56, no. 44 (December 2000): 18.

76. For more on the impact of Phyllis Schlafly, see Donald T. Critchlow, *Phyllis Schlafly and Grassroots Conservatism: A Woman's Crusade* (Princeton, NJ: Princeton University Press, 2005).

77. "A 'Transformative Moment' in SBC Political Activity," August 20, 2010, https:// ethicsdaily.com/a-transformative-moment-in-sbc-political-activity-cms-16555/; Miller Center, "Building a Movement Party," September 18, 2018, https://millercenter.org/ rivalry-and-reform/building-movement-party.

78. V. Messori, *The Ratzinger Report: An Exclusive Interview on the State of the Church* (San Francisco: Ignatius Press, 1985).

79. Charles E. Curran, "A Place for Dissent," *Commonweal* 132, no. 9 (May 6, 2005): 18–20; Laurie Goodstein, "Vatican Is Said to Force Jesuit off Magazine," *New York Times*, May 7, 2005.

80. John Cassidy, "The Disastrous Influence of Pope Benedict XVI," *New Yorker*, February 12, 2013, https://www.newyorker.com/news/john-cassidy/the-disastrous -influence-of-pope-benedict-xvi#:~:text=By%20setting%20its%20face%20against ,brought%20up%20in%20its%20teachings.

81. Rosie McCall, "Far-Right Bootcamp with Ties to Steve Bannon Evicted from

Italian Monastery Due to Lease Issues," *Newsweek*, October 11, 2019, https://www
.newsweek.com/far-right-bootcamp-steve-bannon-evicted-monestary-1464705.

82. Paul Axton, "Have the Dark Ages Returned?," Forging Ploughshares, January 9,
2020, https://forgingploughshares.org/2020/01/09/have-the-dark-ages-returned/.

83. "About," Napa Institute," accessed June 2, 2020, http://napa-institute.org/about/.

84. Heidi Schlumpf, "Tim Busch, Napa Institute Tout 'Authentic Reform' at Upcoming Event," *National Catholic Reporter*, September 15, 2018.

85. Napa Institute, "50 Years after Humanae Vitae: Where Do We Stand in Heeding
the Directive given to Scientists, Doctors, and Nurses?," January 26, 2018, http://
napa-institute.org/2018/01/26/50-years-after-humanae-vitae-where-do-we-stand-in
-heeding-the-directive-given-to-scientists-doctors-and-nurses/.

86. Magis Center, Leadership and Staff, accessed June 4, 2023, https://www
.magiscenter.com/leadership-and-staff.

87. Heidi Schlumpf, "The Rise of EWTN: From Piety to Partisanship," *National
Catholic Reporter*, July 16, 2019, https://www.ncronline.org/culture/rise-ewtn-piety
-partisanship.

88. Heidi Schlumpf, "How Mother Angelica's 'Miracle of God' Became a Global
Media Empire," *National Catholic Reporter*, July 19, 2019, https://www.ncronline.org/
culture/guest-voices/how-mother-angelicas-miracle-god-became-global-media-empire.

89. Heidi Schlumpf, "The Rise of EWTN: From Piety to Partisanship," *National
Catholic Reporter*, July 16, 2019, https://www.ncronline.org/culture/rise-ewtn-piety
-partisanship.

90. "Religious Group Voting and the 2020 Election," Gallup.com, November 13,
2020, https://news.gallup.com/opinion/polling-matters/324410/religious-group
-voting-2020-election.aspx.

CONCLUSION

1. Ann Gerhart and Lucio Villa, "Rose Garden Ceremony Attendees Who
Tested Positive for Coronavirus," *Washington Post*, October 3, 2020, https://www
.washingtonpost.com/graphics/2020/politics/coronavirus-attendees-barrett
-nomination-ceremony/; United States Senate Committee on the Judiciary, "Senate
Confirms Amy Coney Barrett to the Supreme Court|," October 26, 2020, https://www
.judiciary.senate.gov/press/rep/releases/senate-confirms-amy-coney-barrett-to-the
-supreme-court.

2. *U.S. News and World Report*, "Anti-Roe Justices a Part of Catholicism's Conservative
Wing," June 30, 2022, https://www.usnews.com/news/politics/articles/2022-06-30/
anti-roe-justices-a-part-of-catholicisms-conservative-wing.

3. Molly Olmstead, "Today Is a Major Victory," *Slate*, June 24, 2022, https://slate
.com/news-and-politics/2022/06/dobbs-ruling-christian-right-roe-wade-overturned
.html.

4. Nancy Pelosi, "Pope Francis Is a Pope for the People," *National Catholic Reporter*, March 15, 2023, https://www.ncronline.org/opinion/guest-voices/nancy-pelosi-pope-francis-pope-people; "Biden Is America's Most Prominent Catholic. The Church's Most Conservative Wish He Wasn't," NBC News, October 30, 2021, https://www.nbcnews.com/politics/politics-news/biden-america-s-most-prominent-catholic-church-s-most-conservative-n1282753.

5. Giulia Heyward, "Why Do Some Catholic Bishops Want to Deny Joe Biden Communion?," *New York Times*, October 29, 2021, https://www.nytimes.com/article/joe-biden-communion-catholic-church.html; Ed Kilgore, "Denied Communion at Home, Pelosi Receives It at the Vatican," *Intelligencer*, June 29, 2022, https://nymag.com/intelligencer/2022/06/denied-communion-at-home-pelosi-receives-it-at-the-vatican.html.

6. "Plowshares Disarmament Chronology," accessed May 31, 2023, https://ickevald.net/plowshares/plowshares-chronology-1980-2018; Catholic Left Draft Board Raids, accessed June 24, 2023, http://hillelarnold.com/draft-board-raids/.

7. See Sean T. Dempsey, *City of Dignity: Christianity, Liberalism, and the Making of Global Los Angeles* (Chicago: University of Chicago Press, 2023), for a study of how Christian liberalism shaped metropolitan politics between 1945 and 2000. See Mark Wild, *Renewal: Liberal Protestants and the American City after World War II* (Chicago: University of Chicago Press, 2019), for an investigation of the late twentieth-century "renewal movement" in mainline American Protestant churches.

8. Heidi Schlumpf, "Progressive Catholic Women Join 'Pink Wave' of New Political Candidates," *National Catholic Reporter*, July 9, 2018, https://www.ncronline.org/news/progressive-catholic-women-join-pink-wave-new-political-candidates.

9. R. Jahanbegloo, "Gandhi and the Global Satyagraha," *Social Change* 51, no. 1 (2021): 38–50.

10. John Dear, "Thomas Merton and the Wisdom of Non-Violence," accessed June 25, 2023, https://johndear.org/thomas-merton-and-the-wisdom-of-nonviolence-2/.

11. "Merely ecclesiastical laws bind those who have been baptized in the Catholic Church or received into it, possess the sufficient use of reason, and, unless the law expressly provides otherwise, have completed seven years of age," Code of Canon Law, c. 11 § 1, accessed June 21, 2023, https://www.vatican.va/archive/cod-iuris-canonici/eng/documents/cic_lib1-cann7-22_en.html.

12. Ann Walsh, interview by author, February 14, 2022, part 2, 9.

13. "Frida Berrigan and Patrick Sheehan-Gaumer, Vows," *New York Times*, July 15, 2011, https://www.nytimes.com/2011/07/17/fashion/weddings/frida-berrigan-and-patrick-sheehan-gaumer-vows.html. See also Frida Berrigan, *It Runs in the Family: On Being Raised by Radicals and Growing into Rebellious Motherhood* (New York: OR Books, 2014).

14. Aaron Earles, "More Churches Closed Than Opened in 2019. Then Came the

Pandemic," *Christianity Today*, May 25, 2021, https://www.christianitytoday.com/news/2021/may/lifeway-church-close-open-2019-planting-revitalization.html; Jeffrey Jones, "U.S. Church Membership Falls below Majority for the First Time," *Gallup*, March 29, 2021, https://news.gallup.com/poll/341963/church-membership-falls-below-majority-first-time.aspx.

15. Travis Mitchell, "About Three-in-Ten U.S. Adults Are Now Religiously Unaffiliated," *Pew Research Center's Religion & Public Life Project* (blog), December 14, 2021, https://www.pewresearch.org/religion/2021/12/14/about-three-in-ten-u-s-adults-are-now-religiously-unaffiliated/; United States Conference of Catholic Bishops, Committee on Evangelization and Catechesis, "Discussion Guide: Outreach to Unaffiliated," 2020, https://www.usccb.org/resources/Discussion%20Guide--Outreach%20to%20Unaffiliated.pdf.

16. Josh Packard and Ashleigh Hope, *Church Refugees: Sociologists Reveal Why People Are Done with Church but Not Their Faith* (Loveland, CO: Group Publishing, 2015), 26.

17. Packard and Hope, *Church Refugees*, 21, 22, 25, 50.

18. Shadi Hamid, "America without God," *Atlantic*, March 10, 2021, https://www.theatlantic.com/magazine/archive/2021/04/america-politics-religion/618072/.

19. "Berrigan Sheehan-Gaumer," *New York Times*, July 15, 2011.

INDEX

Note: Page numbers in *italics* refer to illustrations.

Abdoo, Jayma, 4, *146*; and defense committee efforts, 132–33, 138, 141; as late addition to Camden raid, 121; plea deal refusal, 124; posttrial activity, 181; and pretrial motions, 148

Abernathy, Ralph David, Sr., 7

abortion and birth control, 189–90, 193, 195, 197

African Americans: disproportionate representation of in draft system, 21, 44; and Johnson Cemetery, 136; population of in Camden, 78–79. *See also* civil rights movement

aggiornamente, 52–53

aggiornamento, 5, 52

Alianza para el Progreso (Alliance for Progress), 59

America (magazine), 188

American Civil Liberties Union (ACLU), 129

American Friends Service Committee, 167

Anderson, W. B., 107

Anderson, William, 4, 107–8, 149

Angelica, Mother, 195–96

antiabortion movement, 189–90, 193, 195

Any Day Now (community), 61

Aquinas, Thomas, 25, 170

Arendt, Hannah, 188

Arrupe, Pedro, 9

ash symbolism, 134–36

Augustine, Saint, 25, 212n47

Ayers, Bill, 63

Baltimore Four, 15–16, 18, 23

Bannon, Steve, 195

Banoff, Barbara, 192

Barrett, Amy Coney, 197

Barry, John: approval of trial verdict, 176; plea deal negotiations, 147–48; trial cross-examinations, 163, 164–65; trial direct examinations, 156; trial objections, 157, 163, 165–66, 172

Baskir, L. M., 4, 21

Beaver 55, 49

Begin, Joe, 60

Benedict XVI (pope), 188, 194–95

Bernardin, George, 187

Berrigan, Daniel, 9, *48*; on abortion, 189–90; *Bow in the Clouds*, 34; *The Bride*, 34; and CALCAV, 139; in Catonsville Nine, 47, 51; and Day, 42; as expert witness in Camden 28 trial, 170; fundraising efforts, 161; at Gethsemani retreat, 32–33, 101; and John Peter Grady, 70; at Iron Mountain, 58, 61; and Merton, 32; and patriarchal authority, 50, 51; Plowshares activism, 185; sermon on peace, 165–66; and Spellman, 29; *The Trial of the Catonsville Nine*, 133

Berrigan, Frida, 200

INDEX

Berrigan, Philip, 9; in Baltimore Four, 15–16, 18; in Catonsville Nine, 23, 47, 48, 51; and Day, 43; as expert witness in Camden 28 trial, 170–71; at Gethsemani retreat, 32–33, 101; and John Peter Grady, 70; at Iron Mountain, 58; and Merton, 32; and patriarchal authority, 50–51; Plowshares activism, 185; relationship with McAlister, 66–68, 171; in Society of St. Joseph, 45; on violent resistance, 43–44

Bertino, Anna, 150

Biden, Joseph, 196, 198

Big Lake One, 49

Billman, Milo, 4, 145; assignment during raid, 93, 109; FBI arrest of, *99*; and pretrial motions, 148

birth control and abortion, 189–90, 193, 195, 197

Bivins, Jason, 190–91

Black, Hugo, 127

Black Panthers, 7, 43, 80, 104, 125

Black people. *See* African Americans

Black People's Unity Movement (BPUM), 79–80, 91, 154

Black power, 43, 79

Blaszczyk, Eleanor, 150

blood, religious symbolism of, 15–17, 18, 184

Bloody Sunday, 45–46

Blough, Ruth, 150

Boston Eight, 49

Boston Globe (newspaper), 23

Bower, Daniel, 150

BPUM (Black People's Unity Movement), 79–80, 91, 154

Braithwaite, Sam, 150, *152*, 153, 165, 171, 176

Bread Community, 62–63, 64

Broege, E. Carl, 64, 125, 144, 145, 155–56, 179

Bronx draft board raids, 11

Brown, Rap, 79

Bruskewitz, Fabien, 187–88

Buchanan, Pat, 105

Buckalew, Kathy, 61

Buckalew, Terry, 4, 145; FBI arrest of, *99*; and John Peter Grady, 92–93; introduction to Catholic Left, 61–62; juror

questions for, *152*; posttrial activity, 182–83; and pretrial motions, 147–48; trial direct examinations, 168

Burns, Ken, 2

Busch, Timothy, 195

Butterbaugh, Jane, 150

Cain, Mary, 53, 54, 65–66, 82

Cajka, Peter, 68

CALCAV (Clergy and Laity Concerned about Vietnam), 139

Call to Action (CTA), 187–88

Camden, New Jersey: industrial development in, 77–78; Johnson Cemetery, 136; socioeconomic challenges in, 5, 73–74, 78–82, 87, 154, 179–80; and Vietnam comparison, 163

Camden 28 Defense Committee (CDC), 131–32, 133, 136–38, 139–41, 160–62

Camden 28 raid: executing, 93–94, *94*, *95*, 111; FBI arrests, 95–96, *98*, *99*, 111–12, 114; FBI surveillance and investigation, 88, 90–91, *94*, 106–11, 123; planning, 70–71, 75–76, 85, 89; sites of action, *86*

Camden 28 trial: bail proceedings, 124; defense challenges, 123–24; defense committee efforts, 131–32, 133, 136–38, 139–41, 160–62; defense legal team, 125, 138–39, 155–56; defense strategy, 125–26, 127–28, 129, 144; defense witnesses, character and expert, 166–74; defense witnesses, defendants as, 162–66; and governmental overreach, 174–75; Hardy affidavit, 142–44, 148, 155, 164; historic nature of, 146–47; indictment process abuses in, 112–13; judge assigned to, 154–55; and jury nullification, 129–30, 132–33, 160, 162, 174; jury selection process, 137–38, 139, 140–41, *141*, 149–50; motion to sever defendants in, 148–49; opening statements, 122, 145, 150–54, 160; plea deals, 124, 147–48, 149, 165; prosecution witnesses, 156–59; verdict deliberations, 175–76

Camden Civil Rights Ministerium (CCRM), 80, 81

Camp Stoddard, 26

INDEX

Camp Warner, 26
capitalism, 194
Carlin, George, 161
Carmen, Anna Marie, 150
Castillo Arnas, Carlos, 52
Catholic Action, 18
Catholic Church: and communitarianism, 56–57; excommunication from, 6,
58, 67, 68, 187–88, 195; and peace, 7, 9,
29–36, 169–70; sacramentalist worldview, 16–18; and warfare, 24–26, 27–29,
212n47. *See also* Vatican II
Catholic Imagination, as concept, 6, 16,
17. *See also* spirituality
Catholic Left (Catholic Resistance):
Catholicism's influence on, 7, 30–32,
34–36, 38–43; civil rights movement's
influence on, 7, 38, 42, 76, 169; feminism's influence on, 9, 49–50; Gandhi's
influence on, 42, 169; patriarchal and
masculine culture of, 50–51; post-
Vietnam activity, 184–91; prophetic
zeal of, 57; scholarship on, lack of, 2–3;
solidarity and parallels with civil rights
movement, 45–46, 45, 80–81, 87–88;
spiritual dimension of, 6; in twenty-
first century, 198–202; white identity
in, 44; women's contributions to, 51–
54. *See also* Camden 28 raid; Camden
28 trial
Catholic Peace Fellowship (CPF), 170
Catholic Right, 193–96, 197–98
Catholic Social Teaching (CST), 7, 8, 9,
29–30, 34–35, 36, 178
Catholic Worker (newspaper), 39, 40, 41,
188–89, 216n8
Catholic Worker movement, 18, 38–43, 61
Catonsville Nine, 22–24, 47–48, 51, 101,
130
CCRM (Camden Civil Rights Ministerium), 80, 81
CDC (Camden 28 Defense Committee),
131–32, 133, 136–38, 139–41, 160–62
celibacy, 66, 163
Central Intelligence Agency (CIA), 168,
192
Cervantes, Miguel, *Don Quixote*, 163
Chaney, James, 106

Chappel, James, 36
Chesterton, C. K., 188
Chicago 15, 48
Chicago Seven, 166–67
Christ, as model, 17, 18, 23, 29, 30–31, 134,
169, 170
Christianity and Crisis (journal), 23
Christian Right, 193–96, 197–98
Christi Matri (encyclical), 27
Church, Frank, 192
Church Committee (Senate Select
Committee to Study Governmental
Operations with Respect to Intelli-
gence Activities), 192
Church of the Brethren, 26
CIA (Central Intelligence Agency), 168,
192
civil defense drills, 40
Civilian Public Service (CPS) camps, 26
civil rights movement: in Camden, 74,
79–82, 87, 91–92, 154; Catholic Left
solidarity and parallels with, 45–46, 45,
80–81, 87–88; influence on Catholic
Left, 7, 38, 42, 76, 169
Clancy, Charles, III, 166, 167
Clergy and Laity Concerned about Vietnam (CALCAV), 139
CNVA (Committee for Non-Violent
Action), 21
Cohen, Mitchell H., 109, 124
COINTELPRO (FBI Counterintelligence Program), 104–6, 191, 192
colonialism and imperialism, 41–42, 162,
172
Committee for Non-Violent Action
(CNVA), 21
Committee in Solidarity with the People
of El Salvador, 192
Commonweal (periodical), 24, 67, 188
communism and Marxism, 8, 27, 43, 56
communitarianism, 56–57
community dynamics and communal living: Catholic communitarian tradition,
56–57; and development of activist
networks, 59–63; marriages resulting
from, 63–69; sexual tensions resulting
from, 69, 70, 75, 91
Congress of Racial Equality (CORE), 80

250 INDEX

Connolly, Sister, 65
conscience, personal, 68
conscription. *See* draft
conservative Christians, 193–96, 197–98
Coplon, Judith, 103
Corbett, Jim, 186
CORE (Congress of Racial Equality), 80
Cornell, Tom, 32–33
Coughlin, Charles, 196
Couming, Paul, 4, 146; assignment during raid, 93, 94, 157–58; family's testimony during trial, 173; FBI arrest of, 96, 99, 114; FBI surveillance of, 110; introduction to Catholic Left, 63; posttrial activity, 179, 199; and pretrial motions, 148; trial direct examinations, 170; and Zinn, 172
Couming, Rita, 173
Courier-Post (newspaper), 87, 115, 133, 134
court cases. *See* trials
Cox, Archibald, 147
CPF (Catholic Peace Fellowship), 170
CPS (Civilian Public Service) camps, 26
Criterion (newspaper), 24
CST (Catholic Social Teaching), 7, 8, 9, 29–30, 34–35, 36, 178
CTA (Call to Action), 187–88
Cunnane, Robert, 33, 64, 199

Daoust, Joe, 60–61, 115, 168–70
Darst, David, 23, 51
Davidon, William, 100–101, 102
Davis, Angela, 121–22, 137, 160
Davis, Rennie, 167
Day, Dorothy, 7, 32, 38–43, 41, 136, 188, 199, 216n8
D.C. Nine, 46–47, 60
DeBerardinis, Michael, 64
"dechurched" people, 201
defense committees, 46, 47, 131–32, 133, 136–38, 139–41, 160–62
Dellinger, David, 167
Dinan, Terence, 107
Dixon, Eugene, 4; and Ash Wednesday celebration, 136; departure from Camden group, 90–91, 121; and Bob Hardy, 118; and pretrial motions, 148; reconnaissance missions, 89; and St.

Vincent's, 73, 76, 77; trial defense strategy, 125
Dobbs v. Jackson Women's Health Organization, 197
Dobson, Ed, 150
Douglas, Boyd, 66
Dow Chemical raids, 46–47, 49, 60
Doyle, Michael, 4, 64, 89; and Ash Wednesday celebration, 134–36, 135; assignment during raid, 93, 94; background, 85–88; death, 184; FBI arrest of, 99, 114; FBI surveillance of, 88; and Bob Hardy, 115, 118, 119, 142–43; in jail, 124; posttrial activity, 179–80; and pretrial motions, 148; trial defense strategy, 125; trial experience, 177; trial opening statement and testimony, 122, 145, 153–54, 162–63; waiting for trial, 131
draft: burning and destroying draft cards, 19–21, 22, 136; classification and sorting system, 18–19, 19, 21; dismissals from, 3–4; loopholes for avoiding, 19, 20, 21; lottery system, 22; violations of, 3, 4, 22
draft board raids: by Baltimore Four, 15–16, 18, 23; by Big Lake One, 49; by Boston Eight, 49; by Catonsville Nine, 22–24, 47–48, 51, 101, 130; by Chicago 15, 48; by Flower City Conspiracy, 48; Milwaukee 14, 48, 64; scholarship on, lack of, 2–3; and "surfacing" events, 83–84; by Women against Daddy Warbucks, 49. *See also* Camden 28 raid; Camden 28 trial
Dunham, Anne, 4, 65, 146; assignment during raid, 94; FBI arrest of, 98, 99; FBI surveillance of, 109; health struggles, 130–31, 145; posttrial activity, 181–82, 186; relationship with Pommersheim, 63–64; trial cross-examinations, 156–57; trial opening statement and testimony, 151

Eberhardt, Dave, 15–16, 18
Egan, Eileen, 53
Eichmann, Adolf, 31
Eisenhower, Dwight D., 40, 41
Ellsberg, Daniel, 127, 147, 192
Emba, Christine, 44
entrapment, 128, 129, 155, 171, 174

INDEX

251

Eucharist, 16–17
Evangelium Vitae (encyclical), 193
Evening Sun (newspaper), 24
EWTN (Eternal World Television Network), 195–96
excommunication, 6, 58, 67, 68, 187–88, 195

Falwell, Jerry, 194
fascism and totalitarianism, 36
FBI (Federal Bureau of Investigation): agents as trial witnesses, 157–59; arrest of draft board raiders, 95–96, 98, 99, 111–12, 114; and entrapment, 128, 129, 155, 174; Hardy as hostile witness to, 142–44, 148, 155, 164–65; illegal information gathering practices, 103–6, 191–93; Media office, burglary incident at, 100, 101–3, 105, 191; records destroyed by Flower City Conspiracy, 48; surveillance and investigation of draft board raiders, 83, 84, 88, 90–91, 94, 106–11, 123
Feingold, Judi, 101
Fellowship of Reconciliation (FOR), 26–27, 32
feminism, 9, 49–50, 189
Ferry, Wilbur "Ping," 33
FHA (Federal Housing Administration), 78
Fife, John, 186
First Amendment, 127, 231n10
Fisher, Clarkson: background, 154–55; instructions to jury, 174–75; and latitude for the defense, 146–47, 148, 163, 166, 167, 168, 172
FISUR (FBI Physical Surveillance), 110
Flower City Conspiracy, 48
Foley, Michael, 22
folk Mass trend, 76
Fonda, Jane, 136
FOR (Fellowship of Reconciliation), 26–27, 32
Fordi, Peter, 4, 145, 146; assignment during raid, 93, 94; and Daoust, 168; FBI arrest of, 99, 114; FBI surveillance of, 110; trial opening statement and testimony, 151
Foreign Intelligence Surveillance Act of 1978 (FISA), 192

Forrest, Jim, 32–33
Forsyth, Keith, 4, 146; assignment during raid, 93; FBI arrest of, 99; and FBI Media office burglary, 101, 191; and Bob Hardy, 117; introduction to Catholic Left, 62; lock-picking expertise, 85; posttrial activity, 180; and pretrial motions, 148; waiting for trial, 130
Francis (pope), 195
Franco, Francisco, 216n8
Friedan, Betty, 61; *The Feminine Mystique*, 9
Froines, John, 167
fundraising, 131, 133, 161
Furlong, Catherine, 156–57

Gage, Beverly, 103
Gandhi, Mahatma, 42, 169
Geddes, Margaret, 49
gender and sexuality: feminism, 9, 49–50, 189; and marriage among activists, 63–68; patriarchy and sexism, 49–51; power dynamics in sexual relationships, 63, 69, 70, 178; reproductive rights, 189–90, 193, 195, 197; and women's contributions to Catholic Left, 51–54
Gethsemani retreat, 32–33, 64, 101
Gibbons, James, 25
Ginsburg, Ruth Bader, 197
Giocondo, Michael, 4, 89, 146; and Ash Wednesday celebration, 134; assignment during raid, 93, 94; and defense committee efforts, 136; FBI arrest of, 99, 114; FBI surveillance of, 88, 97, 109; and Bob Hardy, 88, 97, 117, 118; posttrial activity, 180–81; and St. Vincent's, 73, 76; trial defense strategy, 125; trial opening statement and testimony, 154
Gonzales, Raphael, 81–82, 86, 91
Good, Betty, 173–74
Good, Bob, 4, 146; assignment during raid, 93, 94; family's testimony during trial, 173–74; FBI arrest of, 99, 114; and Bob Hardy, 117; introduction to Catholic Left, 46–47; posttrial activity, 182; in Thomas Merton Community, 60; trial experience, 177; trial opening statement and testimony, 151

Good, Paul, 173, 174
Goodman, Andrew, 106
Goodwin, Guy, 113–14
Goretti High School, 75, 82, 83
Gorsuch, Neil, 197
Grady, John Peter, 4, 146; assignment during raid, 93, 109; background, 69–70; FBI arrest of, *99*; FBI surveillance of, 88, 107, 109, 110–11; at Gethsemani retreat, 32–33, 101; and Bob Hardy, 89–90, 107–8; at Iron Mountain, 58; personality, 84–85; planning Camden raid, 70–71, 75–76, 85; posttrial activity, 179; and pretrial motions, 148; and Puerto Rican riot, 92–93; sexual relationships, 70, 75, 91, 108, 110; and shared meal before Camden raid, 111; trial opening statement and testimony, 160
Grady, Sandy, 115, 117
Grady, Teresa, 70
Graham, Billy, 28
Great Depression, 78
Greeley, Andrew, 17
Griffin, Mary, 45
Gross, John, 117
Groveline, Bartlett, 150, 175
Grumbles, Donald, 113
Grumbles, Patricia, 113
Guilfoyle, George J., 136
Gutierrez, Gustavo, 185
Gutknecht, David, 22

Hamer, Fannie Lou, 42
Hampton, Fred, 104
Hardy, Billy, 117–18
Hardy, Peggy, 115, 118, 183
Hardy, Robert "Bob": assignment during raid, 93; death, 184; family tragedy, 117–18; as FBI informant, 97, 106, 107–9, 111, 112, 114–17, *116*; guilt and remorse, 119, 142; introduction to Camden group, 88–90; posttrial activity, 183–84; reconnaissance missions, 89, 108; trial affidavit, 143–44, 148, 155, 164; trial testimony, 163–65
Harrisburg Seven, 66, 69
Hayden, Tom, 167
Heidbrink, John, 32

Helmsing, Charles H., 189
Hennessy, Martha, 185
Hersch, Seymour, 191–92
Hershey, Lewis, 21
Hicks, Gary Graham, 21
Higginbotham, A. Leon, 61–62
Hinden, David, 148
Hispanic people. *See* Puerto Ricans
"hit and stay" vs. "hit and split" raids, 18, 54, 58
Hoffa, Jimmy, 44
Hoffman, Abbie, 167
Hoffman, Julius, 167
Hogan, John, 51
HOLC (Home Owners Loan Corporation), 78–79
Hoover, J. Edgar: illegal information gathering practices, 103–6, 191, 192; MEDBURG investigation, 106, 109, 112, 114, 191; targeting draft board raiders, 98–100
Hope, Ashleigh, 201
Horowitz, David, 7
Howard, Thomas, 17
Hull, Cordell, 172
Humanae Vitae (encyclical), 189, 193, 195
Huntington, Samuel P., 168

imperialism and colonialism, 41–42, 162, 172
indictment process abuses, 112–13
Inness, Marge, 4, 94, *98*, *99*, 146
Internal Security Division, Justice Department, 113
Iron Mountain, 11, 58–59, 61, 64
Italian mob, 84

Jägerstätter, Franz, 57
Janson, Donald M., 110, 174–75
Jean, Elbert, 33
Jesuits, 9, 33, 59, 170, 180, 188
Jesus Christ, as model, 17, 18, 23, 29, 30–31, 134, 169, 170
John XXIII (pope), 193; *Pacem in Terris*, 128; *Perfectae Caritatis*, 53–54
John Paul II (pope), 187; *Evangelium Vitae*, 193
Johnson, Elizabeth, 188

INDEX

Johnson, Karen, 18
Johnson, Lyndon, 20, 32, 126
Jonah House, 68, 190–91
Joseph House, 61
Jubilee (magazine), 69–70
jury, in Camden 28 trial: instructions to, from Judge Fisher, 174–75; questions from, 146, *152*, 153, 165, 171; selection process, 137–38, 139, 140–41, *141*, 149–50; verdict deliberations, 175–76
jury nullification, 129–30, 132–33, 160, 162, 174
just war tradition, 25, 212n47

Kairys, David, 145; background, 138–39, 155–56; entrapment defense strategy, 129; and Hardy's affidavit, 142–44; hired for Camden 28 defense team, 125; trial direct examinations, 164
Kaiser, Fred, 150
Kavanaugh, Brett, 197
Kelly, Joseph, 73, 76
Kennedy, John F., 27–28, 29, 59
Kennedy family, 51
Kerry, John, 192
Khanlian, John, 161–62
King, Martin Luther, Jr.: and CALCAV, 139; FBI surveillance of, 104, 191; "I Have a Dream" speech, 76; influence on Catholic Left, 7, 38, 42, 45–46, 61, 169; and "Letter from a Baltimore Jail," 23, 46; "Letter from a Birmingham Jail," 46; position on Vietnam War, 61, 171
Kissinger, Henry, 66, 127
Knights of Columbus, 22, 25
Kosek, Kip, 26
Ku Klux Klan, 24

LaHaye, Timothy, 194
Lambert, Naomi, 69
LaPorte, Roger, 29
Leo XIII (pope), *Rerum novarum*, 9, 34
Lewis, Thomas, 15–16, 18, 23, 51
liberation theology, 8, 185
Life (magazine), 105
liturgical movement, 17–18
liturgy: Ash Wednesday, 133–36; Eucharist, 17; folk trend for, 76

Lomax, Jim, 150, 176
Los Angeles Times (newspaper), 103
lottery system, draft, 22
Loyola University Chicago, 57

Madden, Mel, 4, 93, *99*, 148
Madden, Phil, 73, 76
Magis Center, 195
Maria Goretti High School, 75, 82, 83
Maritain, Jacques, 36, 188
marriage: among activists, 63–68; and reproduction, 190, 193, 195
Martinez, Carmen, 91
Marxism and communism, 8, 27, 43, 56
Maryknolls, 52, 59–60
masculinity, 49, 50–51
Mathis, Anna, 150
Maurin, Peter, 32, 38–39, 40
Mayer, Paul, 67, 68–69
McAlister, Elizabeth, 57–58, 66–68, 171, 185, 190
McCarthy, Joseph, 113
McGovern, George, 103
McGowan, Edward, 4, 146; and Daoust, 168; FBI surveillance of, 110; posttrial activity, 181; and pretrial motions, 147–48, 149; relationship with Anne Walsh, 70; trial defense strategy, 125; trial opening statement and testimony, 151
MEDBURG (FBI investigation), 105, 106–11, 191
media. *See* press and media
Media office burglary incident, 100, 101–3, 105, 191
Medina, Gualberto "Gil", 80–81, 87–88, 91–92
Medsger, Betty, 104–6, 176
Melville, Art, 47
Melville, Cathy, 47
Melville, Marjorie, 23, 51–52
Melville, Thomas, 51, 52
men. *See* gender and sexuality
Mengel, James, 15–16, 18
Mennonites, 26, 56
Merton, Thomas, 7, 30–32, *31*, 42, 199
Miller, Gary, 81
Milwaukee 14, 48, 64
Mische, George, 47, 48, 51, 59–60

Mische, Helene, 59, 60

Mississippi Burning (film), 106

Mitchell, John, 105, 112, 113, 127

Mitchell, Parren, 103

Moccia, Lianne, 4, 146; assignment during raid, 93; death of father, 12; FBI arrest of, *99*; introduction to Catholic Left, 11; posttrial activity, 179; and pretrial motions, 148; relationship with John Peter Grady, 69; waiting for trial, 131; at wedding of Dunham and Pommersheim, 64

Mollin, Marian, 50

Moon, Penelope, 24

Moore, Roy K., 106–7, 109, 110, 112

motions to sever, 148–49

Moylan, Mary, 23, 47–48, 51, 52

Muñoz, Marcos, 62

Mural Arts Project, Philadelphia, 179

Murphy, Ned, 4, 145; and Daoust, 168; posttrial activity, 179, 180; trial direct examinations, 162, 170; and Zinn, 172

Murray, John Courtney, 36

Musi, Barry, 4, 146; assignment during raid, 94; FBI arrest of, *99*; posttrial activity, 179; and Zinn, 172

Muste, A. J., 26, 33, 42, 100–101, 139

Myer, Paul, 47

Mystici Corporis Christi (encyclical), 18

NAACP (National Association for the Advancement of Colored People), 79, 80

Napa Institute, 195

Nardi, Joseph, 92

National Action/Research on the Military-Industrial Complex (NAR-MIC), 167–68

National Catholic Conference for Interracial Justice, 46

National Catholic Reporter (*NCR*), 189

National Catholic War Council, 25–26

National Council of Catholic Bishops (NCCB) (later United States Conference of Catholic Bishops), 26, 128–29, 187

National Emergency Civil Liberties Committee (NECLC), 129

National Jury Project, 137

National Right to Life Committee, 189

NCR (*National Catholic Reporter*), 189

Neist, Terry, 107, 118, 143

Nelson, John Oliver, 33

New Left, 7, 8, 37, 43, 166–67. *See also* Catholic Left

new nuns, 53

Newsweek (magazine), 23

New York Times (newspaper), 105, 110, 127, 191–92

New York Times Co. v. United States, 127

Ngo Dinh Diem, 27, 127, 172

Nhat Hanh, Thich, 151

Nightly News (NBC broadcast), 191

Nixon, Richard, 22, 29, 105, 126, 127, 147, 192

nonviolence. *See* peace movement

Northrop, Edward, 23

Novak, Michael, 194

Novick, Lynn, 2

nuclear attack drills, 40

nullification, jury, 129–30, 132–33, 160, 162, 174

nuns and former nuns: and marriage, 64–68; missions in poor communities, 53–54, 62–63; motivations, as political activists, 163; racial privilege, as political activists, 44, 81

O'Brien, David, 20–21

O'Dell, Marnie, 73, 76

O'Grady, Jim, 50

O'Mally, Andrea, 62–63

Order of Saint Clare, 196

O'Rourke, Joseph, 110, 229n55

Orsi, Robert, 50, 55, 57

Pacem in Terris (encyclical), 128

pacification program, 167–68

pacifism. *See* peace movement

Packard, Josh, 201

patriarchy and sexism, 49–51

patriotism, 24–26, 193–94

Paul VI (pope): *Christi Matri*, 27; *Humanae Vitae*, 189, 193, 195

Pax Christi USA, 53, 128

Peace (magazine), 53

INDEX

Peace Camps, 26

peace churches, 26

peace movement: in Catholic theological tradition, 7, 9, 29–36, 169–70; in Protestant theological tradition, 26–27. *See also* Catholic Left; draft board raids

Pearse, Pádraic, "The Fool," 162–63

Pelosi, Nancy, 198

Pentagon Papers, 126–27, 134–36, 147, 172

Percy, Walker, 24

Perfectae Caritatis (encyclical), 53–54

personalism, 35

Phoenix program, 168

Piehl, Mel, 40

Pius XII (pope), *Mystici Corporis Christi*, 18

Planned Parenthood of Southeastern Pennsylvania v. Casey, 197

plea deals, 124, 147–48, 149, 165

Plowshares movement, 184–85, 198

Pogorelc, Anthony, 187

police brutality, 44, 81–82, 92

Polner, Murray, 50

Pommersheim, Frank, 4, 146; assignment during raid, 93, 157–58; evasion of FBI, 96; posttrial activity, 181–82, 186; and pretrial motions, 148; relationship with Dunham, 63–64; waiting for trial, 130

prayers and penance, public, 22, 40, 41

press and media: and Catholic conservative political activity, 195–96; and Catholic progressive political activity, 40, 188–89; coverage of Baltimore Four and Catonsville Nine raids, 23–24; coverage of Camden 28 raid, 114–15, *116*; coverage of illegal FBI activity, 104–5, 127, 191–92

priests and former priests: as expert witnesses in Camden 28 trial, 168–71; and marriage, 64, 65–68; motivations, as political activists, 163, 170–71; and patriarchal authority, 50–51; privilege, as political activists, 44, 81; and sex abuse crisis, 178, 188

"pro-family" movement, 193, 195

Project Life, 134

Project Share, 69

pro-life movement, 189–90, 193, 195

Protestants: peace and nonviolence theology, 26–27; Social Gospel theology, 35–36, 42

Puerto Ricans: activists and uprising, 5, 80–82, *86*, 87–88, 91–92, *92*, 154; population of in Camden, 78, 79

Quakers, 26, 50, 61, 162, 186

Quest for Peace campaign, 186

Quixote Center, 185–86

racial profiling, 140–41

racial unrest. *See* civil rights movement

radicals, as term, 210n12

Raines, Bonnie, 101, 176

Raines, John C., 101, 176

Rankin, Kenny, 161

Ratzinger, Joseph (Pope Benedict XVI), 188, 194–95

Rauschenbusch, Walter, 35–36; *A Theology for the Social Gospel*, 36

Reagan, Ronald, 3, 7, 194

Reed, David, 20

Reese, Thomas, 188

Reilly, Joan, 4, 146, 155; assignment during raid, 94, 158; FBI arrest of, *99*; introduction to Catholic Left, 58; at Iron Mountain, 58–59; posttrial activity, 179; and pretrial motions, 147–48; relationship with DeBerardinis, 64; and shared meal before Camden raid, 111; trial defense strategy, 125; trial testimony, 165–66

Reilly, Rosemary "Ro Ro", 4; assignment during raid, 93, 94; FBI arrest of, *99*, 114; FBI surveillance of, *94*, 112, 123; introduction to Catholic Left, 58; at Iron Mountain, 58–59; posttrial activity, 179; relationship with Broege, 64; and shared meal before Camden raid, 111; trial cross-examinations, 156; trial defense strategy, 125; trial direct examinations, 165–66, 168; trial experience, 145–46; waiting for trial, 131

Religious of the Sacred Heart of Mary (RSHM), 53, 58

religious revival, 28

reproductive rights, 189–90, 193, 195, 197

Rerum novarum (encyclical), 9, 34
Resistance Books movement, 58–59, 63–64
Reuther, Rosemary, 52
Ricci, Anita, 4; death, 183; and defense committee efforts, 139; FBI surveillance of, 88; planning Camden raid, 75–76; relationship with John Peter Grady, 75, 91, 108, 110; relationship with Kathleen Ridolfi, 75
Rice, Megan, 185
Ridolfi, Kathleen "Cookie", 4, *182*; on abortion, 190; assignment during raid, 93, 94; background, 82–83; and defense committee efforts, 139–40; FBI arrest of, 95, *99*, 114; FBI surveillance of, 83, 84, *94*, 109, 110, 112, 123; introduction to Catholic Left, 46, 54; planning Camden raid, 71, 75–76; posttrial activity, 181; and pretrial motions, 147–48; relationship with John Peter Grady, 75, 91, 108, 110; relationship with Ricci, 75; and support from family and community during trial, 124, 146; trial cross-examinations, 156, 157, 159; trial direct examinations, 170, 171, 172; trial opening statement and testimony, 151–53; waiting for trial, 131; at wedding of Dunham and Pommersheim, 64
Ridolfi, Kitty, 83, 84, 146
Ring, Charles, 33
Rodriguez, Joseph, 92, *92*
Roe v. Wade, 197
Romero, Oscar, 185
Roosevelt, Eleanor, 29
Rosen, Alex, 109, 111
RSHM (Religious of the Sacred Heart of Mary), 53, 58
Rubin, Jerry, 167
Ryan, Paul, 196
Ryman, Michael, 143

sacramentalist worldview, 16–18
Sanctuary movement, 186–87
Satyagraha, 42
Schemeley, Martha, 4, 88; departure from Camden group, 90–91; and pretrial

motions, 149; and St. Vincent's, 73, 76; trial defense strategy, 125
Schlafly, Phyllis, 194
Schloesser, Stephen, 178
Schmelzer, Mary, 139–41
Schulman, Jay, 137, 138
Schwerner, Michael, 106
Scoblick, Tony, 65
SDS (Students for a Democratic Society), 7, 24, 43, 50
Seale, Bobby, 125, 167
Second Vatican Council. *See* Vatican II
Security Index (FBI), 103, 105, 192
segregation, racial, 78–79
selective service. *See* draft
sever, motions to, 148–49
sex abuse crisis, 178, 188
sexism and patriarchy, 49–51
sexuality. *See* gender and sexuality
Sharpe, Poppy, 81, 91
Sheehan, Shawn, 62
Sheehan-Gaumer, Patrick, 200
Sheen, Martin, 180
Shields, Clarence, 80
Shuttlesworth, Fred, 42
Sisters of Notre Dame de Namur (SNDN), 53, 54
Sisters of St. Joseph (SSJ), 53, 62, 64, 65, 200
SJS (systematic or scientific jury selection), 137–38, 139, 140–41, *141*
Smith, Gregory A., 200–201
Smith, Mason, 157
SNAP (Survivors Network of those Abused by Priests), 188
SNCC (Student Nonviolent Coordinating Committee), 43
SNDN (Sisters of Notre Dame de Namur), 53, 54
Social Gospel theology, 35–36, 42
Society of Jesus (Jesuits), 9, 33, 59, 170, 180, 188
Society of St. Joseph of the Sacred Heart, 45
Sojourners (magazine), 189, 190
Sorrells v. United States, 128
Spellman, Francis, 27–29

INDEX 257

spirituality: and ash symbolism, 134–36; and blood symbolism, 15–17, 18, 184; and Catholic Imagination, 6, 16, 17; in Catholic Worker movement, 40; vs. church affiliation, 200, 201; and folk Mass trend, 76; and New Left, 7; and public prayers and penance, 22, 40, 41; and sacramentalism, 16–17; and shared meal before Camden raid, 111

Spitzer, Robert, 195

SSJ (Sisters of St. Joseph), 53, 62, 64, 65, 200

Stearn, Bill, 161

Steck, Robert Neil, 168

Stern, Carl, 191

Stoddard, Camp, 26

Stolar, Martin "Marty" R., 125, 145, 155–56, 159, 231n10

Stop Taking Our Privileges (STOP-ERA) movement, 194

Strauss, W. A., 4, 21

Student Nonviolent Coordinating Committee (SNCC), 43

Students for a Democratic Society (SDS), 7, 24, 43, 50

St. Vincent Pallotti Church, 73, 76–77

Survivors Network of those Abused by Priests (SNAP), 188

Sutherland, Nora, 161

Swinglish, John, 4, 119; assignment during raid, 93; FBI arrest of, 96, 99; fundraising efforts, 161; introduction to Catholic Left, 60; posttrial activity, 178; trial direct examinations, 170

systematic or scientific jury selection (SJS), 137–38, 139, 140–41, 141

Teilhard de Chardin, Pierre, 34

Testa, Salvatore, 84

Tet Offensive (1968), 5, 126

Thomas Aquinas, 25, 170

Thomas Merton Community, 60

Till, Emmet, 130

Time (magazine), 105

Tosi, Sara, 4, 146; assignment during raid, 93; and defense committee efforts, 139; FBI arrest of, 98, 99;

posttrial activity, 179; and pretrial motions, 148

totalitarianism and fascism, 36

transubstantiation, 17

Trial of the Catonsville Nine, The (D. Berrigan), 133

trials: Angela Davis case, 121–22, 137; Baltimore Four case, 23; Catonsville Nine case, 23, 47–48, 130; Chicago Seven case, 166–67; Harrisburg Seven case, 66, 137; as political forums for radicals, 121–22. See also Camden 28 trial

Trump, Donald, 195, 196, 197

Tu, La Ann, 167–68

United States Conference of Catholic Bishops (USCCB) (formerly National Council of Catholic Bishops), 26, 128–29, 187

United States v. Moylan, 130

United States v. Russell, 128, 129, 171

Van Patter, Betty, 7

Vatican II, 5–6; conservative push to move away from, 187, 193, 195; impact on liturgy, 76; impact on women, 52

Venard, Theophane, 41–42

Vietnam War: Catholic Church position on, 27, 128–29; and "pacification" program, 167–68; and Pentagon Papers, 127, 134, 172; and Phoenix program, 168; protests against (see draft board raids); public opposition to, 5, 126–27

Vietnam War, The (documentary), 2

Voices of the Faithful (VOTF), 188

Voting Rights Act (1965), 46

Waller, Robert, 158

Walsh, Anne, 11, 12, 64, 65, 70–71, 179, 199–200

Walsh, Tony, 33

Walter Ferrell Guild, 33

Warner, Camp, 26

War Resistors League, 19–20

Washington, Harold, 181

Washington Post (newspaper), 127, 147

Watergate scandal, 147, 166

Waters, Craig, 134
Weather Underground, 5, 43, 63, 101
Weiner, Lee, 167
Weyrich, Paul, 194
WFP (Witness for Peace), 186
white flight, 79
white privilege, 44, 81
Wicker, Tom, 105, 227n27
Williamson, Robert (Bob), *102*; assignment during raid, 93, 94; family disapproval of, 1, 124; FBI arrest of, 99, 114; and FBI Media office burglary, 101, 191; FBI surveillance of, 110; and Bob Hardy, 117; hunger strike, 167; introduction to Catholic Left, 46, 48, 60–61, 169; in jail, 1, 124–25; posttrial activity, 178; and pretrial motions, 147–48; reflections on Camden 28 activity, 183; resignation to prison sentence, 126,
162; trial cross-examinations, 158; trial direct examinations, 168, 169; waiting for trial, 130
Wilson, Woodrow, 25
Witness for Peace (WFP), 186
women. *See* gender and sexuality
Women against Daddy Warbucks, 49–50
Woodstock Theological Seminary, 59, 64, 168
World War I, 25, 26
World War II, 19–20, 36, 40, 57, 216n8
Worrell, Warren, 81

Yoder, John Howard, 33
Young Lords, 80

Zahn, Gordon, *In Solitary Witness*, 57
Zinn, Howard, 171–72, 173